CARING, GROWING, CHANGING

A History of the Protestant Mission in Korea

by Martha Huntley

Friendship Press • New York

Library of Congress Cataloging in Publication Data

Huntley, Martha, 1941-
Caring, growing, changing.

Includes bibliographical references.
1. Protestant churches—Missions—Korea.
2. Protestant churches—Korea—History. 3. Korea—Church History. I. Title.
BV3460.H87 1984 266'.009519 84-6142
ISBN 0-377-00145-7

CARING, GROWING, CHANGING

Editorial Office: 475 Riverside Drive, Room 772,
New York, NY 10115
Distribution Office: PO Box 37844, Cincinnati,
OH 45237

Printed in the United States of America

Dedication

. . . to the long line of missionaries to Korea, Catholic and Protestant, including my husband, Betts Huntley.

CONTENTS

Acknowledgments

I am deeply indebted to and appreciative of the many who helped to make the publication of this book possible. Special thanks to the children and grandchildren of pioneer missionaries who generously shared their family journals, letters, photographs, books, articles and their own ideas and memories: Dr. Samuel H. Moffett of Seoul and Princeton; Dr. Richard Baird of Duarte, Ca.; Drs. Horace G. and Horace H. Underwood of Seoul; the Rev. John Underwood of Kwangju; Dr. and Mrs. Horace Allen of Black Mountain, N.C.; the late Mrs. Gertrude Swallen Voelkel; Mrs. Ruth Noble Appenzeller Knight; Dr. Allen Clark; Dr Charles Stokes; Mrs. Muriel Morris Lewis. Thanks for the input of Dr. Donald Clark, Dr. Edward Schultz and Donald Bishop; for the encouragement of Jim Magruder, Ward Kaiser, G. Thompson Brown, In-Sik Kim, George Worth, Norman Sibley. For encouragement, funds and prayers, thanks to my family, especially Flora Reid, Roberta Beattie, Susan Brown, and to friends Dr. and Mrs. Russell Matthes, Ruth Matthes, Marjorie Neil, Moneta Prince, Windsor Book Club, Patricia Menk, Helen Bundrant, John and Virginia Somerville, and for all this and typing as well, to Ruth Nieusma. And thanks for the patience of my children, Mary, Susan, Michael and Jennifer Huntley, who for seven years have shared me with this endeavor.

Martha Huntley

Preface

In 1884 and 1885 the foreign missions boards of the Northern branches of the Methodist and Presbyterian churches of America appointed four couples, a bachelor and a middle-aged woman to go to Korea "to start a work." The work — of evangelizing, teaching, rendering medical aid and establishing a Protestant church — is still going on.

This book deals with that work and the workers, the coming of Protestantism to Korea, how it changed Korean life and thought, how Korea influenced Christianity and changed the missionaries. "Mission history," wrote John Fairbank, "is a great and underused research laboratory for the comparative observation of cultural stimulus and response in both directions."

I have attempted to trace some patterns alluded to but not closely examined by other books on missions: the role of missionaries as agents of change, their contribution to the modernization of Korea, including the enfranchisement of butchers, the release of women from lives of seclusion and servitude and the development of nationalism. I was also interested in the problem of messengers bearing a message so much greater than themselves, and in the role of women in the missions and in the church.

Even before the first Protestant missionary arrived, there was a church in Korea in the sense of a century of Catholic witness and martyrdom, in individual Korean believers who had accepted the faith in Manchuria and Japan, and in the Holy Spirit long at work. While the missionaries were catalysts and in some cases enablers, the Koreans were the primary agents of evangelism. Koreans participated in all aspects of the work, laboring beside the missionaries in writing the Bible, compiling hymnals, translating textbooks, teaching classes, caring for the ill, building church buildings, preaching the Word and making the rules. As in the case of women missionaries, Korean church leaders were underpaid and underacknowledged, but they were valued and very real partners in the mission enterprise.

So much for content; as for mechanics, spelling presented the usual difficulties. I followed the original spellings of names and places in all quoted materials and otherwise used the McCune-Reischauer Romanization system (without the diacritical marks which I, for one, invariably trip over). Some place names in Korea have been changed, and I used the names that were common at the time — Fusan for Pusan, Chemulpo for Inchun.

Whenever possible I tried to use the participants' own words as they described their work, with its attendant tragedies, pain, frustrations and victories. I know these pioneers well; I have read their mail and their diaries and their tombstones, and have talked to missionary children and grandchildren and to the children and grandchildren of Korean converts and co-workers. I have heard their voices clearly and movingly, and trust you will too.

Every writer and historian writes from an individual viewpoint, each has a subjective basis, and I have mine. As a practicing Presbyterian, after years of research, I am convinced that the lively saga of the missionaries in Korea is not merely their story, but even more, His story.

Martha Huntley
Kwangju, Korea

CHAPTER I

Strangers at the Gate

A Bad Time for Humanity

The 19th century was not a good one for Korea. As someone said of Europe's 14th century, it was "a bad time for humanity." In fact, the 19th century in Korea and the 14th in Europe had much in common. Both were times when the energies of the past had run out; times when much of the philosophy that had sustained society for long centuries had worn out, and old religions were proving inadequate for new crises. Famines, corruption, peasant uprisings, persecutions and plagues recurred with dismal frequency. In 1812–13 drought and famine produced a record death toll in Korea; it was said that 4.5 million persons died. A million or more perished in cholera epidemics in the summers of 1821 and 1822.[1]

The finances of the country had been thrown into confusion by debasement of the currency and the heavy expenses of palace building. Offices were used unscrupulously, and the limit of taxation and extortion was only that of the people to pay. The main qualification of a successful prefect had become the ability to judge when he had reached the limit of the people's endurance. The common people had no incentive to industry when the products of their labor were ruthlessly appropriated by the nobles and officials.

There was a system of submitting grievances for redress but since petitions would invariably be refused and the lot of the complainant be made worse, the oppressed people could only submit or rebel. In a search for alternatives, many turned to rebellion and religion, and the persecutions of the Catholics increased the unrest. There were large scale revolts in 1804, 1811, 1813, 1817, 1833, 1862 and 1885.

The Yi dynasty, founded in 1392, was under the shadow of an ancient prophecy that said it would not last much longer than 500 years. From 1864, the well-intentioned but much-beleaguered King Kojong was dominated first by his unscrupulous, isolationist father Taewongun, and then by his ambitious wife, Queen Min, and her fractious family.

It was natural in this dark age for Koreans to look backward and idealize the Golden Age of the past. Archeological findings in recent years indicate that Paleolithic man first came to Korea 30,000 or more years ago, and the ancient Choson tribes arose in the Taedong River basin area near Pyongyang during the 4th century B.C. "Korea is an old country. In comparison, America is but of yesterday, 'Old England' is a youth and even Greece and Rome have no antiquity. Only China, India, Babylon and Egypt can trace such an ancient history."[2]

It is hard to pin down ancient Korean history because of its mythological quality. Korea has been very late accepting the 19th century idea that history consists of the compilation of objective facts.[3] Korean historians preferred the Oriental way of reflecting historical truths through myth. James Scarth Gale, who more than any other missionary entered into and appreciated the Korean literary mind, wrote a *History of the Korean People,* beginning at the same place and in much the same style as the Koreans:

"Korea takes its beginnings in the misty ages of the past that elude all attempts at close investigation, ages that lie somewhere between that of man and those of angel and spirit beings, joining heaven on the one hand and earth on the other.

"The first great father of Korea was a being called Tangun. . . . His year date, marked with all the confidence of the Far East, is Wu-Chen of Tang Yao, or 2333 B.C. . . . . Tangun was the first great ruler of Korea, his capital, we are told, being at Pyongyang, which would make that town one of the oldest cities of the world, contemporary with Thebes and Shinar.[4]

Korean history actually begins with Kija, who came over from China in 1122 B.C. with 5,000 followers and introduced Chinese customs and civilization, which were both adopted and adapted. The resulting culture was syncretized, Koreanized, but at the same time in many ways was more Chinese than that of China itself.

The Sam Han or Three Rival Kingdoms followed and in the course of another thousand years were fused into one kingdom called Ko-ryu. The Chinese pronounced it something like "Korea," and so do we, much to the annoyance of James Gale. Gale wrote,

"Koryo happened to be the name of the peninsula from A.D. 918–1392. Its ruling house was very intimate with China, the suzerain state, and so the Chinese learned that name and have continued ever since to call it Kao-li or Korea. We got the name, therefore, from them and have so called it, quite unconscious that the country's first, last and real name is Choson, the 'Land of Morning Freshness,' the name given by Tangun."[5]

Another missionary who had an emotional attachment to the name Choson was Lillias Horton Underwood, who wrote: "We always thought it a most suitable name for Korea, meaning 'Morning Calm' to Koreans but the English 'Chosen' to us. The place God had chosen. . . ."[6]

The Yi dynasty was established in 1392 by King Taejo. The Yi's soon set about to eradicate Buddhism, whose influence they considered baneful on political rather than religious grounds. Confucianism was encouraged and revived. Relations between China and Korea, a "big and little brother" form of subservience, were based on Confucian theories.

Celebrated scholars, wise kings and famous literati flourished. In 1403, King Taejong directed his ministers to develop movable type and there is evidence that type was already present in Korea, perhaps as early as 1232, two centuries before Gutenberg.[7] The next king, the good King Sejong, commissioned the unique Korean alphabet, the first and best phonetic alphabet in Asia, universally praised by linguists. In 1592 the Koreans successfully repelled the Japanese invasion of Hideyoshi, largely due to Admiral Yi Sun-Sin's inspired iron-clad "turtleboat." But a million Koreans died in the seven-year struggle and the resulting misery caused Korea to draw her borders closely around herself and attempt to keep out the hated Japanese and everyone else for nearly 300 years.

Another invasion strongly influenced the course of Korean history and thought. In the 17th century the Mings and Manchus were struggling over the Dragon Throne of China. Korea supported the Mings. The Manchus won, however, and invaded Korea. The resulting Manchurian conquest concluded with sworn friendship between the Manchu prince and the Korean king, and a tightening of bonds with China.

There were a number of factors to account for Korea's xenophobia. One is geographical. Korea juts off the Chinese mainland, just south of Manchuria, east of China and west of Japan. In Korea's case geography has been destiny. The Korean peninsula forms a natural land bridge between its two strong neighbors which has facilitated both the flow of ideas and the marching of armies. In its long history Korea has never invaded another country, but has had to fight off 287 major invasions merely to maintain its own independence. The Korean proverb that "when whales fight, the shrimp's back gets broken" grew out of rueful experience.

The Yi's deliberately chose Chu Hsi's reinterpretation of Confucianism as the guiding principle of their new regime, intending it to be a stabilizing influence. Neo-Confucianism eventually became rigid doctrine, and "was more highly developed in Korea than in China, its homeland. Everything in Korean life, including the individual's way of thinking and social behavior, had to conform to Chu Hsi philosophy; all other ideas were barred and suppressed as heresy."[8] In spite of all efforts to make Chu Hsi teachings the only basis of Korean thought and action, some Koreans had become affected, or in the view of the conservatives, infected by Western ideas, especially the scientific knowledge which was coming into China from Europe.

Curiosity cannot be entirely suppressed. One branch of this new school, the *Sohak* or Western Learning, was represented by Catholicism. Early on, fairly large numbers of Koreans who came into contact with Catholicism through China, and later, through French missionary priests and their converts, were won to the faith. Catholicism, with its teachings of the equality of all classes before God and its appeal to an authority higher than that of the monarch's, attracted many. For the same reasons, it was seen as a source of conflict and potential rebellion. To the establishment, Catholicism meant danger.

Even in the 18th century there had been Korean martyrs. Early believers had made the hazardous journey to the Bishop of Peking to request priests and instruction. Although he was unable to send a priest, the Bishop answered their questions and advised them on the teachings of the church, among other things, that the worship of ancestors was inconsistent with church doctrine.[9] The prohibition of ancestor worship was disastrous for Korean believers. In the Yi dynasty, ancestor worship was the equivalent of a state religion. Its neglect meant abandoning all that a Korean held most sacred—duty to family, traditions, state. But zealous Christian converts tore down their ancestral tablets. This was very serious, for in Korean belief, each person had three souls. These separated at death, one remaining in the grave, one going to the lower world and one entering into the ancestral tablet. These tablets, made of chestnut wood, symbolized the continuation of an unbroken family line, as chestnut wood was thought not to rot until the tree growing from it had borne fruit. It was for the heresy of refusing to offer sacrifices to their ancestors that these first Christians were persecuted and imprisoned, tortured and killed.

The 19th century opened with a bloody massacre of Catholics in 1801. The first Catholic missionary to China, a young Chinese priest, James Chu, gave himself up, hoping to save his Korean converts, and was executed. That year 300 Korean Christians were martyred.

One convert, Hwang Sa-Yang, baptized Alexander Hwang, wrote a desperate letter from the cave where he was hiding to the Bishop of Peking appealing to the Christian nations of Europe to send 60- or 70,000 soldiers to conquer Korea.[10] This document, sewn into the garment of the messenger, was discovered by a government agent. It reinforced suspicions and led to intensified persecution.

The Korean court's viewpoint was expressed in a letter from the king to the Chinese emperor. The king reaffirmed his strict adherence to Confucian orthodoxy and declared that Christianity was "utter blasphemy against heaven (*chon*)." He described Christianity as a heresy which stifled "all feelings of filial piety, abolished sacrifices to the ancestors and burned the memorial tablets." The king described believers as "rebels against their princes."[11]

More persecutions followed until 1866. Sometimes believers were victims of political as well as religious persecution. For instance, the years 1811–13 were a time of crop failure and famine. Lackeys of the magistrate of one county decided to pillage the Christians, assuming they would not, as a proscribed sect, resist. The Christians did resist, however, and were arrested in great numbers for rebellion. Many starved to death in the prisons, since the jailors, who were themselves hungry, stole their food.[12]

But the shepherdless Korean church, estimated at 10,000 adherents in 1801, refused to die. It is believed that 1,000 Korean Christians were martyred during the first 50 years of Catholicism, before the first Protestant missionary ever took up residence in Korea.[13]

In December 1835, Father Pierre Maubant with Korean companions crossed the Yalu on the ice, crawling through the water drain under the city to enter Euiju, reaching Seoul 15 days later in January 1836. The following January, Maubant was joined by Father Jaques Chastan and on January 1, 1838, by Bishop Laurent Marie-Joseph Imbert. The priests baptized 2,000 adults in a single year, but just as the little Christian community seemed as if it might flourish, the 1839 persecution broke out.

The house in which Bishop Imbert was living was raided and all the members of the household were tortured. The officials were particularly incensed that the women had taken vows of celibacy in a culture where every person was expected to marry. They took a group of young women and beat them with clubs and hot irons and pulled their bones from the sockets. The magistrate had them stripped naked and thrown into the jail of common robbers, but none of the men touched them.

Bishop Imbert's legs were bent, torn with clubs and then flayed. He also was beaten. Thinking that if they offered themselves for execution the persecution might subside, Imbert sent word to Chastan and Maubant to give themselves up. All three were tried and executed on September 21, 1839, on the banks of the Han River. Soldiers played at mock warfare, stabbing them from this side and that until they were almost dead, and then decapitated them. In the 1839 persecution 130 Christians, many of them descendants of earlier martyrs, died.[14]

One of the earliest Korean church leaders, Andrew Kim, who had been sent to China by Maubant, was ordained there in 1845. He was seized reentering Korea and executed just a month after his ordination. The only other Korean priest, Thomas Choe, died in 1861 after 12 years of service.

Gradually more French missionaries, in spite of the great dangers and hardships involved, managed to enter Korea, but they had trouble surviving. To avoid detection, they wore Korean mourning garb which included a large hat of bamboo reaching to the shoulders and also a cloth stretched on sticks and held before the face, to indicate the mourner was hiding his face from heaven in shame for allowing the death of a parent or sovereign. Further protection was provided by the custom that mourners refrained from speaking, even when addressed.

Lucius Foote, the American consul, had suggested to Horace Allen on his arrival that he don these clothes, but Allen, a Presbyterian missionary, understandably preferred the camouflage provided by the title of physician to the legation. Bishop C.G. Mutel who came to Korea in 1880 wore this disguise. He said many Korean boys found him out, but never gave his secret away. Korean dogs were a different matter. The barking dogs knew foreigners when they smelled them, and were one of the greatest threats to the disguised priests.[15]

Under constant threat of annihilation, the Korean Catholic Church had grown to 23,000 and had two foreign bishops and 10 priests in 1866 when the last great persecution flared.

There were a number of Catholics at court including Taewongun's wife and young King Kojong's former nurse, Martha Pak. Some of these hoped the French priests could be instrumental in helping to make treaties between Korea and France and England, thinking that such treaties would check the Russian aggression then threatening. Such aid might impress the Korean government and perhaps result in religious toleration. One of the court Christians, Thomas Kim, approached Bishop Simeon

Francois Berneaux who had been in Korea for 10 years to ask him to assist the government in making such treaties.

Berneaux agreed and returned from the country to Seoul to meet Taewongun who at first appeared amenable to the suggestion. Unfortunately, the idea backfired. Taewongun's suspicions of the political motives of the Catholics were aroused and he decided it was all a subversive plot. In spite of his wife's pleas, he had the priests arrested. Their death sentence read that they "rebelled, disobedient, condemned to die after having been tortured." The last clause was added to show that they had not repented nor recanted under interrogation which had included beatings with clubs, dislocation of the bones and other all too familiar tortures.[16]

Of the two bishops and 10 French priests, all but three were executed. The last three to be killed—Daveluy, Huin, Aumaitre—were taken 75 miles south of Seoul and executed on March 30, which happened to be Good Friday. The reason they weren't killed in Seoul is that 14-year-old King Kojong's marriage was at hand and sorcerers in selecting an auspicious day for the ceremony decided torture and execution in the capital would bode ill for the royal nuptials.[17]

In Father Daveluy's case, the executioner, after striking him once with the ax, stopped and haggled over his fee before striking the final blow. Two thousand Korean believers are estimated to have perished in this persecution. The executioner of the missionaries, severing their heads from their bodies, cried, "It is done."[18] So it seemed with the Catholic Church in Korea in 1866.

Yet, by 1884, after 100 years of Korean Catholicism, there were reported to be 319 Christian communities and 17,577 believers. In 50 years, of 26 French missionaries, 12 were martyred, five died in other ways, two were deported, two left voluntarily, and five remained. Many thousands of Korean Christians—men, women and children from all social classes—had been imprisoned, tortured and killed on the banks of the Han and in jails across the country. They died for their faith, but in their executioners' eyes they died because they appeared to be the forerunner of French imperialism, and they carried the contagion of new ideas.

In contrast to the *Sohak* (Western Learning) of which one expression was Catholicism, the *Tonghak* (Eastern Learning) movement grew up. Peasant rebellions broke out all during the 19th century in Korea and the last and greatest of these was the *Tonghak* insurrection which the government finally suppressed with outside help, bringing war to Korea.

The Tonghak sect was founded in 1860 in Kyongju, by the gentle Choe Cheu (1824–1864) who suffered intensely because his idealism misfit him for his time.[19] Choe was an interesting combination of social reformer and traditionalist who made one of his slave girls his foster daughter and married another to his son.[20] He felt strongly that the religious origins of Oriental learning needed to be revived. His teachings, in the Korean pattern, combined and Koreanized elements of Confucianism, Buddhism, Taoism, Shamanism and even Catholicism.

The Tonghak movement was nationalistic in that it was deliberately conceived as an alternative to Western Learning, although it was influenced by the *Sohak* School. It was mystical, in that its founder claimed inspiration and revelation from heaven. Choe's aim was to rehabilitate the minds of the people and to eliminate the corruption so pervasive in society. His philosophy was directed to this world, but he realized that Korea was soul sick and the times called for a spiritual remedy.

This movement was rightly seen by the officials as a threat to their values and they suppressed it as ruthlessly as they had Catholicism. In fact, they thought Choe was a Catholic. Arrested with 20 followers in 1863, he was executed the following year in Taegu, on charges of "disturbing the world and deceiving the people."[21] But the Tonghak movement went underground and lived on.

The *Sohak* and *Tonghak* philosophies were not mere aberrations, exceptions to the prevailing world view. They were essentially cracks in the massive, monolithic structure that was 19th century Korean Confucianism. They indicated the stress the whole system was feeling as the century and the Yi dynasty ground to a close. To understand the Korea that the first Protestant missionaries entered, one needs to look more closely at the Confucian world order itself.

Confucianism was basically a system of subordinations. It rested on the foundation of five relationships which spelled out the duties and attendant virtues of inferiors:

Father and Son—filial piety
Sovereign and People—loyalty
Husband and Wife—deference
Older and Younger Brother—obedience
Friends—faithfulness.

James Gale's assessment was that "Undoubtedly a strong steadying influence has been exercised on the state and on society by the observance of the *o-ryun* (five relations), so that courtiers have been loyal, children filial, wives faithful, age honored and friendships sacred. . . . There has been ceremony, gentleness, deference, kindness, appreciation of fun and humor, but for comparison and conclusion and action there was no room."[22]

Emphasis was laid upon decorum, rites and ceremony. Virtue was often equated with conformity. "The very center of Confucianism was its emphasis on propriety. Courtesy and morality are practically identical throughout the Orient," wrote a scholar on Korean thought. "The Chinese themselves regarded the Korean adherents as more virtuous than themselves, and referred to Korea as 'the country of Eastern decorum.' "[23] Great stress was put on form and "face," and any conduct causing loss of face was exceedingly painful. "Face" was as important to Koreans as "honor" was to Westerners of the period.

The underlying Confucian principle was authority, and as the Five Relationships indicated, authority began at home. The family was a pattern for all society, and the ideological pattern for the state. Because ancestor worship was the taproot of the family system, male children were highly desired and favored. The head of the family was considered a priest as well as a king and a judge. His functions and authority were inherited by his eldest son and could be transmitted only to a son.[24] The son's duty was to perpetuate the family line and to carry on worship of ancestors, which extended filial loyalty to the dead.

Nor was this the only duty of sons; the duties of a son were many and onerous, inculcated from early childhood. Whatever his age, when he left the house, he had to tell his parents where he was going and why. These farewells were long and involved, but if he were married, it was considered bad form to bid his wife goodbye, at least in the presence of others. When he returned, he was obliged to report to his parents on his activities. Each night he was supposed to prepare his parents' bedding and each morning to inquire solicitously about their health. In the presence of an elderly person, he was to walk in a dignified manner and to refrain from clearing his throat, coughing, or blowing his nose. Smoking and drinking in the presence of his elders were strictly prohibited.

When a parent died, a son was supposed to be in mourning for three years, doing no other work and refraining from all social activities. He was expected to wail for days and to go unwashed. The expenses of burying a parent properly were enormous, and the whole period of mourning was so strenuous that a husband was not permitted to divorce a wife who had gone through it with him.

It was considered a virtue for sons to weigh their words carefully before addressing their parents.

A wife was supposed to exercise discretion when talking with her husband; the first three years of marriage she was supposed to speak to him hardly at all. A Korean writer, Younghill Kang, wrote: "There are three ways of speaking in Korea, the first to an older and superior, the second to equals and chronological playmates, the third, to children and dogs. Brides are not supposed to speak disrespectfully even to dogs for the first few days."[25]

In fact, husbands and wives lived in near isolation from each other. In well-to-do homes, they could not sleep in the same room, and to see each other during the day was considered improper. Most men asked their parents' permission to sleep with their wives. "Because of the strict separation of the sexes, husband and wife had little opportunity to meet during the day, and the presence of elders made it impossible to talk. At most, twice a month a lucky date was chosen when the young couple, upon receiving the father-in-law's permission, was allowed to spend a night together."[26]

Until a wife bore a son, her position in the husband's lineage was insecure. Only after the birth of a male heir had the wife fulfilled her duty and acquired the privileges and authority of motherhood. Women were generally restricted to the kitchen, the back courtyard, and the inner rooms. Their family members were not encouraged to visit. Upper class women went out in closed chairs, veiled, in voluminous garments covering all but the eyes and a bit of nose. Women were kept strictly secluded because immoral behavior was presumed if men and women so much as met. The higher the social class, the stricter the seclusion; lower class women had considerably more freedom than their aristocratic sisters.

Women were not allowed to possess money or property of their own. They could not lend anything to others, even to their own parents, without their husbands' consent. A woman was expected to submit to three men in her life: her father, her husband and her son. This was called the "Honor of the Three Submissions."

There were seven commandments for married women:

1. Be obedient to your husband's family, especially his parents.
2. Bear sons.
3. Do not commit obscene acts.
4. Do not be jealous of your husband's concubine(s).
5. Do not contract malignant diseases such as epilepsy, venereal disease, etc.
6. Do not chatter or gossip.
7. Do not steal.

Violations of any of these were considered grounds for divorce, which brought great disgrace upon a woman and her family.[27]

In the West, the unit of society is considered to be the individual but in Korea, it was the group, and above all, the family group. All decisions were considered from the viewpoint of the good of the family. Family life overshadowed and virtually swamped individual life. The extended family was a method and agent of social control and conservatism.

Confucian principles in government included a civil service examination. Theoretically applicants for government office passed the exams on merit. The subject matter was based entirely on Confucian classics and commentaries, the writing of poetry and essays. Skill in calligraphy counted strongly in the competition. But by the 19th century *yangban* could secure official preferment through wealth, bribery and family influence.

The word *yangban* means "the two orders," the orders being civil and military offices, the elite of the Yi dynasty caste system. The *yangban* could be "demoted" only if they committed treason, engaged in industrial or commercial occupations or married a widow or a slave.[28] Since 10 per cent of the population were *yangban* by the late 1800s, there were many more men clamoring for office than there were positions. Thus offices were frequently sold and changed. Each official and his numerous hangers-on had to make their fortunes as quickly as possible, and almost the only source of income was from extortions of their constituency. Bribery, extortion by violence, false legal accusations, staggering illegal taxation were rampant.

Originally, governors and officials had been outstanding scholars. The fact that all the literati held office and all the office holders were intellectuals partially accounts for the long stability of the system and its strong conservative cast. In old Korea the intellectual elite *were* the state, under and yet at a comfortable distance from the fatherhood of the king. But this old order of things was breaking down with the corruption, venality and greed of the times. The representative of government was no longer the virtuous scholar, but was instead the grasping extortionist.

In the 1880s the structure of centuries was collapsing. The outside world was crowding in on Korea. Foreigners were at the doors. A significant element in the confrontation between East and West was their ignorance of each other. George Washington understood that the Chinese were "droll in shape and appearance," but was taken aback in 1785 to learn they were not white. For their part, the Chinese and Koreans considered Americans to be a newer and therefore even more insignificant breed of Europeans—barbarians, intrusive, hairy and malodorous.[29] Foreigners were called *yangui* (Western devils) in Korean.[30]

In 1889, James Gale met the governor of Hwanghae province and in the course of conversation learned that the dignitary did not know the names "America" or "England" but thought the Western world was all one country, Westernland. His world was still flat and in the middle of it all was China, the Great Country, with Japan, Contemptible Dwarf Land, edged off to one side. If you went far enough there were falling off places into nowhere.[31]

Nor did many Westerners know where Korea was. Malcolm Fenwick, a Canadian Baptist who spent most of his life in Korea, told of his boyhood pastor praying for a missionary: "You know, Lord, Corea is an island in the Pacific Ocean." This startled the young Fenwick who thought it was an island in the Mediterranean![32]

Sin Ki-Son, the minister of education in 1896, wrote a kind of last hurrah of the reactionaries which was published as a text-book. Among the passages that shocked foreigners in Korea at the time was his opinion that "Europe and America are far removed from the center of civilization. It would not be too far from the truth to think of Europeans and Americans as more like animals than human beings. Their languages resemble the chirping of birds rather than human languages, so that one finds it hard to understand them. Their religion, called Christianity, is a paganism so full of vulgarities, fallacies and superstitions that it is not worth our attention."

Malcolm Fenwick drew some interesting conclusions in contrasting the minds and values of East and West: "It is a fact that apart from Christ the civilization of China and Korea has done more, very much more, for the peace and happiness of the race as a whole, than the civilization of the West. . . . Race antipathy, which is in us all, I think, is most deeply seated in the Easterner. . . . While treating you with every mark of courtesy, and even smiling, perhaps bowing too, his inner attitude is one of disgust, despising, of loathing the white man. He says to himself, 'The white man is rude; he is arrogant; he does not know how to efface himself; he smells.' And in comparison with the Oriental, it is all true."[33]

But the time had come for the confrontation of East and West in Korea. This meeting of minds would mold not only the history of the Christian missions and church and the modernization of Korea, but would also play an important part in the shaping of the 20th century.

To Start a Work

The 19th century in the West was vastly different from the bad time that Korea experienced. The West was as bustling as Korea was stultified, as confident as Korea was perplexed. While Korea, bankrupt in workable ideas, was clinging to the glories of its past, the West was bounding, with more enthusiasm than knowledge, into its future. And among the countries of the West, none was so energetic as young America.

To America, the 19th century was a time of national adolescence, of idealism and expansion. After 1865, with the freeing of the slaves and the salvation of the Union, America was looking for more people to save, more people to free. The spirit of the age was a missionary spirit.

The United States enjoyed a Manifest Destiny and knew Providence had decreed her development. The American church was itself a product of missions. Its transition from receiving missionaries to sending them began on a summer day in 1806, when a band of pious students at Williams College caught in a thunderstorm huddled under a haystack to keep dry, and held a prayer meeting. By the time the downpour had ceased they had vowed to carry the Christian message overseas. From its unlikely beginning at what became known as the Haystack Prayer Meeting, the U.S. Protestant missionary movement was youthful and intense. But young people alone weren't involved. Women's organizations were founded primarily for the promotion and support of foreign missions. The chief purpose of church publications was to keep their readers abreast of news from distant mission fields.

Church people believed that faith must be incarnated. Missionaries, it was understood, went out as "ideas with their skins on." Those ideas, almost universally held by members of mainline denominations, were called the Gospel.

Protestant missions were already thriving in China and in Japan, and the first calls to start a work in Korea came from missionaries in these countries after the American-Korean treaty was signed in 1882. The Rev. George W. Knox, a Presbyterian missionary in Japan, wrote his board in 1883 urging: "Is no one ready for this opening in Corea? A missionary school, started at once would have every promise of the highest success . . . . The missionary should be on the ground by April next. Cannot our church send three men, two clergymen and a physician, to open this field? If our church cannot, will not some other church obey the call?" This letter was printed in the January 1884 *Foreign Missionary*, indicating the mission board was willing to pass the challenge on to potential contributors.

From China, the Rev. Gilbert Reid wrote in 1884: "I am still enthusiastically interested in the immediate occupation of Corea. I base my opinion on intelligence received from the Japanese side, the China side, the Manchurian side, and from Corea itself . . . men are needed to labor not as missionaries as much as in the capacity of a teacher and a physician . . . . I urge the sending of two such men this autumn. Foreigners are already pressing into the capital and ports, and some, with their disreputable lives, would do immense harm to our western civilization, unless at once counteracted by the pure, benevolent, intelligent activity of Christianity." Reid seemed to view missionary activity partially at least as an antidote to the corrupting influence of Western ideas and activities on the culture and people of the East.

A petition to "the churches in America" to begin mission work in Korea appeared in the March 1884 *Missionary Review of the World,* written by a Korean who had been converted to Christianity in Japan, called Rijutei by the Japanese. This intriguing gentleman was Yi Su-Jong, an early progressive. He was influenced by a Christian named Tsuda and was baptized in April, 1883. To the missionaries, as Henry Loomis of the American Bible Society wrote, Rijutei seemed "almost too good to be true."[34]

About 40 years old, Yi Su-Jong was a *yangban,* an accomplished Chinese scholar, gifted poet, calligrapher and artist, who was one of the court officials who prepared the Chinese-Korean test papers for the national state examinations. He spoke Japanese fluently enough to preach in it shortly after his baptism.

He also preached to other Koreans residing in Japan and took them to Christian services. During this period the Korean reformers were in favor of the introduction of Christianity to Korea, as an "uplifting" or "civilizing" influence. They considered Christianity progressive. Their mentor Fukuzawa Yukichi had taken a pragmatic view of religion, once recommending that Japan adopt Christianity as a state religion in order to get out from under her unequal treaty status vis-a-vis the Western nations.

Although Rijutei himself first became interested in Christianity while in Japan, 18 years earlier one of his relatives and closest friends had been executed in the Catholic persecutions. The unfortunate man had been suspended by ropes from a cross, had had his arms and legs cut off and, after a period of great suffering, had been beheaded. The Korean nobleman fully expected to be killed if he returned as a Christian to Korea. In 1883 he told the missionaries that "no Corean can become a Christian except at the risk of his life." For whatever reason, when he did return to Korea in May 1886 he was put to death by the reactionary government.[35]

It was through studying Scripture, especially the Sermon on the Mount, that Rijutei had become a believer. His great desire was to participate in the preparation of the Bible for his people. During the time he was studying the Bible in Chinese, he had had a dream so compelling that he was convinced it was a revelation from heaven. In Yi's dream, two men, one tall and the other short, came to him with a basket of books. He asked them what the books were, and they replied, "These books are the most important of all books for your country." When he asked what book it was, he was told, "It is the Bible."[36]

So when he was approached by the American Bible Society with a proposal to prepare a "Chino-Corean" translation, Rijutei gladly agreed and began at once, starting with Matthew and Mark. Those Gospels and Acts were published in Yokohama in 1884 in Chinese with Korean endings indicated by certain Chinese characters printed at the side. The following year, the Gospel of Mark in mixed Chinese and Korean characters was issued.

Thus it was that when the first two American Protestant minister-missionaries to Korea, Horace G. Underwood and Henry G. Appenzeller, the one short, the other tall, arrived in Japan enroute to their new field in 1885, the work of translating the Scriptures into Korean had already begun.

The significance of Rijutei's work lies not in its accuracy or its adequacy. No part of these early translations was incorporated into the later Korean translations. Rijutei knew no Hebrew or Greek and his biblical background was sketchy at best. But to have such whole-hearted participation in Bible translation by a Korean, "indigenized" Scripture from the beginning, was a promise of great things to come in the relationship of the Korean believers to the Bible.

The urgent appeals of missionaries from Japan and China and from the baptized Rijutei could not long go unheeded. It was inevitable in the Christian tenor of the time that there would be a response to their challenge. Although the senior secretary of the Presbyterian Foreign Missions Board advised delay, a young board secretary, F.F. Ellinwood, favored immediate occupancy. It was Ellinwood who convinced David W. McWilliams of Brooklyn to contribute a gift of $6,000 to start missionary work in Korea. A young physician "of excellent training and devoted spirit" Dr. John W. Heron, from Tennessee, was appointed the first Presbyterian missionary to Korea although he did not arrive on the field until June 1885, after Horace Allen and Horace G. Underwood.[37]

The Methodists responded even earlier. President John F. Goucher, president of Goucher College in Baltimore, happened to be traveling on the same eastbound train in September 1883 as the first Korean Embassy to the United States which was heading for New York and Washington. Thus he had met Min Yong-Ik, Hong Yong-Sik, So Kwang-Bom and the others and had struck up an acquaintance with them. Impressed by the Koreans and fascinated by what he learned from them of Korea and its possibilities as a mission field, he wrote the Board of Foreign Missions of the Methodist Episcopal Church offering $2,000 if they deemed it expedient to extend their work to Korea. Then as now mission boards were not quick to commit themselves to new work. Nothing happened. Goucher had more success in approaching the Rev. Robert S. Maclay, superintendent of the Methodist mission in Japan, in a letter dated January 31, 1884, suggesting he "make a trip to Korea, prospect the land, and locate the mission."[38]

Maclay and his wife were receptive to the idea and made the visit the following June. He had met Kim Ok-Kyun in Japan and through him was able to bring a letter written in Japanese to submit to King Kojong, requesting permission to open a school and to begin medical work in Korea. This petition was presented on the last day of June, and on July 3 Kim Ok-Kyun assured Maclay that the king was favorably disposed for Maclay's "society" to "commence hospital and school work in Korea," and that the Methodists could "proceed at once to initiate the work."[39]

Maclay was able to recommend to his mission board that they "begin education and medical work, using no disguise as to the ultimate object being evangelization." He assured the board that fears of opposition by the Korean government were unfounded, that "schools would be welcome, and hospitals are a necessity."[40]

The Maclays had stayed—and overstayed their welcome—with American Minister Lucius Foote on this visit. Since they had received no official permission to rent or purchase property, they asked Foote to buy land for the Methodist mission near the legation. This Foote agreed to do.

Over the months, appeals continued to appear in the Methodist church press and Dr. Goucher's gift had been supplemented. During 1883 no fewer than 15 articles on Korea appeared in the *Christian Advocate* and the many resulting donations ranged from two gifts of $1,000 to $9 from a nine-year-old girl in California. C.H. Fowler, then corresponding secretary of the Methodist Mission Society, pressed upon the mission authorities the desirability of the project, and the General Missionary Committee formally decided to begin the work;[41] finally, in December 1884, $5,000 was added to the Japan Mission appropriation to start a mission in Korea.

The first Methodist appointee to Korea, like the first Presbyterian, was a physician, Dr. William B. Scranton. Accompanying him, his wife and infant daughter to Korea was his 52-year-old mother, Mary F. Scranton. A woman of ability and grit, Mrs. Scranton had been general secretary of the Methodist Women's Foreign Missionary Society and was appointed by that group as its first missionary to Korea. She served 25 full years as a missionary until her death in 1910. She began Ewha School on May 31, 1886, with "Mrs." Kim, her first student, the concubine of an official who hoped she could become interpreter to the queen.

The Koreans respectfully called Mrs. Scranton "The Old Lady," and some referred to her as the Princess Scranton, thinking she was a daughter of the Royal House of America.[42] She had great dignity, yet could work hard and relate to people from all walks of life. She is credited with having astonishing energy, great executive ability and steadfast, earnest faith. In 1886, Presbyterian Dr. John Heron wrote his board that "Mrs. Scranton is a tower of strength to her own mission and no small help to us."

Her practical streak proved useful. Since the sexes were strictly segregated from the age of seven, it was Mrs. Scranton's idea to hang a curtain in the churches with men on one side, women on the other, so that the women could attend services. She was keen on cleanliness, and this carried over into all her work. A sense of her personality as well as her priorities comes through in an article she wrote for *The Heathen Women's Friend* for July 1887:

"When the invitation was sent it had a strange addendum. The guests were told they must come in *clean clothes*! These women met all the requirements yesterday. Their light blue and white and green dresses were as spotless as I could ask.

"If you imagine that the seven invited guests alone came, you are not thoroughly acquainted with Korean 'tricks and manners.' Every mother told her mother, if she had one. If there was no relative of this sort, she managed to find a sister or a sister-in-law, or some one a little further removed, to bring; and I found, when my guests were all assembled, that 20 had been added to the list invited. I did not care, however, for I felt as if I got just that nearer the heart of Korea."[43]

Dr. Scranton's wife was destined to be "the other Mrs. Scranton" all the days of her life in Korea, overshadowed by her dynamic mother-in-law. She once described how she had come to Korea:

"Some one, I think Dr. Maclay, came to see Mrs. Scranton in Cleveland, probably in 1884. Meeting me in the hall he asked if I felt like going to Korea as a missionary. I stared at him in amazement. I had no knowledge of foreign missions, all my small activities having been concerned with home missions, Red Indians and those working for them. So I replied, 'Good gracious! Of course not.'

" 'Then,' he said, 'You had better not go.'

" 'But I have never thought of going.'

"Nothing more was said and I thought no more of it. In early summer Dr. Scranton had a very bad attack of typhoid fever, and as our baby was seriously ill at the same time, I saw nothing of my husband, who was nursed by his mother. After he recovered, we were driving out, and he said he had something to tell me that might prove a shock and told me he had offered himself as a missionary to go anywhere except Central Africa. After a moment I said, 'Wither thou goest, I will go' and after a pause, 'and there will I be buried.' "[44]

William B. Scranton was 28 at the time of his missionary appointment. He liked ritual and felt the Koreans did too. Thus he believed missionaries should have ritualistic services in the highest Methodist forms. Methodism meant a great deal to him and he was more denominationally minded than most of the other missionaries; it was over the issue of union work with Presbyterians that he would terminate his missionary career. In points of dress, he was said to be "the only one among the Methodists who would be recognized as a clergyman."[45]

The Scrantons' cook and later evangelistic helper went on to become one of the most popular preachers in Seoul and one of the most compelling personalities in the Korean Methodist Church. But no one had known what kind of missionary Scranton would make when Bishop Fowler, oblivious of events taking place in Korea, ordained the young doctor "to deacon's and elder's orders for the purpose of missionary propaganda," on Dec. 4, 1884.

"Undy" and "Appen"

Although Drs. John Heron and William B. Scranton were the first appointees respectively of the Presbyterian and Methodist mission boards, and Dr. Horace N. Allen was the first Protestant missionary actually to reside in Korea, the pioneer missionaries most often cited are Horace G. Underwood and Henry G. Appenzeller, who arrived together on Easter Sunday, April 5, 1885.

These two ordained ministers were zealous and evangelical; they stayed a lifetime, and each gave his life for the cause. They were also both followed by their children. The force of their personalities influenced almost every aspect of mission work in Korea, and continues to do so today. No one could be a more "compleate missionary" than Underwood and Appenzeller, who called each other "Undy" and "Appen."

Yet each of these superb missionaries had trouble in getting appointed and had planned to go to another field.

Horace Grant Underwood was born in London, July 19, 1859, the fourth of six children of John and Elisabeth Underwood. Religious interdenominationalism and energy seem to have run in the family. A great-grandfather, Alexander Waugh of Scotland, in the 1790s founded a union committee of Episcopalians, Presbyterians, Baptists, Independents and Methodists to start a religious periodical, and later a mission society. Underwood's father John, a devout Christian, was a manufacturing chemist who invented safety check paper on which writing could not be altered, an ink which would make 75 copies, and the first copiable ink. He also pioneered in typewriter design and improved on typewriter ribbons.

When Horace was only six, his mother died with her last baby. At 10, he was sent with his older brother Fred to a Catholic boarding school in France for two years. His biographer and wife, Lillias Horton Underwood, shunned Romanism, but described Horace's boarding school as "a Roman Catholic school carried on by a Professor Die, who the boys found to be good, wise and kind . . . . No attempt at proselyting was made; the boys attended their own English church and kept their Protestant faith unshaken, but learned, too, a certain tolerance and good feelings toward Christians of that other church."[46]

The Underwood boys, though lively, were unusually pious. The first night at boarding school they knelt beside their beds and said their prayers as always, undeterred by the pillows, shoes and other missiles derisive dormitory mates showered upon them. This they continued to do until, one by one, all the boys in the dorm followed their example. In their late teens, the boys habitually made the round of the town saloons to distribute religious tracts.

Horace was 12 when he joined his family who had emigrated to New Durham, New Jersey. He was sent to Hasbrooke Seminary and later tutored in Greek and other subjects by a scholarly local minister. He entered New York University in 1877, walking seven miles to classes each day. He graduated in 1881, and entered the Dutch Reformed Theological Seminary. During these years, he slept five hours and worked 19, attending and leading seven or eight different religious services each Sunday. He was active in the Salvation Army. He admired their engagement in the world so much that his family feared he would join. In later years, in passing a little Salvation Army group at a street corner, he would join in the singing and prayers with zest.[47]

Underwood had decided to become a missionary at the tender age of four, after hearing a stirring address by a man from India. To go to India was his settled decision when be began studying for the ministry, and he had already spent a year in medical study to prepare. Naturally he joined the Student Volunteer Movement for prospective missionaries.

During his second year in seminary, the American-Korean treaty was signed and a classmate presented a paper on the Hermit Kingdom. Underwood wrote, "the thought of a year or more having passed without a move on the part of the church so stirred me that I determined to set to work and find someone to go . . . yet, do what I would, urge as I might, and still no one had offered, no church seemed ready to enter . . . then the message came home to me, 'Why not go yourself?' "

There were many discouragements. "Twice I applied to the Dutch Reformed Church but lack of funds compelled them to decline. Twice I applied to the Presbyterian Board, only to be told it was useless."

Horace reluctantly accepted a call as pastor of a church in New York and was about to drop his letter of acceptance in the mail box when he seemed to hear a voice saying, "No one for Korea. How about Korea?" He wrote, "I drew back the letter in my hand, determined to make another effort Koreaward and turned my face once again toward 23 Center Street, the old Presbyterian Board rooms. This time the secretary that I had previously seen was out and I saw a new face, F.F. Ellinwood, who assured me of his interest. In a few days I was notified that I should be appointed."[48] He was appointed on July 28, 1884, just six days after the board's cable authorizing Horace Allen to move from China to Korea.

His decision was not without cost. His fiancee flatly refused to go to Korea and their engagement was broken. The 25-year-old Horace started off with his luggage, a typewriter, and a large camera. His oldest brother, John T., who built up the Underwood typewriter company and financially underwrote much of the Presbyterian work in Korea, accompanied him as far as Chicago. The brothers always considered themselves to be in partnership in the Gospel.

Horace sailed from San Francisco on December 16, arriving in Yokohama about a month later where he stayed with the J.C. Hepburns, longtime missionaries to Japan. Unable to get a steamer to Korea until late March, he held evangelistic services for sailors, began studying Korean with Rijutei and some of the refugee Koreans, teaching them English in return.

He met General and Mrs. Lucius Foote, who were on their way home. Foote assured Underwood that it would be perfectly safe to go to Korea now and that the way for mission work was open.

Henry Loomis of the American Bible Society wrote the Presbyterian Board in January, "I am rejoiced to see Rev. Mr. Underwood here, and he seems to be the right man for the field, but he should have brought a wife." Horace Allen agreed; he wrote Underwood that if by waiting in Japan he could "go into the country married it would be best to wait."[49]

During the next two years a number of people urged matrimony on Horace, partially because they thought a wife would have a steadying influence on the impulsive, enthusiastic young minister, and partly because they were aware that Koreans married early and looked with suspicion on single adults. In fact, an unmarried man or woman of whatever age in Korea was called "a big child." Celibacy was considered unnatural.

Henry Appenzeller did bring a wife, but it didn't help him enter Korea any faster. But that is getting ahead of our story.

Born on February 6, 1858, Appenzeller came from a Pennsylvania German-Swiss farming family. He was a member of the Reformed Church, where he was converted at the age of 18, and he annually celebrated the date as his spiritual birthday. Three years later he changed his membership from the Reformed to the Methodist Church, remarking in his journal, "Since my conversion I have been among the Methodists most of the time and feel more at home than I did in the Reformed Church."[50]

Licensed to preach while a student at Franklin and Marshall College, Appenzeller was a good-humored, enthusiastic orator who enjoyed using colorful phrases. After his graduation in 1882, he entered Drew Theological Seminary. In his last year there he preached at Green Village, regarded as the best appointment open to Drew students. Both Appenzeller and Underwood were delegates to the Inter-Seminary Alliance in Hartford, Conn. in 1883. One of the aims of the Alliance was the "stimulation of a livelier missionary spirit among the students."

Henry's Drew roommate, Julian S. Wadsworth, a lifetime friend and correspondent, wanted to go to Korea as a missionary, and Appenzeller applied to the Methodist board for appointment to Japan. A September 1884 letter from board secretary J.M. Reid is the first clue that Appenzeller might be asked to go instead to Korea: "I am very glad to receive the assurance that you are still faithful to the call to Japan. As you observe, the Japan field will in the spring be extended to Corea."[51]

The next month, Reid wrote again. Another minister had decided against going to Korea, and Reid broached the subject of Appenzeller's changing fields: "Now the question is upon whom the honor and responsibility of founding that mission must rest. Dr. William B. Scranton will go out this winter to Japan, and stay there long enough to learn something of missionary work and something of the Korean language. Then he will go to Korea. We need a preacher also. Somehow or other my heart has turned toward you for this great work. I am almost overburdened with anxiety to do the right thing. I want you to think about this work and pray about it, and write to the lady (his fiancee, Ella Dodge) about it; and in a very few days I may be in Madison or have you come here for an earnest and anxious session on this subject . . . . Dr. Scranton, our medical man for this work has a wife and little child, and a devoted and enterprising widowed mother. They will all go, so you will have a little circle there to begin with. At first there will be much temporal business. Your beginning will be largely on the line of teaching and medical work. If I could only feel that God will help you to be adequate to all these exigencies, I would not hesitate a moment."

Henry Appenzeller agreed to go to Korea, although he was disappointed that he would not be going with Wadsworth, who was unable to go for health reasons. But there was a long delay in his appointment, apparently because President Goucher, who had contributed much of the money for opening the Korea mission, felt its founder should be mature and experienced. Goucher, who had been impressed by the dignity and poise of the Korean members of the first Embassy to the U.S., may have found the earnest, enthusiastic Appenzeller a bit callow in comparison.

Finally, on December 20, Reid wrote: "Bishop Fowler has just come in and announced to me that he and Brother Goucher have decided to appoint you missionary to Korea. I will be glad to have you report for duty at any time . . . . I suppose you have noticed the changes reported in Korea—the report of the king being driven from the country. I fear the anti-foreign party is in the ascendant. But it was only a brief newspaper dispatch which may be contradicted next week."

These were busy days for Appenzeller. The letter of his appointment was written just a few days after his marriage. He completed the three-year course a semester early and took his final examinations in January, graduating *in absentia*.

Unlike Underwood, Appenzeller did not have the support of his family. His father bluntly declared that he was "throwing himself away." His mother was upset by recurring dreams and visions that he would drown in Korea (which he did, in 1902, four years after her death).[52]

"Physically he was one of the stalwarts," said a classmate. James Gale said he was "gifted with a superabundance of life that constantly overflowed . . . . His hair grew gray, for however much the ringing laugh sounded out . . . . no one gave more heart and soul to this all-important work."[53]

The truth of this can be traced on Appenzeller's records at the Methodist Board. On his arrival in Korea in 1885, he was 5'11½" tall, weighed 200 lbs., was "rugged and muscular," with brown hair and gray eyes. At the time of his first furlough in 1892, he was 31 years old and weighed 140 lbs. In 1900, at the time of his second and final furlough, he was 42 years old, weighed 131 lbs., was gray and bent, and his best friends did not recognize him.[54]

On January 15, 1885, Reid wrote a nine-page letter of advice and instructions for opening a new mission work in an uncertain situation. He directed the Appenzellers to proceed to Tokyo and report to R.S. Maclay. "You will be expected to remain some little time in Japan, unless in the judgment of Dr. Maclay you ought to proceed at once to Korea . . . .It would hardly seem to me to be wise to enter the Kingdom until the American minister shall have found it possible himself to return . . .

"Very large discretion must necessarily be given you at this early period in the history of the Korean mission . . . . You are sent with the understanding that the country is not formally opened to Christianity; but we have had every assurance that medical work and teaching would be highly acceptable to the Koreans. Therefore this will doubtless be your first work. By the time suitable buildings have been purchased, I hope you will have gained sufficient knowledge of the language to be able to superintend the school and students will be found for instruction . . . I do not know how God will open the work before you." Reid wrote that Appenzeller would be responsible for purchase of real estate, saying blithely, "the American minister can assist."

He told the Appenzellers to read carefully the *Discipline* on missionaries, also the charter, constitution and by-laws "and you will govern yourself by the laws laid down, and be subject in all things to the proper authorities of the church. Send us a report once a quarter, and for the first year or so, I trust you will write us by every mail, giving as much detail as possible. We will also be glad if you will write sometimes for the press in this country."

On February 2, 1885, Appenzeller was ordained by Bishop Fowler in San Francisco and the following day he and his bride sailed with the Scrantons for Korea and had a very stormy passage.

CHAPTER II
The Honeymoon

First Impressions

Henry Appenzeller's biographer, in the rhetoric once used for missionaries, wrote of his arrival in Korea, "The coming of a live, typical American Christian in 1885 into the mysterious hermit kingdom was like an invincible stream of light."[1] One day it might seem that way, but Appenzeller felt nothing if not vincible. He wrote Maclay that he was puzzled by "the dangers of crippling the work by endeavoring to start it!"

William Scranton described the uncertain beginnings. "We were all greeted with 'go slow,' 'be cautious,' 'no rights,' and like expressions . . . We therefore went to work cautiously but without apology and in the spirit in which every late comer has been minded on his arrival . . . '*now* something is going to be done.' "[2]

Mary Scranton added, "We were not expected to make manifest in any way the designs we had in coming to the country . . . . What then? An effort to win hearts and acquire the language. But if we came too close, there'd be a rapid closing of doors and speedy retreat behind screens . . . . As for language learning, there were no books, no teachers worthy of the name, and no interpreters whose knowledge went further than the simplest forms of speech.

"Whether we won the people's hearts or no, it is certain that they won ours, and the desire grew more intense to be a blessing to them."[3]

The Appenzellers lived their first month in Korea in a packing-box shanty in Chemulpo, awaiting accommodations in Seoul. The Scrantons were with the Allens, a difficult situation since the two doctors had already fallen out over the hospital. It must have been a relief to all concerned when the Methodists were able to buy their own land and move. Their first residences were far from grand, however.

Mary Scranton wrote, "There was no window glass anywhere to let in brightness and sunshine until one happy day Mr. George C. Foulk, our charge d'affaires, made me a present of three photograph plates. These I thankfully, if not proudly, inserted in the window near my desk and rejoiced at being able to see at least with one eye at a time the light of heaven again.

"I suppose missionaries ought to be so far above the earth as never to think of 'what shall we eat' . . . . in this the first representatives to Korea signally failed. The meal in the barrel turned sour . . . . Beef was forbidden, on account of disease among the cattle; of potatoes and other vegetables there were none. We ate chickens and eggs, quite different from their American counterparts . . . Yet a day was never so dark, but that at its close we could honestly say, 'We are glad to be in Korea.' "[4]

The foreign residents had similarly unfavorable impressions of Pusan (then called Fusan), Chemulpo and Seoul. Appenzeller, straining to get a first glimpse of Korea while sitting on deck in the Fusan harbor, found the mud walls and thatched roofs of the homes blended into the earth so thoroughly that he could hardly see the village at all. He wrote, "the houses seem more like large beehives than anything else."[5]

First impressions are strong. Rosetta Sherwood, coming to Korea as a young doctor five years later, recorded hers in a letter home written scroll fashion on 34 yards of six-inch wide Korean rice paper: "Today, October 10, 1890, we come in sight of the coast of Korea. As we draw nearer, I look with considerable interest at this country which promises to be my home for some time to come. I can't say it looks very inviting, though I am bound to make the best of it."[6]

Seoul was not much more imposing. Allen, looking down on it from a hill, thought it resembled a collection of hay stacks that had wintered out.[7] Interspersed among the thatched roofs of the poor he could see the tiled roofs of the gentry, surrounded by small patches of green trees and grass.

Lillias Underwood described narrow, filthy streets, flanked by low mud houses with roofs of thatch or tile. She thought Seoul looked somewhat like a vast bed of mushrooms.

The walls of the city, built of great ivy-covered blocks of stone, and its huge gates were impressive, however. When the curfew bell, with its "extremely sweet and solemn, low and yet penetrating tones,"[8] tolled, the ponderous gates to the city were swung to and barred for the night. "The first impressions we had of Seoul were of the bell in the center of the city which used to ring and the legations were shut down for the night. Then we raised our eyes to Nam San (South Mountain) and saw the fires burning there assuring us that all was at peace in the rest of Korea. When the bell was rung and the gates shut, the men stayed at home and the women came out and called on their friends. It was impolite for men to be out on the streets at night . . . but we foreigners allowed ourselves to go out as exceptions to the rule. We would walk down the Main Street . . . and see only the lights showing through the cracks in the boards in front of the stores and perhaps a little boy carrying a one-candlepower lantern in front of some old lady."[9]

More than the adjustments to and impressions of their physical surroundings, the new missionaries were painfully aware of their helplessness in not knowing the language. Well educated, articulate, opinionated adults, they suddenly found themselves speechless. The greatest culture shock was to discover they were illiterate. To be ignorant and mute is difficult for anyone, but these people had come to preach the Gospel; they were "ideas with the skins on," and how could they express the first idea, the purpose of their being in Korea, without a language? The first major task for all was to tackle Korean. A few, such as Horace Allen, were indifferent students; others, such as Horace Underwood, were gifted and enthusiastic. Most simply struggled through.

Appenzeller studied with a tutor five hours a day. He sandwiched his study into a daily schedule that began at 5:30 a.m. and continued until 7 p.m. and began again after supper, meanwhile supervising all the building and business of his mission. There were no language institutes, no textbooks nor English-Korean dictionaries, only a French-Korean dictionary prepared earlier by the Roman Catholic priests. "I am getting quite a knowledge of the French," admitted Appenzeller ruefully.[10]

John Heron began studying the language within a week of his arrival. In his first letter to the board, he wrote, "I cannot forget that my mission is to tell of the Great Physician, not simply to exercise my own skill. I long to tell these people of the dear Savior who died for them."

The struggle with the language did something to the missionaries. It defeated a few; it equipped many. Although it may not have added much to their self-confidence, it undeniably contributed to their humility. It knocked off a lot of arrogance. Language study took long hours, and eventually long years, of sacrifice and self-discipline. Annie Baird conscientiously studied Korean all her life. She warned against the temptation of becoming lazy in continuing language study: "It is a pity to be satisfied with mediocrity of effort and nowhere so much as on the mission field. To keep learning Korean it will be necessary to relinquish the delights of omnivorous reading in English."[11] She advised new missionaries to "Avoid the mistake of thinking that you can gratify all your literary and social tastes and learn Korean too . . . you will never talk Korean as the Koreans do without some sacrifice . . . . Drudge faithfully through the first three years, and at the end of that time, the promised land, though yet far distant, will be in view."[12]

Not only did language study strengthen the characters of the missionaries, it underscored, for some at least, the necessity of having to live their message, as well as to convey it verbally. It gave them great opportunities to practice patience. And it brought them into proximity with Koreans, language teachers, who in many cases became their first converts, their closest friends, and some of the earliest church leaders. Through their efforts to learn the language, the missionaries learned much more, absorbing many of the thought patterns and ideas of the Korean people.

The missionaries' desire and attempt to learn the language accomplished something for Korea as well. Allen in his first letter to Ellinwood in 1884 wrote, "The better classes all understand the Chinese characters and read them readily . . . . As the Corean written language is not much thought of, a good knowledge of the Chinese character will be most essential to an educational work." The board secretary probably did not grasp the full implication of that observation. The fact was that a knowledge of Chinese was not only the core but also the goal of education in Korea; not only the means, but the end. In Korea, as in China, as John Fairbank has said, "The Chinese language had the character of an institution, rather than a tool, of society. The Chinese written language, rather than an open door through which China's peasantry could find truth and light, was a heavy barrier pressing against any upward advance and requiring real effort to overcome—a hindrance, not a help, in learning."[13]

There were significant social and cultural by-products of the traditional Chinese-Korean educational system as well. The universal method of memorizing before understanding was a natural matrix for authoritarian thinking. The resulting separation of the hands and the brain was probably one factor responsible for the retardation of technology. But the main drawback of the system was that it closed the learning process to the majority of the people; this was as true of the missionaries as of the Korean common folk. Foreign adults, with a few rare exceptions like James Gale, could not in their lifetimes hope to master the intricacies of Chinese.

The missionaries were not only forced, but thrilled, to find an excellent linguistic tool in the native Korean alphabet, *hangul*. An easily learned, phonetic alphabet, *hangul* was developed for the people in 1446 A.D. after three years' work by the sages of King Sejong's court. Unfortunately, it was spurned by scholars who had already invested their lives in the joys and challenges of the Chinese character. They did not want an alphabet "that any woman could learn."

Other obstacles to the use of *hangul*, which at that time was ignominiously called *unmun* or "vulgar script," included political conservatism. Language reform was opposed on the grounds cited by a Chinese scholar, who said an easily learned alphabet could unleash the patriotic zeal of the masses and enable hundreds of millions of Chinese to write letters and to send telegrams to Chinese officials, demanding things.

It was one of those unintended consequences of history that the missionaries in their search for a key to simplify communication in Korean, unearthed and seized upon a hidden treasure, *unmun*. The rediscovery and increasing use of the Korean alphabet was revolutionary, opening the doors of literacy not merely to missionaries but to women and to the entire citizenry of Korea. *Hangul* ultimately became not only a key to communication and education, but to Korean hearts; to the missionary, it turned out to be one key to the kingdom.

Besides becoming acquainted with a new country, culture and language, the missionaries had first impressions of their coworkers. The warmhearted, unsophisticated Appenzellers were teamed with the more reserved Scrantons and seemed to work harmoniously, if not with the personal compatibility that Appenzeller and Underwood shared. The tensions between Scranton and Allen were largely relieved when Scranton began his own work. Allen showed a grudging respect tinged with genuine liking for Underwood, except intermittently when the latter did or said something with which the doctor didn't agree.

Allen's first impressions of the Herons were favorable. He wrote in his diary, "This afternoon Dr. Heron and his wife came to us . . . . We like them very much. They are Southern people, very polite and pleasant." To Ellinwood he wrote, "We are very much pleased with our new friends . . . . They seem grateful that it so happened that I . . . had a place open for them and do not seem to blame me for having been first."[14]

Heron probably never foresaw the coming friction with Allen. But Allen's domineering, jealous attitudes and Heron's sensitive, sometimes hot-headed, temperament spelled trouble. These troubles—of personality conflicts, of less than perfect charity—are illustrative of another of the chief adjustments the new missionaries and those who followed them had to make. Not only did they have to contend with strange surroundings, customs, culture, language and other missionaries, they also had to confront their own sinfulness, inadequacies and failings. To face themselves may have been the most difficult adjustment of all.

Lillias Underwood wrote of her disappointment in discovering that neither she nor other missionaries were perfect: "Missionaries are like other real Christians, no better, no worse . . . . There are the usual shortcomings: Some of us are domineering and seem to want to run things; some are quick-tempered; some are selfish; some are narrow and bigoted."[15] In a letter home she described her surprise that becoming a missionary had not automatically cured her faults. She had always had such an exalted opinion of missionaries, she said, that she had felt they were far removed from the failings and spiritual feebleness of other people, and without reasoning it out, she must have thought that in setting foot on Asian soil she would find she had left all her defects behind.[16]

More than anything, the missionaries wanted to do good and to be good. Their daily small failings, and occasional spectacular ones, discouraged them. Like the language, the accomplishment of goodness came more readily to some than to others, but was a continuing struggle for all. It was as sinners, not as saints, that the missionaries made their contributions to Korea. That fact, after all, was at the core of their message, theologically and practically. It was part of the meaning of being "an idea with the skin on." The idea must be transmitted through a flawed instrument, less than perfect personalities and physiques, through sometimes fumbling lips and lives.

Strife

Annie Ellers, sent out as physician to Queen Min, wrote Presbyterian board secretary Ellinwood shortly after her arrival in Seoul, "My short stop in Japan opened my eyes with regard to missionaries. We're not all angels!"[17] After a few months in Korea, she was ready to believe missionaries, far from being angelic, were demonic. Nowhere is the fallible—or, from a theological viewpoint, depraved—nature of man more evident than in the squabbling that rent and almost destroyed the Presbyterian mission in 1886 and 1887.

This most bitter of all missionary disagreements on the Korean field is an unpleasant story. Disheartening as it is, however, the Allen-Heron conflict is important to Korean mission history for several reasons, one being that it almost ended it. When every Presbyterian missionary on the field resigned in 1886, the work of the Presbyterians which was to become the predominant Protestant denomination in Korea came dangerously close to dying at birth.

The results of the feud indicate that missionary personalities and relationships are important in the conduct of the work. The altercation also pointed out the crucial role sometimes played by board secretaries. The secretaries served for many years as a kind of umbilical cord of the missionaries to their home church. Their decisions and letters affected conditions on the field for better or for worse.

The Allen-Heron conflict revealed the different schools of thought on how to conduct missionary work that were there from the beginning. These opinions influenced mission policy for years to come. Without being fully conscious of it, the Presbyterian missionaries in their heated actions and reactions of 1886 and 1887 were debating missionary policy. Some of the resulting institutions, embryos of great schools and hospitals still in existence, were not so much thought out, as fought out.

By saving the life of Prince Min Yong-Ik in the abortive coup of 1884, Horace Allen early established himself under the aegis of the Korean king and court. He had sought and was determined to keep government patronage for the hospital he founded and directed, which he perceived as an "instrument of civilization." He felt Christianity should start at the top and work down, extending no further than the government could support it. The century of Catholic martyrdom was a telling argument; because of the opposition of the authorities, the Catholic church in Korea had nearly been wiped out. The last great persecution which had taken place only 20 years earlier was vividly remembered. Allen's views were colored also by his experiences in China, where he had seen missionary work blighted by the hostility or indifference of the influential official class.

Underwood, on the other hand, did not idealize the elevating influences of "civilization." He saw missionary work primarily as proclamation, "spreading the Gospel," but also in terms of doing something to relieve the miserable plight of the poor, the ignorant, the ill. Always an optimist, he felt the Korean government's opposition to Christianity was unfounded, weak, and temporary; that the officials would be won over by the good works that missionaries do. Underwood came into contact with all classes of Korean society; he was the first, and for a while, the only missionary who could speak freely with Koreans in their own language, and so he had more knowledge of the ordinary person's concerns.

John and Harriet Heron had heard of Allen's wonderful treatment of the severely wounded Prince Min Yong-Ik and his heroic opening of the Korean field and were looking forward "with pride and delight" to joining him. In Japan they received kind letters from the Allens and on their arrival in Seoul a warm reception. Heron was a little surprised to find Allen even younger and less medically experienced than himself; "I had expected to find in him a fatherly counselor," but he consoled himself with the prospect of "a friend and companion, helpful and genial."[18] How vastly disappointed he became!

Secretary Ellinwood had made a serious mistake, when he notified Allen of Heron's appointment "to assist you in your work." Unfortunately, Allen considered Heron his assistant ever after. Heron had to struggle constantly for "equal rights in things in which we are equally interested," as he wrote Ellinwood early in 1887. "If you had told me when I left New York that I was to be Dr. Allen's assistant, then I'd have understood my position, but instead I came out here thinking I was to be Dr. Allen's partner."

The first recorded mention of troubles between the two doctors is Allen's diary entry only two months after the Herons' arrival. Allen had received a proposition from Moellendorff to do, along with his mission work, customs medical work for $720 a year. Apparently Allen had crowed over this arrangement and the Herons resented it. It ended with Allen's "announcing my intention of resigning from the mission. Mrs. Heron took it up and denounced me as unfit for a missionary and said I simply used this as a pretext to resign and work for money. This really and rightfully angered me and wears heavily on Mrs. Allen who has so long longed for a woman friend and had learned to love Mrs. Heron; she was unconscious of any trouble between Dr. Heron and myself."

Allen showed a curious self-deception in this incident. He had written several times, even before the Herons' arrival in Korea, that he wanted to quit mission work, and his letters and diary prove that he was looking for a better salaried position. At any rate, his first resignation was sent to the board on September 2, 1885, citing "Heron's professional jealousy" as the cause. He requested to be sent to Fusan or to be allowed to come home "and study missionary character from a distance." Ellinwood wrote a soothing reply and the resignation was shelved. For a while.

By December 20, Allen was once more fuming. "Heron and I have again fallen out. He is eaten up with jealousy. I have written home to be relieved and sent home on sick leave. Don't think I will send it."[19]

In episodes large and small, unkindnesses and frustrations abounded in the Heron-Allen relationship, often overflowing to include Underwood. The Allens refused to allow the Herons and Underwood to draw water from the well located on Allen property, though other water was inconveniently located and dangerous to drink. There were wrangles over horses, who could use the stables, and the cost of stable repairs. Allen ordered all the drugs for the government hospital and foreign patients and kept them locked in his office. Heron, who had no financial responsibility at the hospital, once resorted to sneaking into Allen's office to examine his accounts.

Heron was indignant to find that Allen was charging gifts for officials and wine and beer for his own and his guests' consumption to the medical accounts. Since these funds came from his medical work among the customs staff and other foreigners, Allen considered their use should be completely at his discretion, and his alone. "Of course," wrote Heron, "it may be said that this is only right since he brings in the funds. But in order to give him time for this, I do all or nearly all the Korean practice and very frequently take his turn at the hospital while he is attending some foreigners. I feel that I partly earn this money."[20] Allen was enraged to find that Heron had snooped into his accounts. Heron, on the other hand, was angry that the medical accounts were closed to him, and unhappy with the way the money was used.

Allen did not consult Heron on hospital matters, even major ones such as plans for a new building. When Heron asked to be allowed to take some of the palace medical calls, Allen replied brusquely that he, Allen, was the king's physician. Yet he expected Heron to take his place any time palace duties interfered with his being at the hospital. After this had happened several times, Heron refused to do it again, infuriating Allen. Heron suspected—unjustly—that Allen was deliberately excluding him from palace social functions and honors extended to the doctors of the government hospital.

When angry, Allen wrote scathingly sarcastic notes to Heron and Underwood. He criticized Heron and slighted him in the presence of Koreans and foreigners. In his letters to Ellinwood, he frequently belittled both Underwood and Heron, harping on what he considered their shortcomings and intransigence. Heron eventually found out about some of these remarks.

Allen's high-handedness in mission affairs was exemplified by the opening of the medical school connected with the royal hospital in January, 1886. Horace Underwood said the school "developed out of a suggestion made to me by a Korean suggesting that I conduct the government school in English. While speaking to Dr. Allen I said if such were the case it would be well to make more than a simple case of teaching English out of it and introduce English in all the branches. To this Dr. Allen acceded and drawing up a proposal spoke of it to some of the Koreans. The proposal could not be carried out because of the coming of the American teachers. The concept was changed into a medical school in connection with the hospital.

"Dr. Allen made all the arrangements concerning the number of students, the rules, the buildings, etc. and we heard nothing further till one day he sent us a note asking whether we could begin to teach on the following Monday."

Underwood and Heron, highly trained adults with busy schedules and minds of their own, were taken aback to be asked, almost ordered on such short notice to teach students, subjects and hours chosen by Dr. Allen. They reacted, said Underwood, by asking Allen to call a meeting of the mission. "Dr. Allen seemed not to understand what we should want to know for, but upon our pressing a resolution requesting him to let us know all that had been done he read a letter and explained matters. When we were adjourning with hard feelings against each other it was suggested by someone that we close the meeting with prayer. This was done and we parted apparent friends."[21]

Allen's account of the incident was somewhat different. He wrote in his diary on January 22, 1886, "The new Medical and Scientific School of the Royal Hospital commences today with Rev. Underwood, Dr. Heron and myself as professors. The scheme originated with me, and I put it through. Had the antagonism of my co-workers to deal with. We had a meeting the other day in which these gentlemen wished to use me up, but it gave me an opportunity to tell them that Underwood was a hypocrite and a tattler, that Heron was an envious, pouting man. They were taken aback. Couldn't deny my special charges. We ended with a prayer meeting and the past month has been quite pleasant."

Although Heron and Underwood continued to teach an hour or two daily in the royal hospital medical school, there was a residue of dissatisfaction. In August, Allen complained in his diary and in a letter to Ellinwood, "Heron and Underwood were so obstinate about teaching in the school because it came through me that I had to threaten to hand the whole thing over to the Methodists."

Matters came to a climax the next month in an ugly scene after Heron first heard about a new hospital building from another foreigner. In the ensuing confrontation, the two doctors almost came to blows. According to Allen, each called the other an ass. "Heron said he was not jealous of me and shook his fist in my face. He accused me of being apostate though beer and cigars were the only charges he could get. I drink beer in summer and it has done me much good this season. I always smoke a little. I said, 'Well, Heron, we must split.' He said, 'Yes, we must and that right soon.' "[22] Allen ordered Heron out of his office, and after this the men didn't speak to each other for a long time.

Both Heron and Underwood sent in their resignations in mid-September. Perhaps inspired by Allen's threat a month earlier to "hand the government hospital over to the Methodists," they asked to be dismissed to that mission.

"My reasons for resigning," wrote Underwood, "are that I do not think it right that I should remain in a mission where the only way to get along with a certain fellow missionary is to have nothing to do with him nor with any work with which he is conected and yet this is the only way to get along with Dr. Allen." Underwood summed up the difficulties neatly when he wrote they had "come from the most part from Dr. Allen arrogating to himself powers and rights that we cannot concede to him."

Heron wrote, "It is impossible for us on the field to do any missionary work under Allen's direction." He added, "I am simply a machine for relieving suffering, placed in the hands of a man who uses his success only for his own aggrandizement."

Allen wrote Ellinwood on October 2, "I must and *will* get out of the mess. I am disappointed in missionaries. . . . I am willing to withdraw if you like for good or temporarily." After learning of his associates' resignations from George Foulk who heard it from Ella Appenzeller, he wrote again, "This makes it more imperative that you should do something with me. For whatever may be my private opinion of these men I am sure they will do more in real soul-saving work than I can. Therefore I think it best for the mission for me to step out." In his heart of hearts, Allen knew he was not missionary material.

Annie Ellers could not help being drawn into the quarrel. She wrote Ellinwood, "Well, it was you told me not to take sides. I did not on reading those words fully comprehend but now I do—I have not nor will I take sides," she said, "but the position here is not only deplorable but disgraceful to mission work."

She wrote again in a few weeks, "Dr. Heron and Mr. Underwood informed me of their sending in their resignations and their intention of joining the Methodists . . . then there will be a very small chance for a Presbyterian mission here. In that case Dr. Allen would accept the government position and I would be here alone. I am not usually a coward, but such a position would I fear drive me out of the field." She suggested that "if Dr. Allen were called home for a year the trouble might be done away with and on his return all might go well."

With the resignations of Heron and Underwood, the chronic resignation of Allen, and the conditional resignation of Annie Ellers, the ball was now in the board's court. They made it clear that they did not want to lose Dr. Allen. The first replies from Ellinwood to Underwood in late October and to Heron in early November neither accepted their resignations nor dealt with their dissatisfactions. Allen wrote in his diary, "Letter from board fully sanctions my action and censures others. Allow them to leave or stay as they choose."

Ellinwood appeared to have accepted Allen's characterization of Heron as a jealous man, counseling him, "Your position has evidently been a trying one in respect to Dr. Allen. He has received many honors from the government as a result of his great success. This he could not help. Possibly, sometimes he may have been unduly exalted thereby." Since Heron had never mentioned feeling any lack of honors or any slight from the king or government, he could readily guess where Ellinwood had gotten the idea that the problem involved status.

Ellinwood's letters to the field tended to reflect, almost echo, opinions he received from Allen's lengthy, frank, interesting and often caustic letters; for instance, his fear that the Methodists' coming might "jeopardize matters," and his cautioning Underwood to discard "ministerial garb" were in obvious response to Allen's earlier comments to him. By the time Ellinwood's advice, colored by Allen's concerns, was received on the field, it was not always relevant, helpful, or appreciated.

Ellinwood was horrified that Heron and Underwood would consider joining the Methodists: "The idea of your leaving the mission and going over to the Methodists would amount to a betrayal of a great and sacred trust, and I hope you will consider this very calmly before taking so disastrous a step . . . would it not be a grievous sin in the sight of God, if you were to subordinate so unspeakable an interest to the paltry considerations which are wholly personal to yourselves?" Ellinwood summed up, "My belief is that you are only considering one thing, namely that of getting away from Dr. Allen."

He advised Heron to study the language diligently, for, "by so far as you can gain a knowledge of the language, you have an opportunity to excel Dr. Allen," and, "Don't act hastily . . . let time go by . . . pray that God will give you grace to understand each other better . . . to set before a heathen nation a better example than that of rending the mission which has been formed by personal dissentions."[23]

The next move in the drama was made by the Allens. At a

December meeting of the mission, Allen submitted a letter: "I now declare my settled intention for leaving for America October next . . . . I put the date thus far ahead for two reasons. First our infant cannot be weaned from its Korean nurse before that time. Secondly, I wish so far as is possible to evince my good faith by turning over all the hospital, school, palace and foreign work to my successor, Dr. Heron. This action is taken voluntarily and from the same motives that induced me to devote six years at school in preparation for the work of a medical missionary. I am strongly urged by the board to stay at my post but I feel that the position is better understood by myself than by them. And I feel sure from past experience that more trouble will arise if I remain." (This letter, addressed to his co-workers rather than the board, is neither in Allen's handwriting nor his style and was probably written by his wife.)

The other Presbyterians, taken by surprise, voted "as such a matter could not be decided upon hastily, it be laid on the table," and also that "said communication be sent home (to the board)."

Allen was correct in his assessment that he knew the situation better than the mission board. Also, he was negotiating a good position which was pretty sure to come through by the following October. "Adm. Shufeldt, Judge Denny and Lt. Foulk have urged the U.S. Department to make me Secretary of the legation here," he confided to Ellinwood in a letter written on December 13, the same day as the letter of resignation to the mission.

By now all the foreigners in Korea knew of the troubles in the Presbyterian mission. Two wrote earnest letters to the board in December.

George Foulk wrote that Allen "is brave, energetic, skillful, broad in his views, thoroughly unselfish, and has conducted himself here in such a manner as to commend the respect and affection of almost without exception those who know him . . . Dr. Allen is the only missionary in Korea who has been a true pioneer . . . Like every other man, Dr. Allen makes mistakes . . . natural enough and especially so for a man with the keen intelligence and great energy and impulsiveness he has—the very qualifications to produce the most effective work."

Foulk explained that he himself was "an old Presbyterian school boy," and had hoped "the government should join himself to the missionary to do all he could to make his work effective and receive the missionary's help in establishing among the people the highest regard for the Christian civilization of his country. My idea has been a failure," he sadly concluded, "because of the unwholesome quarrels and wrangles directly in the face of the gentle Savior—who is *my* Savior too, though I don't know the difference between a Methodist and a Presbyterian."

Foulk felt that philosophical differences in the approach to mission work divided the Presbyterians: "The differences between Dr. Allen and Messrs. Heron and Underwood with regard to methods of working here may be explained as follows: Dr. Allen aimed at influencing the official class—the king and the nobles. Messrs. Heron and Underwood, not being able to take positions such as Dr. Allen held among the higher Koreans, and influenced by feelings of impulsive ambitions, not altogether unselfish, have parted from his line of action . . . and tend to direct their work among the people of the lower orders . . . to Korean eyes the *wrong* side—because the governing officials will maintain and use their power to bend the people to their will. . . ."

One of the government teachers, George Gilmore, wrote on Christmas Eve to say that in his opinion the resignation of Allen would be a "calamity," that Dr. Allen "is a politic and longheaded man." Although "I have found Dr. Heron a most noble man, extremely self-sacrificial," Dr. Allen "has gained prominence here." Like Foulk, he felt Allen's approach to missionary work would be the successful one. "I think that Dr. Heron and Mr. Underwood totally misapprehend the nature of the work here in the *fundamental* particular the Koreans must be converted from the *head* downward."

In January 1887 Underwood presented a plan for settling some of the difficulties among the Presbyterian missionaries, to which all agreed. His plan called for regular meetings for departments within the mission. The three doctors working in the government hospital would be an advisory board with equal powers and votes. Medical orders would be subject to its approval. The key point was "in all the work of the mission where two or more are engaged and do equal work, equal powers shall be visited."[24] This plan was in keeping with standard Presbyterian missionary practice. Under the plan, relations among the missionaries went along smoothly for several months, especially since Allen had begun the new year resolved to do "everything in my power to remove all causes of offense."[25]

Meanwhile, the Presbyterian board was considering sending two or three missionaries including the beloved and respected Dr. J.C. Hepburn from Japan to mediate. As relationships on the field seemed much improved by February, it was decided the trip was unnecessary and the men did not go, but Dr. Hepburn wrote Ellinwood an insightful letter:

"In regard to the whole trouble, I took very much the same view that you have. That on the one side there was an unconscious assumption of authority naturally fostered by longer residence, acquired reputation and social position, where the finer instincts of the Christian gentleman were perhaps wanting, as well as forgetfulness of what was due to a brother, an equal, indeed I dare to say, a superior in medical education and general culture, tender sensibilities and high-toned Christian principles. Dr. Heron and wife sojourned with me some time when enroute to Korea. . . . I formed a high opinion of them in every respect and anticipated for them a useful career. . . . I advised the Doctor and Mr. Underwood to be patient, withdraw their resignations, to remember they were servants of Christ . . . to study the language . . . not to seek high things for themselves . . . not to look too minutely into the affairs nor mind the manners of Dr. Allen. I advised Dr. Heron if he found his position in the Government Hospital under Dr. Allen disagreeable, he should open one for himself, quite independent and having more of a missionary character. . . . I have no doubts that jealousy, that bane of missions, had begun to enter into [their] hearts."[26]

Heron replied to Hepburn's advice by writing him, "You are very right and I am very wrong." Dr. Hepburn wrote further to Ellinwood, "I feel sorry for Dr. Allen. His Christian principles are so fearfully tried. The world and Satan are just as powerful and busy in that poor and miserable kingdom of Korea as they are in New York City."

He ended by commiserating, "It requires strong faith and trust in God in the secretaries of our board to enable them to hold on when they see so much of the weakness and infirmities of the laborers sent into the vineyard."

By the time this letter was received, the board had made another major mistake. Still hoping to keep Allen in the mission, they "earnestly requested Dr. Allen to relinguish his intention of withdrawing from the mission even temporarily" and stated that Allen was to be considered physician in chief of the hospital, though they advised that he "consult with his assistant physician in all important matters."

The cheerful tone which had characterized letters from Korea since January when Underwood's "equal powers" plan had been adopted abruptly ceased and a new spate of hurt and outraged correspondence began. Heron and Underwood resigned again. Allen wrote that he was unable "to do anything with Dr. Heron who is obstinately silent or downright insulting," but urged the board to keep Underwood who "cannot be spared . . . he is the best Korean scholar here and will be a valuable missionary once he quiets down."[27] The Methodist Dr. Scranton wrote a sympathetic letter to Heron, offering him a place in his mission.[28]

George Gilmore, who had written Ellinwood in December that to lose Allen would be "a calamity," now wrote to say he thought Dr. Ellinwood had been "extremely prejudiced" in Allen's favor, causing trouble "to loom up again" in the mission. "A letter lately received gives absolute control to Dr. Allen," he wrote, and quoted Allen as saying, "You know I can do as I please now." Gilmore urged the board to rescind its action, and concluded that "The difficulties might all have been solved by giving Dr. Allen and Dr. Heron equal powers."[29]

The altercation was finally quietened by Allen's acceptance of King Kojong's invitation to accompany as secretary a Korean mission to the United States. He wrote Ellinwood of the offer in August 1887, and said he'd accept "unless the board cables 'Allen Korea No.' " The cable was not sent. At a Seoul Presbyterian mission meeting, Allen, seconded by Annie Ellers Bunker, moved that the mission reinstate the plan of work Underwood had presented in January; the vote to work by the "equality" plan was unanimous.

Although Allen had some misgivings about accompanying the Korean embassy—"With two small babies and a lot of fool Koreans to look after it will be far from agreeable. While here I am without doubt the strongest foreigner in the country so far as influence with the king is concerned"[30]—he began making preparations to leave. Heron did not know of Allen's plans until early September. Then he encouraged him to stay, saying he could not be spared from the work. Heron withdrew his resignation, almost a year after first submitting it.

Underwood, however, still intended to resign. The board had not approved the appropriations for his March trip to Japan, because of a letter Allen had written suggesting Underwood was malingering or taking the trip for courting purposes.[31] Underwood had not been well, and all three Presbyterian doctors had "voted and urged" that he go to Japan for a period of rest and recuperation. There his health had improved and he had published his and Appenzeller's revised translation of Mark. The board's inference that he had misused funds to go on a pleasure trip was, he said, "uncharitable, unjust, and unChristian."

Now Allen wrote Ellinwood, advising him to make peace with Underwood. "Just as I was congratulating us on the bright prospects of our mission, I learned Underwood has not withdrawn his resignation and will not unless charges made in connection with his recent trip to Japan are withdrawn. He was not sick but presented other reasons of sufficient weight to cause the mission to grant him leave. . . . At any rate, the trip was taken with mission sanction and cannot be recalled. . . . It is unfortunate that you have alienated Mr. Underwood just at present. He seems Presbyterian as opposed to Methodist and is a very valuable man, knowing the language better than any other in Korea. It will be wise to concede to him a little. The Methodists are active but we have better material if we can just get it into harmonious action."[32]

Underwood finally withdrew his resignation on September 30, and on October 25, on the eve of his departure for the States, Allen presented his but added, "I shall expect to come to Korea again under your (mission board) auspices."

By the end of 1887, Dr. Heron was writing Ellinwood of his work at the palace, in the government hospital and school, and among the foreigners, complaining about the other missionaries, and begging for reinforcements. His letters sounded quite like Allen's as he began to grapple with some of the same situations and problems. Things were back to normal in the Presbyterian mission.

Foundations

In spite of the squabbling among the missionaries, an amazing amount of work was begun.

As early as July 1886, Appenzeller was writing Methodist Secretary Reid cheerfully, "The end of our first year in Korea finds us safely 'out of the woods:' Dr. Scranton no longer mixes his medicine in a 8′ square room with a stove box for a table; his mother no longer lives in a paper house and I am permitted to meet my pupils, not in the dining room, but in another specially fitted for the purpose."

The next January, he asked for $7,000 for his school. The following month, Heron wrote his board, "Our Methodist friends have made us almost envious when they told us $26,000 was appropriated for their work this year." These funds provided a great forward thrust in the Methodist work.

At this time Appenzeller had 45 students in his school, by no means all from the lowest class. "I am glad I have the three classes represented," he said, "and that from a literary point of view there is no difference between them."[33]

Underwood was eager for the Presbyterians to open a school for older boys. He had already taken younger boys into an orphanage, a project he began in January, 1886. Foulk had asked that a formal request for permission to open an orphanage be submitted, signed by the three Presbyterian men. A few days later Underwood was delighted to receive a more positive reply than he had dared to hope from the government:

". . . In their desire to benefit our people, Dr. Allen, Dr. Heron, and Mr. Underwood propose to establish a home for orphans and homeless children in Seoul, at which they may be fed and clothed, taught Chinese and Unmun, and ways of supporting themselves. What on this earth is more worthy of the consideration of this government than this proposition? Who, hearing of it, would not approve?" Signed by Kim Yun-Sik, President of the Foreign Office, on February 14, 1886.[34]

Underwood sent copies of the petition and its reply to Ellinwood with the remark that his idea was "meeting with approval on all sides." All sides but one, anyway. Although Heron expressed his aspirations for the new work, "which we hope will be a center of light in this land, our first *real* missionary enterprise,"[35] Allen was not enthused. He didn't want what he considered a "flighty" scheme of Underwood's to interfere with his own brand new "Medical and Scientific School." Also, he thought the proposed orphanage should be operated in the same way as the hospital, under government sponsorship.

Allen's philosophy of mission is nowhere better expressed than in a letter to Ellinwood: "I like to see the government work for itself, and I think in regard to their orphanage that government help should be accepted. It is better in my mind to instruct a government in these institutions of civilization and secure their adoption than to carry on a feeble proselyting concern. Christianity always goes with the missionary."

So the orphanage-school got underway in faith, hope and controversy. A few months later Allen was writing, "The orphanage is not a success,"[36] while Underwood was saying, "The orphanage is going along very nicely."[37] Underwood continued, "We have now 10 on the roll but one is away sick. . . . The people cannot understand how anything can be done without a selfish motive and have already put around many stories about what we are going to do with the boys, such as 'send them to America as slaves,' 'fattening them up for the table,' etc. We know we must expect this."

Earlier there had been considerable apprehension about possible government opposition to mission schools. According to Appenzeller's diary, "the whole school waited on me in a body and requested that my school be put on a government basis as the report had gone forth that this was a mission school. Three students left, one permanently . . .because they are afraid they will be persecuted (which here means beheading) if they remain in a school of this kind. I shall do all I can to give the school a proper standing, but it seems to me the very thing which ought to distinguish it is what gives the offense."

But surprisingly, just two months later, Appenzeller's school received royal recognition when an emissary of the king came and bestowed a name and name plaque on the school: "Today the name of our mission school given it by His Majesty and the President of the Foreign Office was sent to me. It is Pae Jae Hak Dang ("Hall for Rearing Useful Men"). This gives us a recognition by the government and a standing before the Koreans we hitherto did not have. . . . The nameplate has been properly framed and now hangs over the large front gate; the silent guardian of our educational work. It is the proclamation that the school has royal endorsement and encouragement. It is our charter."[38]

Within a month, student enrollment increased from 30 to 43, and by the end of the year, to 63. In May construction began on a school building including a chapel, four classrooms, a library, office and basement for an industrial department. It was, wrote Appenzeller, "one story, of brick, best material inside, entirely foreign style of architecture, the first and only one of its kind in Korea."[39]

Mrs. Scranton's fledgling school for girls and Dr. Scranton's hospital also were honored with names and signboards from the palace. The girls' school was designated "Ewha," or "Pear Blossom" school by Queen Min who chose the royal insignia she favored; and the hospital, "the Universal Relief Hospital."

Henry Appenzeller, a warm and successful orator by the standards of his day, loved to preach and longed to do direct evangelistic work. Teaching always took second place in his heart. For that reason, Pae Jae, the work he was to be best remembered by, was to be his burden as well as his greatest achievement. In July 1887 he asked his board to send teachers so that he could be freed for more evangelistic work. He continued to make the request, but was never able to escape his duties at Pae Jae. Methodism, like the first Methodist missionary, has been indelibly associated with education in Korea.

To Appenzeller, Pae Jae school stood for evangelical Christianity, liberal Christian education, and the raising up of a "native ministry" for Korea. For him, nothing else justified the school's existence.[40] "I want the students who come here to get converted," he wrote frankly.

And they did. By the spring of 1887, Appenzeller had begun to teach Christianity to interested students. He wrote of a student, Han Yong-Kyung, who had "come over after dark to see light."[42] The next month when there were three such seekers, he distributed the catechism in Korean for the first time. The first Korean he baptized, in July 1887, was Pak Choong-Sang, a Pae Jae student; and the student Han was baptized in October.[43]

Earlier baptisms had taken place, however. On Easter Sunday, 1886, a year after his arrival, Appenzeller baptized his own infant daughter Alice, the first Caucasian child born in Korea, and the Scrantons' baby, Marian Fitch. In his diary Appenzeller called it "a blessed day for us missionaries here. . . . After the babies were in this way given unto the Lord, I baptized Hayakawa Tatzye, an attache to the Japanese legation."

The following July, Appenzeller wrote, "Brother Underwood baptized the first Korean convert in the Protestant mission, Mr. No Toh-Sa. I had the pleasure of assisting in the service. The man takes a great risk in thus exposing himself to the wrath of the Koreans but we pray he may be kept by him who has called him to a new life. At the same time, at which I also assisted, the Herons' little daughter Sarah Anne was baptized by Bro. Underwood. These services were held at Dr. Heron's house."

On September 12, 1886, Appenzeller baptized the Allen's four-month-old son Maurice at the American legation. The Scrantons' third daughter, Catherine Anne, was baptized the next year.

Besides baptizing their own babies, the missionaries were seeing an encouraging response from the Koreans to the Gospel. In 1886, both Appenzeller and Underwood had several men coming to their homes to study Christianity. Appenzeller wrote prophetically in his diary, "We seem to be all right as long as we do not try to do the very work for which we are sent here, but the Lord will open a door which no one can shut." In January, 1887, Underwood informed Ellinwood that "We are to have several baptisms next Sunday—the men who have applied seem to be thoroughly in earnest. They are some of the offshoots of Ross' work in the North. . . . We examined three the other day and they passed a good examination. . . . They seem to realize they will be taking their lives in their hands—we cannot say them nay. . . . These men have been having services on the Sabbath and witnessing."

The Methodists reported four baptisms in 1887 and the Presbyterians more. Heron wrote, "Do you not feel like shouting over these baptisms?"[44] But the news disturbed rather than delighted Ellinwood. Although he had written to Horace Allen in September 1886, advising him to "Rejoice with Underwood in the encouragement he receives in his direct Christian work," and to Underwood the same day, saying he considered the baptism of No Toh-Sa the "first dawn of spiritual success . . . the first streak of dawn, and of the full day," by the following spring he was urging caution. "As to the baptisms of which you speak, we should have been a little inclined to tremble. Better to bear on the side of safety than to run the risk of an explosion."[45]

In January 1887, Allen wrote a stiff letter to Underwood protesting the proposed baptisms—"you are in danger of totally ruining the present work and future prospects of yourselves and others and of laying the men liable to persecution and destruction. "This (baptizing) is missionary work proper and last night I heard your representative state to the British representative that there was no mission work proper being carried on here and that it would not be allowed." Allen concluded, "As it is in violation of the laws of this country, I cannot as a Korean official[46] give my consent to the proceeding."

Underwood replied that if baptizing was "mission work proper," it was "no more so than many other things being done;" and that baptisms took place regularly in China where there were government restrictions. As for the risk of the men's martyrdom: "They realize and are willing to take the risk—why should we refuse? . . . When God points out something for us to do, we have nothing to do with the apparent results. We must leave them with God and do the work placed in our hands."

As for ruining the work, Underwood said, "I cannot see how the baptism of these men in my house will in any way affect that of our friends or the hospital. The hospital cannot be said to be doing the work of proselyting. In the school there is always a Korean official who would at once report were I to teach Christianity." And he concluded, "I dare not deny baptism to these three men who have sought me out for it. I find no warrant for denying them baptism in the history of missions, in the acts of the Apostles, or in the teaching of Christ."[47]

Heron reported in September 1887, in a letter to Ellinwood that "There are 30 persons wanting baptism 100 miles from Seoul, 12 in Seoul either Christians or inquirers which makes our hearts glad. Last Sabbath Mr. Underwood baptized three. We have 11 baptized. We do it very quietly."

Very quietly indeed. The services were solemn occasions, with Homer Hulbert watching at the door. In the fall of 1887 Underwood made one of his memorable trips, to the village of Sorae, where he baptized seven men and found the village "tempered with the Christian spirit."[48]

It is important to remember that there was already a beginning, a basis of Christian witness in Korea even before the arrival of the first Protestant missionaries. In addition to the century of Catholicism, the appeals of Korean converts in Japan and the Rijutei translation of scripture had had an early influence.

Even earlier, in the autumn of 1873 and again the next year, Scotch Presbyterian missionary John Ross[49] of Newchwang, Manchuria, had ventured about 40 miles from Euiju to the gate on the border between Manchuria and North Korea. On his second visit, Ross met a Korean pedlar, Yi Ung-Chan who had lost his wares and livelihood in a shipwreck. Yi agreed to teach Korean to Ross and his colleague John MacIntyre. Yi was baptized by MacIntyre and is believed to be the first Korean Protestant Christian.[50] He later helped the Manchurian missionaries translate the Gospel of Luke into Korean.

Another Yi, Yi Chung-Song, a bankrupt Korean herb dealer, turned up at Ross' home as a beggar. Hired to work with the Chinese printers in preparing the Gospel of Luke for publication, he too became a Christian.

Rumors of a special book being printed in Manchuria reached Seoul and underlings attached to the annual embassy bringing tribute to the Chinese court soon began dropping in to check on its progress. One of them began taking an interest in the work, and was hired as the compositor. This released Yi Chung-Song to work as a colporteur and in 1882 Ross sent him back to his native village with a few hundred copies of Luke and some tracts. All had been sold, and were being read with deep interest, he reported on his return, and already some villagers wanted to be baptized. Ross could hardly credit such good results and thought Yi's report was made only to please him. He sent him out again, however, and Yi returned six months later with a similar report.

Ross set out in November to see for himself the results of Yi's work and baptized 75 Koreans in four valleys in Northeastern Manchuria. Ross was much impressed with the Koreans he encountered. Shortly after his arrival at an inn in the first Korean village he reached, "in marched a body of about a dozen Koreans, gentlemanly in appearance, garments, manners and speech. They came in to welcome us. This they did with a smile lighting up their faces, as though welcoming long-lost and very dear friends. . . . We were conducted to the house of the principal farmer, in whose guest room we found a crowd of men filling the warm, close room. . . .

"Next morning we prepared to receive applicants for baptism. About 30 villagers appeared . . . all well clad. They were all farmers and heads of families. The women and children were, they said, believers; but they thought the younger people would not be received, and their women, for social reasons, could not present themselves where the men met. . . . Some were baptized and some postponed for further Christian instruction . . . We were informed that in each of the 28 valleys which lay between us and the long, white mountain 400 miles to the northeast, there were believers waiting to be received into the church."[51]

Two brothers who were to become famous in the annals of Korean Christianity, So Sang-Yun and So Kyong-Jo, had travelled to Manchuria to peddle merchandise in 1878. After a series of misadventures, they met Ross and MacIntyre. So Sang-Yun, who was ill, was taken into the hospital where he recovered, and both brothers became Christians. After Sang-Yun's baptism in 1879, he assisted with the Bible translation and printing. Later he, too, returned to Korea as a colporteur, settling in Sorae where he was instrumental in the conversion of many of his neighbors, some of whom were baptized there in 1887 by Underwood. The younger brother, So Kyong-Jo was baptized in 1887 in Seoul and in 1907 became one of the first seven Presbyterian ministers to be ordained in Korea.

After the failure of the 1884 coup, some of the progressives had fled to Manchuria. A few of these men happened across the valleys Yi had visited; curious about the new teaching they heard there and having nothing better to do, they slowly wended their way to Newchwang and John Ross. They introduced themselves as having read his book and said they were praying to the God of Heaven. These men eventually were baptized. One of them, a young scholar, returned to Seoul to instruct his friends and relatives in his new faith. A year later, he wrote Ross asking him to come to the capital as 13 of his friends desired to be formed into a congregation. The next year he wrote again, saying there were 79 believers eager to be baptized.

Ross arrived in Seoul in September 1887, on the same day that Underwood organized the first Protestant [Presbyterian] church. Ross wrote that he accompanied Underwood and Heron through the dark city to find a company of 14 well-dressed, intelligent-looking men. One was baptized that night, but the principal business was the election as elders of two men, cousins of the young revolutionary. They had been believers for six years. Ross was told there were over 300 men, *yangban* in Seoul who, though not yet prepared to join the church publicly, were believers.[52]

In these early years, though the surface of Korean life seemed unchanged, there was a good deal of spiritual ferment going on underneath. Underwood knew the government was aware of this but was willing to look the other way. In November 1887 he wrote, "The prevalent idea that the government is opposed is not so. It is passive. Korea is as open to work today as Japan."[53]

That fall Appenzeller bought a house to use for Sunday services, calling it Bethel Chapel. He baptized the first Korean woman Protestant, the 29-year-old wife of a colporteur, in a service in his home.[54] In November, the Methodists licensed two Korean local preachers.

The highlight of the year for Appenzeller was Christmas Day when he preached for the first time in Korean. The text was Matthew 1:21, "Thou shalt call his name Jesus." Although he read the sermon "and closely," he wrote, "This was the first Methodist sermon in Korean in Korea and *perhaps* the first formal sermon by any Protestant minister. Of this however I am not positive as Mr. Underwood who knows more Korean than I do 'talks' to his people. I can hardly realize that in less than two and a half years of living in Korea I not only hold meetings but am actually trying to preach to the people in their own tongue. It is poor preaching I admit, but as it is done in the name of the Lord, I trust He will bless this effort. It will be a happy day when I can preach with some degree of comfort to myself and the hearers."[55]

By 1890 the Methodists counted 165 adherents (inquirers, catechumens, baptized members) and the Presbyterians had baptized more than 100. This increase was by no means solely the fruit of the foreign missionaries' labors. Most of the converts were made by Koreans.

The reactions of the first Koreans to work with foreigners are interesting. Curiosity was often the catalyst for making acquaintance. Kim Chang-Sik, who became an outstanding Methodist church leader, recounted that he was 29 when he first saw a foreigner in Seoul: "I thought him unmannerly and savage-like. I had heard that Westerners caught children and ate them. I doubted this, but wanted to prove whether it was so or not, so I secured work with a foreigner."[56] As gatekeeper for Methodist missionary Franklin Ohlinger, "I carefully observed his daily life and that of Mrs. Ohlinger, but found nothing evil in them."

Choe Pyung-Hyun was introduced as a possible language teacher to 20-year-old George Heber Jones in 1888. Choe's first reaction to the foreigner was of distaste and he remembered thinking, "In their faces they show they are animals. How could one reason with them on the Five Relationships or on the Three Bonds between Sovereign and Subject?" He refused to work for such a species until one day when he saw a foreigner gently carry a sick beggar to the small new mission hospital. In appreciation for this kindness he agreed to teach George Heber Jones, and thus began a long and fruitful partnership.[57]

Gradually such matches were made, of mind and soul mates, between Koreans and missionaries. Daniel Gifford, in writing of the early years of mission work, said the first 10 years was a period of preparation; "We were learning Korean, and what is still more important, Koreans."[58] Beyond policy, principles and practice were people and their relationships to each other. This, too, became one of the strong foundations of the Protestant church and mission in Korea.

The Newlyweds

The Methodist ranks were reinforced in 1887 and the first half of 1888 with a doctor, Meta Howard, and teacher, Louisa Rothweiler, who arrived together in October; China veterans the Rev.

and Mrs. Franklin Ohlinger with their three children, in January; and young George Heber Jones in May.

Dr. Meta Howard began medical practice among women immediately, working with William Scranton until November 1888 when the Methodists opened a separate hospital for women. In the fall of 1889, her health broke down and she returned to the States.

Miss Rothweiler, too, plunged at once into the work. The experienced and able schoolteacher was stricken with smallpox in December 1888, which left her eyes permanently damaged, and in 1892 her health also failed, necessitating a medical leave to America.

The Ohlingers, who had been 12 years in China, moved into the first brick residence in Korea, constructed for them at a cost of $3,000, a scandalous sum to the hard-pressed Presbyterians. Ohlinger was put in charge of the Methodists' Trilingual Press, which began quite humbly, chiefly to provide employment and training to Pae Jae students. Ohlinger wrote of its facilities in 1890, "This building doubtless answers some purpose but a good-sized hollow tree would do nearly as well for a press building."

Tragedy struck the Ohlinger family in 1893 when two of their children died of kidney complications following colds. Their son Bertie, 12, was buried on May 30 and their 10-year-old daughter on June 3, and the parents with their surviving son left Korea.

The longest and strongest service of the new recruits would prove to be that of George Heber Jones, as he signed himself. Just 20 when he arrived in Korea, Jones was a graduate of American University in Tennessee. A cheerful, dynamic man with sandy reddish-blond hair which thinned early, he can be identified in many photographs by the brimless hat, something like a skull cap, he often wore. He built up the Chemulpo circuit, considered one of the most successful in self-support and self-propagation among the Methodists. Missionary historian George Paik credits the circuit's achievements to the wise guidance of Jones, who laid special emphasis on the instruction of class leaders, exhorters, and local preachers and sent them out to preach among their neighbors.[59]

During this period, the Presbyterians were struggling along with no reinforcements, operating on a financial and personnel shoestring. Underwood's vast energy enabled him to do the work of several people, and Heron, through sheer determination, managed to do almost as much. Both men's letters make poignant reading in their repeated pleas for help. To his friends, the J.C. Hepburns in Japan, Underwood woefully admitted, "I have about given up all hope in stirring the board. I have written letter after letter. . . . They seem almost to have forgotten they have a mission here at all. We must have more workers."[60]

Heron's situation was especially difficult. All work had increased and he was doing more than he and Allen had previously done together, plus taking up the work of Annie Ellers who withdrew from medical practice after her marriage. Like Allen, Heron found the palace work gratifying to the ego, but hard on the constitution. It required full formal dress whatever the weather; each call could take half a day, and could come at all hours of the night. In addition, he was in charge of the hospital school, working without an interpreter.

In the midst of the hot, trying summer of 1888, a second daughter, Jessie, was born to the Herons. This meant they could not leave the sweltering, unsanitary city for rest or a change. Mrs. Heron became ill and hovered frighteningly close to death for a full year. Heron, too, was unwell. He wrote that "Were it not for the hope of winning Corea for Christ, I would not live here a day,"[61] and "The summer work is too hard for anyone . . .for the past three weeks I have hardly been able to drag. I do not believe when I left home you could have ever sent out a man with a better constitution or more robust health than I had. It is just 9 a.m. and already I have seen nine patients and that is a fair sample. . . .I do not want to break down—I should feel disgraced to go home now."[62]

In addition to his work load and his wife's illness, Heron was weighed down with financial worries. In fact, all the missionaries were having a hard time making ends meet. Appenzeller wrote to the Methodist board to ask them to remit Dr. Scranton's debt of $166.54. "I *know* this debt he owes the mission hangs over him like a dark cloud. He cannot save enough to pay it and he *worries* about it. I don't believe he would approve of my writing to you about him in this way, but I really feel the mission society can afford to cancel this burden better than have him worry out his life trying to pay it."[63] The Methodist board canceled the debt. Underwood wrote his board requesting a raise in March 1888, saying he could not keep house on his salary; his request, too, was granted.

But when Heron, whose outside work was bringing in several thousand dollars a year, several times his salary, to the mission, asked to be able to keep enough to pay off his debts and to insure his life, the request was denied, on the advice of Horace Allen who wrote from Washington, "I am perfectly confident that your allowance is ample."[64]

Added to Heron's woes was the death of his beloved father in the spring of 1888; he wrote Ellinwood, "It was a great trial to me to be in Korea at a time when as both a son and as a physician, he needed me so sorely and only the knowledge that I was about my 'Master's work' kept me up." Harriet's father died not long after.

Aside from the load of work and worries, Heron's experiences paralleled a number of Allen's earlier ones. The Allens went through the 1884 coup, the Herons were on hand for the 1888 baby riots. So unnerved were they, especially since Harriet was eight months pregnant, by the wave of antiforeign riots that for years afterward Mrs. Heron kept a hatchet by her bed and John kept his gun handy.[65]

Heron accomplished a notable cure for another Min, cousin of the queen. The unfortunate man had a skin disease which precluded his admittance to the palace. After 10 days treatment, he was sufficiently recovered to appear before the king, who was so delighted that he sent the doctor a very handsome official's cap, valued at about $40.[66]

There were a number of other generous gifts from the palace, and Heron, like his predecessor, found himself the startled beneficiary of a bevy of dancing girls, 14 of them between the ages of 16 and 18, who arrived one day in 14 palanquins carried by 56 bearers.[67] Although Heron, like Allen, thought they might be trained as nurses for the hospital, Harriet objected and the whole lot of giggling girls was returned to the palace, declined with thanks.

For Horace Underwood, the arrival of the next Presbyterian missionary was especially welcome. The other missionaries had for some time been urging matrimony on him, and Underwood had obligingly courted a girl or two. But the arrival of Lillias Horton, M.D., settled the issue. Although 37-year-old Lillie was eight years older than Horace, the pretty doctor caught his eye at once. She was small, even tiny; in fact, she was just Queen Min's size, less than 5 feet tall, and she wore size 5 gloves and 1½ shoes. Lillie appeared frail, but she was fiercely resolute.

Her childhood had been clouded by a seige of rheumatic fever with a relapse that prevented her graduation from high school. On the eve of her departure for Vassar, someone persuaded her mother that a college education would ruin a devout, impressionable young lady like Lillie, and her mother refused to let her go. Perhaps in rebellion for having the dream of college snatched from her, Lillie resisted her mother's desire, almost an obsession, that she become a foreign missionary.

About the time Mrs. Horton became reconciled to the idea that her older daughter was not going to be a missionary, Lillie met an Englishwoman from India. As she excitedly announced to her family, "She told me such awful stories of the condition and needs of women there that I have decided to study medicine and go there, too!"[68]

Her sister Leonora noted that "Mama wasn't as jubilant as I would have expected." The family wondered how their Lillie, fastidious to the point of being finicky, could ever endure the rigors of a medical education. Her sister wrote that Lillie grew up "with very acute sensibilities, a shuddering hatred of raw bloody things, of things not meant to be seen, of imperfections in flesh and blood creatures whether malformed by nature or ruined by nature or ruined by accident, and of smells. How she loathed them! She hated to hear operations described, dead things were revolting, and yet we saw her go through the dissecting of dead human beings, spending days in the dissecting room, without faltering or a word of complaint. When anyone asked her how she stood it she had only one answer, 'I can do all things through Christ who strengtheneth me.' It was a visible miracle."

Although she was 30 and had been out of school for 12 years, Lillie did very well in her medical studies, graduating with honors from the Women's Medical College of Northwestern University in three years and doing post-graduate work at the Hospital for Women and Children in Chicago.

Appointed for missionary service in April 1887, she was packing to go to India when the board asked her to go instead to Korea. She agreed, leaving home in February 1888. According to her sister, "Our house was desolate . . . . Papa went as far as Kansas City with her . . . . Mama took to her bed and remained there until Lillie's first letter came." Enroute, Lillie was annoyed by the predictions of the other missionaries that she would soon marry, and wrote home, "You know, mama, I'm not going to marry. I am dedicated to Christ and his work."[69]

The day after her arrival in Seoul, Lillie went to work at the hospital. Her colleagues praised her ability and fervor, but were concerned that she would break down. Heron wrote two weeks after her arrival, "She is, I think, working too hard on the language, considering she's not yet over the effects of her trip,"[70] and Underwood, "The only fault we find with her is that she insists on working just as hard in the hot weather when she is not well as she did in the spring when she was."[71]

From May 1888, until September, all religious activities among the Koreans, including morning prayers at schools and Sunday services were halted. Anti-foreign feeling had been stirred up by the construction of the Catholic cathedral on a prominent site overlooking the palace. Horace Underwood and Henry Appenzeller had started out on a two-month evangelistic foray north, getting as far as Pyongyang, when they were recalled to Seoul by American Minister Hugh Dinsmore and their missions. Tensions culminated in the so-called Baby Riots of June 10-25.

As in China, it was rumored that the Western barbarians were kidnapping and eating children, and using their eyes in cameras. Koreans, who did not milk cows, generally believed that to get the condensed milk they used, foreigners caught Korean women and cut off their breasts. The hospital was suspected of butchering children, and the orphanage of fattening them up for immoral purposes.

In China, officials had spread just such rumors, stirring up mob action resulting in the deaths of a number of missionaries.[72] In Korea, although there was public unrest, wild rumors and instances of several hapless Koreans killed by mobs, there were no foreign casualties.

According to a letter marked confidential from Horace Allen which was taken from reports received by the Korean embassy in Washington, "a mob has killed a few Koreans and caused sufficient excitement to cause the summoning of the Marines from ships at Chemulpo to guard the legations. It had nothing to do with the missionaries and was caused by the unnatural act of a father in selling his son to the Japanese for immoral purposes. The populace became so angered that, taking justice into their own hands, they killed the father and before they were quieted some others were killed . . . . It amounted to little more, or perhaps not so much, than a lynching . . . . I regard it as a most favorable sign that the mob was dispersed without having made any attempts to injure the missionaries."[73]

The mob's restraint was particularly impressive, said Allen, "as the Koreans firmly believe that the young boys at Underwood's house are for purposes unnatural." One of the orphanage boys, he said, had been dismissed because he'd been caught engaging in sodomy with the servants. "It is very doubtful," added Allen, "that it pays to send unmarried men to Korea since the people will not believe in our morality." Even so, Allen was convinced that "Foreigners are safer in Seoul than in New York," and felt the newspaper accounts played up the Korean "outrages" too much.[74]

During the riots, Lillie Horton refused to stay home from work. Returning one day from the clinic, her chair was surrounded by ruffians who warned the bearers they should all be killed if they took her to the hospital again. So the following days she rode horseback, escorted through the troubled city by Horace Underwood.

Such experiences were not reassuring to her nervous mother. After receiving a letter from Lillie saying that she thought she'd heard one of the tigers still occasionally sighted in Seoul on her roof the night before, Mrs. Horton insisted a pistol be sent to her immediately. Mr. Horton asked the head of his hardware store's cutlery department to see to it and a few days later the accommodating employee came up with his idea of the perfect weapon — "a really pretty little pearl handled pistol and a stiletto with a handle to match the pistol! On the small plate was inscribed, 'From pa and ma. May God protect thee!' "[75]

Her family in Chicago began hearing more and more of Horace Underwood. He took Lillie to prayer meeting. He took her skating. He took her horseback riding. He was always sending flowers. One charming example of the flower-sending was recounted by Lillie, who, she said, "loved a virginal white honeysuckle best of all flowers because one spring evening when it had been pouring rain all day, and she had been shut in, feeling a little lonely and homesick, at 9 p.m. a great spray of this lovely vine, dripping with rain, was handed in at her door with a note saying, 'Compliments of the rain and Namsan.' The handwriting was the Captain's," Lillie's pet name for Horace.

Her sister finally suggested that maybe Lillie was thinking about marrying Mr. Underwood. "Never," said her mother. When at last the inevitable letter came, "It certainly was a terrible blow to mama. She seemed almost stunned. She said . . . that it had been easier to give her up to God than to give her to a man, which papa and I thought wicked . . . . Of course, she got over her dismay; she finally even came to think it a good thing."[77]

Lillie's mother wasn't the only one dismayed. Heron had obviously not considered that a "middle-aged" lady of almost 38 would consider marriage. He wrote a half-joking, half-serious letter to Ellinwood, "I am discouraged . . . . Just when we get a good woman physician, here comes along Mr. U. and takes her away from her work to help in his . . . Mr. Underwood needed a wife badly enough but he might have found one without spoiling a good doctor to get one."[78] Heron was, he said, baffled as whether or not to request still another woman physician since they seemed to have the habit of marrying within a year.

Lillie was not called to the palace for six months after her arrival because of the anti-foreign feeling in the capital, but when she did meet Queen Min in the autumn of 1888, each woman immediately liked the other. They had much in common, petite and stout-hearted, fragile-looking yet determined; both were intelligent and conservative, and both would be doting mothers.

When Lillie and Horace Underwood were married on March 13, 1889, the Queen showed her regard by sending as a wedding gift a whole train of little pack ponies laden with one million Korean coins called cash.[79]

At dawn the next morning, bride and groom set out on a nine-week, 1000-mile-long honeymoon trip. There were groups of believers from Seoul to the Yalu River who needed oversight and encouragement, and who wished baptism. For more than two years, all the Seoul missionaries had wanted to begin work in Pyongyang, and someone was needed to go there and scout out that field. But everything except force was resorted to by the foreigners in Seoul to prevent the Underwoods from taking this journey.

No European woman and few men had yet been outside Seoul and the port cities. Heron warned Underwood that his wife would not be able to withstand such a trip. American Minister Hugh Dinsmore was opposed to venturing into the interior, feeling it would further antagonize the Koreans when anti-foreign feeling was running high. He refused to issue Underwood a passport to the country except on the condition that he neither teach nor baptize. Despite these warnings and restrictions, the newlyweds felt the journey was well worth its dangers, a great adventure. Lillie said, "It seemed to me no honeymoon so rich in delight could ever have been planned before."

Horace Underwood wrote Ellinwood, "Our missionary trip is going to be a test in a sense. Dr. Heron thinks it altogether too hard for Dr. Horton, but he has never taken the trip. Mr. Appenzeller of the Methodist Mission who also agrees with him is one of those men who do not know how to look out and take all the food they can when they go . . . . My experiences have taught me how to travel with more comfort and less comforts than he can." He explained that they would take their own bedding, "a small Scotch oven" that they could find flour, rice, chickens, eggs, beef, onions and turnips "anywhere," and that they were taking other food in plenty as well. He admitted, "It will not be an *easy* trip," but felt, "The women of this land can only be reached by women and sooner or later they must begin to travel."

He wrote that Lillie would have preferred to go on horseback but since only "the low dancing girls travel in this way, Dr. Horton will travel in a native Korean chair and will I think do a good deal of walking." This native chair had a wooden box frame and was high enough for Lillie to sit upright "in Turkish fashion," with a roof of bamboo covered with oiled paper, sides closed in blue muslin and little windows of stained glass on either side. There were cushions beneath and behind, a shawl draped about the inside to keep out draughts and a hot-water bottle and foot muff at her feet. "I felt positively steeped in luxury, and quite too babified for a hardy missionary,"[80] she wrote.

With the chair went, of course, chair coolies, "two who carried, and two who, by placing a strong rod under the chair, lifted its weight from the tired shoulders for half a minute or so, once every 10 minutes, changing places every three miles." Lillie said the carriers were "a very rough set of customers," full of fun and spirits, who told long and fishy yarns to the country folks to beguile the tedium of the road. "There was nothing, according to them, that we could not do, or had not got, 'Why even a boat,' said they, 'is in that trunk. It folds up very small, but one blows into it, and it gradually grows hard and large and lo! a boat.' Thus was magnified our rubber bath tub."

Lillie walked as much as possible, but spent many weary miles in the chair. "The ordinary road soon came to be tolerable, but when the bearers in the half light of early dawn (or worst still, the evening, when tired) picked their way over the narrow foot-paths, slippery with clay, between half-submerged rice fields, or jumped across intervening ditches, the rear man going wholly by faith, I must say it was not easy or pleasant."[81]

It was quite a crowd for a honeymoon. Lillie in her chair, and the four carriers; Horace on his horse with a groom to lead it; grooms for the three ponies with their loads of medicines, Chinese tracts and books, food, cooking utensils, bedding, blankets and bathtub. In addition, there were a Christian assistant, a cook and a Kesu or private soldier.

Lillie left a vivid portrait of Horace Underwood's mode of operation: "When we traveled together, I often wondered at his vigor and indefatigability . . . . After a long day's trip, I usually felt very tired and sleepy, and found it hard to present the Gospel to a lot of rough peasant women who crowded close around me in the wildest curiosity. It was a distinct effort to sing and show pictures and tell them about a future, and their need of salvation. But he seemed as lively as when he started. He would get the packs unloaded and everything settled for the night, closely overseeing the cooking arrangements which he always personally took charge of in the country, all the time making jokes, telling stories, petting the children, saying pleasant things to the housewife and servants, and chumming up with the inn keeper. Then after lunch or supper, he would sit down in the men's sitting room with a crowd around him and talk with them by the hour, or hold a meeting out under the stars at the top of some little hill or high gateway, where he would preach and sell books without the least signs of weariness, and start on again early the next day and so on and on."[82]

On this particular trip, they encountered many curious, eager crowds and a few hostile ones, friendly and unfriendly magistrates, two robber bands and one group who badly beat some of their Korean helpers. They passed through wild territory and some frightful weather. Once in a remote village when the newlyweds at last managed to take a moonlit walk in delicious privacy, they realized the strange pens they'd been seeing were tiger traps. They returned "with less lover-like and more business-like pace" to their little room.[83] Medicine, books and tracts meant for the entire trip were distributed within a few days and they sent for more from Seoul. Lillie treated over 600 patients, and they talked with hundreds of people. Horace Underwood crossed over the river into China to baptize 33 villagers and to celebrate Holy Communion.

Lillie wrote, "Perhaps Mr. Underwood was not so cautious as worldly wisdom would have dictated. Did he trust God too much? Was he reckless as well as brave? I sometimes think he was reckless of himself and us when he was bent on duty, but at any rate, no harm ever came, though at times it seemed near.[84]

Since there was no Christian constituency with whom they could lodge, they stayed in dirty inns or occasionally in magistracies. Numbers of dogs, cats, chickens, pigs and ducks were underfoot in the courtyards, and ponies noisily fed and sometimes fought in the stalls next to their rooms. A major problem everywhere was sightseers crowding about the paper doors and windows. "Every door was full of holes made by dampening the finger and placing it with gentle pressure against the paper. It was dismaying, when we fancied ourselves quite alone, to see all those holes filled with hungry eyes."[85] Some honeymoon!

The helpers, cook, and chair bearers slept like sardines in a can or beansprouts in a barrel in the general quarters. The newlyweds usually were given the room reserved for women. They sent out for bundles of fresh clean straw thatch, piling them a foot or more high to foil the ever-present industrious vermin, and spread their bedding on top.[86] "In this way," said Lillie, "we slept peacefully, except when the heated floor became intolerably hot, and our bed correspondingly so, then we rose, piled our straw in another place, remade our couch, and composed ourselves again to slumber. We never did this more than three times in one night, and it was a mere diversion."

After the long miles and large crowds, it must have been a relief even to Horace, to withdraw with his bride into their mown hay-scented chamber, read a few lines from the Bible, surely some from the Song of Songs, and to blow out the candle.

Extending the Boundaries

In 1890 both Protestant missions were finally able to strike out from Seoul. The Presbyterians gained one of their greatest assets with the arrival of Samuel Austin Moffett.

Moffett is difficult to describe. No single personality trait stands out. He was positive, though not so enthusiastic as Underwood; judicial and discriminating, but not thorny like Allen; quieter in his zeal than Appenzeller; neither brilliant nor creative in the sense Gale was, but highly intelligent, steady and focussed. A marvel of balance, Samuel Moffett was a genial man, liked by all.

A recent discussion on successful executives posed the question, "How do you spot a leader?" and answered, "They come in all ages, shapes and conditions. Some are poor administrators, some are not overly bright. One clue: the true leader can be recognized because somehow his people consistently turn in superior performances."[87] Moffett, who *was* bright and an excellent administrator, was a leader from the time he set foot on Korean soil; a trademark of his career was that any group he was in performed better.

The first mission meeting after his arrival was the most businesslike and forward-looking the Presbyterians had had. Although it was a traumatic year, riddled by sickness, John Heron's death and Horace Allen's resignation, Gifford wrote in October, "Our mission policy is taking the shape of more aggressive, systematized evangelical work,"[88] and much of this was due to Moffett. Korean Christians, who gave nicknames to the missionaries, had a particularly apt one for him: "the looking-up-the-road man."

Moffett arrived in Seoul on January 25, 1890, his 26th birthday. He wrote that his first impression, "deepened as time goes by, was that the people show an utter lack of positive happiness. The seem to have a look of settled submission to an unsatisfactory life. The first happy face I saw was that of our native evangelist and the contrast impressed me very strongly."[89]

He also wrote that everyone was overworked, "There is work enough now for a dozen."[90] For this reason, Moffett was immediately given supervision of the orphanage, and with James Gale's help, managed within a year to bring order out of chaos and turn it into a functioning boys' school with Chinese and Bible as the core curriculum and a strong Christian emphasis. To avoid attracting "rice Christians," he required the scholars to provide partial support; weeded out students who did poorly; dismissed the inept staff, and hired two competent, committed Christian Korean teachers.

He began studying Korean two days after his arrival, and his approach—as with everything—was straightforward. "The language is difficult; but it seems to me that in three years one should be able to use it quite effectively, to do so in less than two years will be very exceptional."[91] Yet a year later, Horace Underwood reported, "Mr. Moffett passed an exceptionally fine examination . . . and bids fair to be one of the first students of the language."[92]

Although the Presbyterians and Methodists had planned from the beginning to open stations all over the peninsula, the only Protestant missionaries who had yet lived outside the capital were the Horace Allens who spent seven months in Chemulpo and James Gale who was 10 months in Fusan.

In the Methodist tradition of circuit-riding Henry Appenzeller made a yearly trip north and in late summer, 1890, Samuel Moffett went along on his first trip to Pyongyang. "As yet it is not open to foreign residence," he wrote. "Very little evangelistic work has been done. Roman Catholics are said to number 3,000 with a French priest living as a Korean in a small place south of here. The Methodists have had a local preacher here for some time and at their meeting there were 18 men present . . . . Our own work consists of three baptized men, three reported believers, and several interested friends of these. They are without direction or leadership and have no regular meetings. It is in this province that a great deal of our colporteurage work has been done and where Mr. Ross of Moukden and his followers have labored. Here I have been visited by men from six or seven cities. The people are larger, hardier, more independent and have more spirit than those in the south."

Moffett reported that his Korean teacher, and he were all managing to live on $1 a day. "I have been here 10 days, living quietly in a Korean inn—going on the street every day exciting considerable interest. The people greatly dislike the Japanese and their manner towards me changes as soon as they know I am an American. A great many have visited me in my room, many of whom have read considerable of the Bible and some tracts while here; with many I have talked of Christ and with others my teacher has talked."[93]

These were scouting years, and almost every letter of both Methodists and Presbyterians referred to the opportunities for expansion and pled for more missionaries and money to start work outside of Seoul. The boards, too, urged their missionaries to "get somewhere a foothold outside of Seoul."[94]

The problem of expansion remained lack of personnel and means. Moffett wrote Ellinwood, "In your letter you say 'we ought not to put all our eggs in one basket'—but—it depends on how many eggs you have. We certainly need not less than five missionaries in Seoul. Seoul will always be the center of the work. The Methodist realize this and are to open four preaching places in Seoul this fall and have their educational work and press underway, with five people and all the money they want . . . . We have but three and no physician. Mr. Underwood alone has the language."

The Methodists, too, had their dreams before they opened new stations. Appenzeller wrote his board in 1889 that he had taken a short trip to Songdo (Kaesong) with the Rev. Mr. Ohlinger, "to spy out the land." Being "thoroughly Methodistic" he had taken collections at services. "We have endless work to do in Seoul, but we want to reach the regions beyond."[95] There was no further itineration that spring, however, because "Our minister has refused to ask for a passport for me unless I promised to refrain from preaching."[96]

Methodist work in Seoul was growing too. By January 1891, Appenzeller estimated 120 persons were hearing the gospel in Korean every Sunday morning and in the evening, Appenzeller preached at Chongno and Ohlinger at a service at the Ladies' Home "up on the hill." After the Methodist annual meeting in June 1891, Appenzeller wrote, " 'Great gains' and 'rapid strides' as far as the natural eye sees are not visible, but we are moving forward, our congregations are increasing, more books are sold, and the medical work is enlarging, and the truth is entering the hearts of some men and women here."

The 1891 annual meeting of the Presbyterian mission was delayed so that William and Annie Baird, who arrived on February 2, could take part in the five-day sessions which began the next day. The first *rules and by laws* of the mission"[97] were read and adopted indicating that the mission was pulling itself together. Moffett was behind this, hoping "to avoid friction which has resulted from having no settled policy."[98]

Also during the meeting, Underwood and Baird were directed to select a site in Fusan for a new station and Moffett was authorized to buy property in Pyongyang.[99]

Moffett set out on February 25 with James Gale, a Canadian who had come to Korea in 1888 as an independent missionary. They traveled with the Korean evangelist, and four other Koreans with two pack ponies. Their accounts are filled with the joy they experienced as they left mission responsibilities, petty grievances and paperwork behind. Zest for new experiences, appreciation of the people and challenges met along the way, as well as for the beauty of the countryside, shines through their reports. (Never mind the bed bugs, sandstorms and lack of comforts.)

At one inn an old grandmother asked if they had books with them, saying, "I know of the Western book and I know westerners are good people and that they have not come to harm us." Gale had a run-in at this inn, when he borrowed the family fishing pole. The grandfather took exception and called for him to return the rod. "I pretended not to hear. The storm would blow over in a little . . . but a whirlwind suddenly caught me, in which I lost line, fish, interest and everything. When I came to, an old Korean, 70 years of age, was carefully putting a fish-rod back in its place, while an American was pretending to dig wild onions on the bank of the river, the village people meanwhile looking on."[100]

Moffett wrote of preaching the gospel in cities, towns and villages all along the way. They stayed in Ping Yang five days having service there on Sunday. The mission had authorized him to purchase a house there under the $400 appropriation of the board, but since there was no missionary to put in charge the purchase was not made. "I was again impressed with the desirability of having a Christian worker there and have some hopes that one of the two professing Christians there will develop into a trustworthy leader. We found several inquirers, but the people are still suspicious of foreigners and afraid of Christian books."[101]

They crossed the Yalu into China, visiting John Ross in Mukden. With information obtained there they visited the Korean valleys and decided that the work could be better done from China than from Korea as the valleys are almost unapproachable from the South. They spent two weeks in the mountains of China and North Korea, finding the region sparsely settled, poor and so nearly destitute of food that they gave it the name Starvation Camp and lived on boiled oats and millet most of the time.

Moffett wrote that "From an evangelistic point of view, the journey was most successful. We preached to hundreds of people who had never heard the gospel. We found them ready to listen . . . . We had not an unpleasant experience on the whole trip, the people and officials being very courteous although their curiosity was so great that we could hardly get a half hour alone. The North is open for successful work."[102]

On their long trip, the two friends must have shared a good many confidences. Perhaps they discussed James Gale's affairs of the heart, for when he began the journey, Gale was engaged to a girl in Canada. Somewhere along the way, he decided that he had made a mistake, wrote explaining his feelings, that his heart belonged elsewhere (to Harriet Heron), and the engagement was broken. Moffett was an admirer of Mrs. Heron, and may have been in love with her himself, but after he and Gale returned to Seoul about May 20, it was Gale who wooed and won her, writing Ellinwood in September, "I hope to be married the coming year, but not to the person of whom I wrote you."

The board decided Gale was dangerously fickle. Not only did they closely question the circumstances of his broken engagement, but they expressed displeasure with his work plans as well. Having spent three years in the country, Gale wanted to settle down and work in Seoul; the mission unanimously wanted him there. But the board was expecting "a man to work in the interior who is not encumbered with a family."[103] The board came very close to rejecting Gale, though the other missionaries wrote to praise and endorse him. Even Horace Allen wrote, "I congratulate you on getting Mr. Gale. He is a No. 1 man whether he marries Mrs. Heron or not."[104]

Correspondence on the matter continued for six months. Moffett wrote in late December, "Your letters of November 19 have taken us completely by surprise and have been the occasion of much pain and regret . . . . Gale is a thorough Presbyterian, a firm believer in Scripture, the Calvinistic system of theology, and the necessity of the Holy Spirit's presence for success in the work. He speaks the Korean language better than anyone else on the field and is just finishing a translation of Acts which bids fair to be the best translation of any book yet given to us judging from the Koreans' comments . . . .

Gale's appointment as a Presbyterian missionary was secured, and he was married to Harriet, a happy match, in April.

When Moffett and Gale had headed north in February of 1891, Underwood and Baird had started south to buy property in Fusan. They were told by local authorities that permission to sell land would have to come from Seoul. Underwood wired Allen who had become secretary of the American legation, and after many delays and difficulties, Minister Augustine Heard was able to wrest permission from the reluctant Koreans.[105] Heard wrote Baird, "Your land was the first yielded to foreigners, as foreigners, by the Korean government."[106]

Besides the problems of when and how and who to start work outside Seoul, the Presbyterians had another problem, one still recurring in mission circles: how to withdraw from work once begun. The mission had wanted for some time to reorganize the government hospital into a truly evangelistic institution, or failing that, to start in its stead a new mission hospital. Heron's death and Allen's return to the royal hospital prevented them from taking those steps. After receiving a number of letters from Seoul, Ellinwood wrote Allen requesting him to turn the hospital over to the mission. Allen refused to do so until he could pass it to another physician. In January 1891, the mission asked R.A. Hardie to take charge. Hardie and his wife were a newly-arrived couple sent out by the Toronto YMCA and, like Annie Ellers, Hardie did not actually have an M.D. degree. According to Allen, "The Koreans absolutely refused to have him after a month."[107]

The government hospital had no physician for two months until the April 3 arrival of Cadwallader Vinton and his bride, Letitia. Vinton began work at the hospital in mid-April, but felt frustrated from the start that no evangelism was permitted. Even the religious books, tracts and gospel protions he left lying around the hospital were confiscated by ubiquitous government officials. No government funds ever reached Vinton. More than half of the hospital appropriations continued to go into the pockets of the officials. Vinton, "in accordance with the unanimous feeling of the mission and the formal advice of its voting members," severed his connection with the royal hospital, putting the key in his pocket and walking away.[108]

Allen was furious. He wrote Ellinwood, "It seems that your first and only success in Korea has slipped through your fingers. Dr. Vinton came with Mr. Gifford today to inform me that the mission had decided to drop the hospital. Reason: there was not enough opportunity to do mission work. But as none of them has ever tried to do such work, how can they know anything about it?" Allen did not attempt a confrontation with the mission, but he wrote the board and also appealed to American minister Augustine Heard to use his influence to urge Vinton to stay on at the hospital. Vinton continued to doubt the value of the hospital to mission work, explaining, "It is not a hospital where severe cases can be relieved and treated to best advantage, but a dispensary where the physician must only expect to give out medicines to applicants, to be used or misused as may result."[109]

Meanwhile the board had written that "we were very surprised at the suddenness with which the hospital terminated the hospital work . . . . You expect too much in the way of ethics from the Koreans . . . . We sympathize with the earnest desire to have our medical work more of a distinctly missionary effort but question that measures to sever the hospital connection will achieve this end." The mission was instructed not to surrender the hospital, nor to take "any important step of this kind" in the future without consulting the board.

Allen wrote, "The hospital has been saved entirely by the action of the American legation against the machinations of the Presbyterian Mission."[110]

During the month that Horace Underwood was away with Baird in Fusan trying to buy property, his wife's health failed alarmingly. The mission doctors said the only hope for her survival was to go to the States. Six coolies carried Lillie on a long steamer chair 26 miles to the boat, and Annie Ellers Bunker and Louisa Rothweiler, both only recently returned from health leaves, accompanied her in case she needed emergency medical attention on the way. "I can never tell with what regret, shame and pain I left Korea," Lillie wrote, "to go *now*, a *failure*, to leave my work scarcely begun, perhaps never to return, was bitter. But more bitter still was the thought that I was dragging my husband back from a life of usefulness."[111]

Underwood wrote plaintively from San Francisco, "The final

decision to return was very sudden. My wife had a sort of collapse . . . . It was a great trial to us to have to leave our work . . . . We hope the Lord may have something for us to do in America."

And that was the case. Underwood's dynamic energy was put to excellent use in the States. A compelling and popular speaker, he had a good story to tell of missionary work begun with impressive results. His love for the Korean people and his vision of a strong Korean church, "a light in the East," as well as his contagious enthusiasm were all communicated. The importance of this cannot be overemphasized, because there are two sides to missionary endeavor, the field and home support; one cannot exist without the other, and the relative efficiency and enthusiasm of one side affects the other.

Very soon after his arrival in the States, his brother John offered salaries for six missionaries in Korea. Ellinwood wrote Horace Underwood that the board had agreed to accept his brother's offer, but admitted that he didn't know where one was to be found. He suggested that Underwood visit McCormick Seminary "and plead the cause of Korea . . . You can plead as no one else can. I shall pray for your success."

Underwood made the visit at once, recruiting two students who would ultimately be indispensable members of the Pyongyang team—Graham Lee and W.L. Swallen. The next month Underwood spoke at the Inter-Seminary Missionary Alliance in Nashville, Tenn.

Horace Underwood on this one health leave was eventually able to recruit seven young people to open the Southern Presbyterian mission, and six persons for the Northern Presbyterians, all of whom were sent out and salaried with funds provided by his brother. Among the latter group were a woman teacher, Ellen Strong and an outstanding doctor, O.R. Avison and his family.

One very unpleasant by-product of Underwood's well-publicized speaking tour was Malcolm Fenwick's famous attack, printed about the time the Underwoods returned to Korea, in an 1893 issue of a premillenarian publication called *The Truth*.

The independent missionary Fenwick was a holy terror. Though Canadian, Fenwick's ancestry was Scotch, one might say "hot" Scotch. His childhood had been a rugged one, as he was only five when his father died leaving 11 children. Unable to attend college, he was heavily influenced by the Student Volunteer Movement and the Niagara Bible Conferences. He studied the Bible at night and preached every chance he got. Without denominational affiliation or backing, without college or seminary training, Fenwick felt both unwilling and unable to go as a missionary, yet continued to feel called to Korea. He was stirred to hear a missionary from India say that a man dying of thirst did not care whether water was given him in a fine cut-glass goblet, but would gladly drink from a rusty, battered can and live. "That simple illustration made me willing," said Fenwick. "I could at least be a battered, rusty can and carry the life-giving water."[112]

Fenwick secured financial backing from a group of individuals in Toronto, and arrived in Seoul in November 1889. After 10 months of language study in the capital, he went with Korean friends to Sorae. Fenwick built a Korean-style house there in 1891 and gardened while continuing to study Korean. It was from Sorae that he wrote the letter maligning Horace Underwood, accusing him of exaggerating mission successes in Korea and of baptizing converts willy-nilly.

Taking exception to what he had heard of Underwood's speeches in America, Fenwick wrote to a friend, J.H. Brookes, printed in *The Truth* and later reprinted in a book on missions by James Johnston, the letter sparked controversy for a decade. Fenwick wrote: "Two years ago a man named Underwood returned from this field to America, and has since been spreading exaggerated stories throughout the churches in the United States . . . . Let me give you an account of his converting work in a village where I afterward lived, as given me by one whom he baptized on the occasion mentioned.

"A native who received mission money was directed by Mr. Underwood to get together at least 40 or 50, and he would be along at such a time. Rather perplexed at the number demanded, the native set to work to gather his friends, but could muster only nine. The missionary arrived, and after exhortation at considerable length, asked the natives to remove their hats. 'What for?' said one. 'Oh, never mind,' coaxingly pleaded the native friend: 'take off your hats' and with the politeness so characteristic of the Easterner, they removed their hats, and then the Rev. Mr. Underwood, D.D. administered baptism to these nine men, none of whom, with the possible exception of one, he had ever seen."[113]

The Underwoods and their board were aghast. "(Fenwick) ought to be trounced," wrote Ellinwood.[114] Lillie called the story a slander.[115] *Truth* made partial amends by publishing Underwood's letter of refutation with an editorial commending him. The Toronto committee discontinued Fenwick's support and suggested he withdraw from the field.

The next year, Fenwick stated in *The Missionary Review of the World*, that he was deeply sorry he ever wrote the letter but claimed his charges were true. "The letter was penned under conviction that the Church of Christ in America was given to exacting glowing reports from missionaries to bolster up their methods of raising money."[116]

The story, whatever its origin, was false. The missionaries had been very skeptical of easy conversions and attempted to be sure that anyone baptized knew the essentials of the biblical faith. This wasn't always possible—as one missionary wrote, "No one in these modern days but the Pope lays claim to infallibility of discernment. That some black sheep have gotten into the church is evidenced by the fact that we have had to put them out."[117] Underwood's reports may have seemed overly optimistic but he had the experience and facts to support his claims of the responsiveness of the Koreans.

Fenwick's letter was significant in that it has influenced mission policy up to the present. All missionaries became even more cautious about whom they baptized, and a waiting period of months and often years was required before baptism. During the probation period, the seeker was required to observe the Sabbath, study the Bible and church polity, pass examinations on these subjects and on his personal faith, abstain from alcohol, tithe, learn to read if illiterate, read the Bible and introduce others to Christ. In most Korean Protestant churches today these remain the requirements for baptism.

CHAPTER III

Turning the World Upside Down

Sam Moore and the Butchers

By 1895 many different kinds of leaven were at work in the Korean social lump. Nothing would ever be exactly back again to its old routine.

Samuel Moffett, in a letter written that August, described some of the many changes he had seen in his five years in Korea. Foremost was the dismantling of the Gate of Welcoming Grace which had been erected in 1539 to welcome the annual embassy coming from China to collect tribute. This was a tangible sign that Chinese influence had left Korea.

Moffett wrote that the gate "was a momument which filled the heart of every intelligent Korean with awe. . . . as I approached the capital through the Pekin Pass I confess to some of the feelings of a Korean as I gazed upon the two large stone pillars, all that was left of the gate which for years had stood as a monument to Korea's dependence upon China. . . . one of the most interesting and picturesque objects around Seoul because of its conspicuously isolated position on the most important road, and because of what it represented. Under this gate the King of Korea and the Imperial Messenger of China met, the former prostrating himself three times, with three knocks of the head to the ground. . . . The Koreans acknowledge China's defeat altho they are dumbfounded to account for the fact that the once despised Japanese were able effectually to overcome the long revered Chinese [who had] furnished the only perfect standard in religion, literature, morals, customs, rites and ceremonies."[1]

Other changes were evident. Moffett wrote that the flowing garment of the aristocracy had disappeared, to be replaced by black robes for officials and that leather shoes had become popular. There was a new coinage, a silver five *yang* (one dollar) piece and a one *yang* piece.

For the first time since 1456 Buddhist monks were allowed to enter the capital. In fact, a new Buddhist temple was being built on the site of a very ancient marble pagoda in the center of the city.

Many Japanese were coming into Seoul and buying up long lines of houses, converting them into shops. Moffett wrote that "the Koreans look on with mingled feelings of respect, fear, alarm and suppressed anger as they see the recently despised and hated Japanese effecting this transformation."

In Pyongyang the first railroad, a very small one, was under construction, and "the Japanese merchants who followed the army to Pyongyang have not been at all loath to stay. As we know from them that the city will soon to open to foreign residents, we plan our mission work accordingly." Moffett foresaw that the Japanese "will soon control so much of the trade and monopolize so many lines of industry that the Korean will find himself without a trade, forced in order to live to become 'hewers of wood and drawers of water' to his recently found friends and protectors, the Japanese."

Changes were being brought about by the Christian influence also, some of them the unintentional consequences of 10 years of Protestant missionary effort. One example was that of Sam Moore and the butchers.

Some missionaries were sensitive observers and recorders of Korean culture and mores, but not Samuel Moore. He was a very different kind of man, single-minded, first and last an evangelist. As one of his colleagues said, he was "constant in season, and sometimes, even out of season."[2] Yet inadvertently and almost singlehandedly he managed to demolish a pillar of the centuries-old Korean caste system.

Sam Moore was 32 when he arrived in Korea from Illinois, a graduate of McCormick Seminary, with his wife Rose. He plunged into language study, immediately putting to use any scrap of Korean he learned. He never did achieve much knowledge *of* the language, as the Presbyterian language committee repeatedly pointed out, but he quickly gained an exceptional speaking ability. He spent each day in a small Korean house several miles from his home to isolate himself from foreigners and to surround himself with Koreans. His incentive was to be able to speak well enough to present the gospel, which he considered the happiest of work. He made his first convert—the Moores' cook—only a few weeks after his arrival; by the time he had been six months on the field, he had "given the native brethren a little talk" and led prayer in church.[3]

Each morning Sam Moore met with 20 or 30 men, talking with them and teaching Bible. Every afternoon he walked around Seoul, on the main streets, or in the villages along the Han River. "I go with a pack of books. . . . If I begin to read aloud from a Korean book, a crowd gathers at once to listen and they are always unanimous in saying that our doctrine is right and their idol and demon worship folly."[4] The trips along the river (which he later made in a houseboat named "The Glad Tidings") resulted in 25 congregations by 1900, with a membership of over 850 adults, 100 of whom he baptized in a single year. He also founded two churches in Seoul's western suburbs.[5]

After the government hospital was reopened by Dr. O.R. Avison, Moore and his teacher preached there regularly. In 1893, his second year on the field, Moore organized a group of believers into Seoul's second Presbyterian Church with a charter membership of 16; the church grew to 43 its first year.

Moore began a boys' school the same year with six boys from "heathen" families. The school had 20 students in 1896 and by then most of the parents had been baptized. The school budget was minimal—$1.50 a month for wood and $75 a year for the teacher. The boys studied Christian books and Korean history in Chinese and Moore taught them geography.

The missionary was sometimes more zealous than wise. In 1893 the American legation received a complaint that Moore had smashed some temple idols on a visit to a monastary; Moore denied the report. Horace Allen said he had been present, at a distance, and knew it was true. Moore claimed that "not even one image was cracked or injured in the slightest degree. It was only when the chief priest of the temple had agreed with me that the images were a lot of rubbish and ought to be thrown away that I lightly tapped one as illustrating their inanity."[6]

The most controversial aspect of Moore's work began in 1894 with the conversion of a single man, Pak the butcher. Pak had first heard of God through the Catholics. He had considered sending his son to a Catholic school but did not want to pay the tuition, so sent him instead to Sam Moore's day school. When Pak came down with typhus fever,[7] no Korean would have anything to do with him, but Dr. Avison visited him and was credited with saving his life. That Avison, physician to the king, would come to a butcher's home impressed Pak, who gladly listened to his doctrine and accepted it. His entire family was converted. The son, Pak Tong-Jul, did well in school and in 1907 became one of the first seven medical doctors graduated from Severance

Union Medical College. His daughter graduated valedictorian of the Presbyterian girls' school. Pak himself became a banker, an evangelist to the butchers, and an elder in the Presbyterian church. His story was like hundreds of others taking place in Korea except for the significant difference that Pak came from the despised outcaste butcher or *paekchong* class, considered for more than 500 years lower than low—beneath the slaves and prostitutes.

During the Yi dynasty, butchers were regarded as far beneath common people as commoners were below the *yangban*. For five centuries they had been Korean society's scapegoats. *Paekchong* were not allowed to live in tiled roof houses, wear silken clothes or even straw shoes, nor could they smoke or drink in the presence of others. They were expected to step aside and wait humbly in the street for their betters to pass. They could not even walk normally, but had to "bow and jump as if they were running. If they did not bow, they could be hanged."[8]

All the traditional honors of Korean life were denied to butchers. They could not wear the topknot, nor bind up their hair until a son was born to them. They were forbidden to wear rings, the Korean hat, or the *manggun* beneath it. A butcher bridegroom going to his wedding had to ride a cow rather than a horse; his bride, instead of being carried in a fine palanquin, was carried on a board to her own wedding.

Butchers were forbidden on the pain of death to bestow such favored names as *In* ("Mercy"), *Ye* ("Courtesy"), or *Ui* ("Righteousness") on their children, and sometimes could not use even their family names. They had to speak "up," using honorific language, and bow down to everyone, including slaves and children.

It was the matter of language which most troubled the butchers; one of whom said it was easier to endure the ignominy of going hatless and *manggun*less than the grievous trial of being addressed in low talk by boys.[9]

The origin of these restrictions seems to have been derived from custom rather than from any Buddhist or Confucian text. Presumably they were the result of the Buddhist abhorrence of taking life. There was also a Confucian saying that "Since men cannot bear to listen to the dying cries of animals all the noble and wise agree that the slaughter house should be far from their dwellings."

The gruesome butchering methods of the day might partially account for people's distaste for butchers. These were graphically described by Isabella Bishop. Visiting Korean markets she found "the pieces of bleeding meat blackening in the sun perfectly sickening. This aspect of meat, produced by the mode of killing it, has made foreigners entirely dependent on the Japanese butchers. The

Koreans cut the throat of the animal and insert a peg. Then the butcher takes a hatchet and beats the animal on the rump until it dies. The process takes an hour, and the beast suffers agonies of pain. Very little blood is lost; the beef is full of it, and its heavier weight is to the advantage of the vendor."[10]

The seven outcaste groups had been classified in the mid-15th century by Hwang Hui, a prime minister of the Yi dynasty, who held office under the great reformer King Sejong. The outcastes included servants of the sheriff; buffoons, traveling singers or entertainers; butchers; basket makers; *mudang* or women sorcerers; *kisaeng* or dancing girls; and makers of leather shoes.

How the butchers came to be at the very bottom of this list is difficult to understand, particularly in light of their usefulness. There were five great animal sacrifices annually, one each season and one at the end of the year. At each of these 70 to 90 head of oxen, sheep and pigs were slaughtered. In addition, sacrifices of 10 pigs were offered twice monthly to the ancestral spirits, and sacrifices several times a month were offered to the palace gods as well as a monthly sacrifice to a legendary Chinese general who aided Korea against Japan in the 16th century. There were also frequent special sacrifices, bi-monthly ones to Confucius and others to the great spirit of the heavens when a change in weather was requested. The slaughtering required by each of these sacrifices was done by butchers without pay. For their labor the butchers were exempt from taxation, but this meant that they were not enrolled on national records, and their status as non-persons was reinforced.

Nor was there any escape. Butchers were not allowed to enter other fields of work; their children could only become butchers and were allowed to marry only other butchers' children. They had no legal rights. Thus for a butcher like Pak to participate freely in the church community was unheard of. To Pak, becoming a Christian meant becoming a man.

What it meant to the church was something else.

Just a week after Pak's baptism in 1895, Moore wrote to Ellinwood describing the effect it had on the congregation, and his own reaction: "Our little church is flourishing. Four baptized last week makes a membership of 20. One was Mr. Pak, a butcher. It wasn't known he was a butcher for several weeks. . . . A Korean explained to me one might take a beggar up and make a man of him but the butcher can never rise. Yesterday at church half a dozen regular attendants were absent. . . . they felt they could not belong to the same church as a butcher."

Moore's helper Yi said they would probably build a chapel somewhere or meet for worship at home. "I said that I thought it strange that children of one Father could not sit down together in one room. Then the butcher could keep still no longer but came and sat before them and asked what sin he had committed against their highnesses. Had he not always used the highest talk in addressing them? When he came here he thought our religion was one that took up low, lost and dying sinners and lifted them to heaven . . . .The *yangban's* religion would permit only the highest classes to go to heaven. . . . Yi lost his temper and began to speak very loudly and abusively. When I told him to hush up the *yangban* all went out together, and two or three of them did a good bit of talking while I started a song, 'Jesus Loves Me' with the few who remained.

"The *yangbans* went off without saying goodbye to me and told my teacher that they were never coming back. At first I was disposed to think them sinners above most all others, but when another missionary reminded me that at home also there were Christian people who would not allow low people or colored brethren to meet with them for worship, and I remembered that these have only just come out of the darkest heathenism, I felt more lenient. Just a week earlier the group had sacrificially given enough to send out a Korean worker. I had been considering two men for the position, one the butcher. All seemed so promising and now about half the members are gone."[11]

About a month later some of the *yangban* returned. Moore wrote, "They acknowledged themselves in the wrong and promised to do better. Mr. Shin, however, says that he can only return to the church on one condition, that a custom be established giving the *yangban* seats of honor and the butchers the back seat of the room as per Korean custom."[12] When Moore refused to agree to such an arrangement, Shin replied that he could not return to the church, but that he would remain a Christian and observe the Sabbath at home.

By summer, there were six more butchers in the church, meeting daily at Pak's home for Bible study. The increasing number and participation of butchers in the church proved to be more than the gentry could bear. Saying they were "dissatisfied with the attitudes of the missionaries toward temporal affairs,"[13] they left and started amother congregation, the Hong Mun Suk Kol church. But in only three years, the two congregations reunited to form Central Church. During its first four years, 108 adults were baptized, 30 of whom were butchers. Presbyterian historians have written that this church was stigmatized for years because of the large numbers of butchers in its membership, and did not grow as fast as other Seoul churches.[14]

The conversion of the butchers affected far more than the feelings of church members. As Moore and Avison came to know Pak and to discuss with him the discrimination experienced by butchers, they not only sympathized but urged him to appeal to the government. In April 1895, Mr. Choe, an old-fashioned scholar and teacher in Moore's day school, helped Pak petition the Home Department for redress of the butchers' grievances. The petition concluded, "that henceforth your humble servants shall be allowed to wear the hat and manggun and that the servants of the magistrates are forbidden from this time forth to maltreat us, your humble servants."[15]

A few days later the petition was answered: "Your desire is granted. Wear the hat and manggun, dress like other men, and be on common level. Take heed, however . . . . consider carefully your inward prosperity. If the servants of the magistracies come to oppress you, be careful—do not quarrel with them but show them this decree."

Moore recorded that "the joy of the Negroes on hearing of President Lincoln's Emancipation Proclamation was not greater than that of the Korean butchers when the decree went forth that they should be allowed to wear hats. In some instances they were so elated that they wore their hats day and night."[16]

Just as the Emancipation Proclamation did not abolish slavery in America overnight, the butchers' situation wasn't immediately ameliorated. In many places the posters notifying the people of the new law were not put up, and where they were the public sentiment in favor of the ancient customs was so strong that the butchers dared not put on their hats. Another petition from the butchers in November, that orders be issued "that the new law be observed in Chungchong province as in the other provinces," was answered brusquely, "Since we have already issued the decree do not trouble us any further," perhaps because the government was just then preoccupied with the queen's murder and its aftermath.

The following March the butchers petitioned again, this time asking to be included in the census and other national registries. The government could not deny the reasonableness of their request and replied, "Since all are alike subjects, how can your request be refused, and your grievance left unremoved?"

Pak, who had been elected president of the butcher's guild, took several Christian butchers with him visiting groups of butchers all over the country and "assisted them in donning their hats." On these trips, the Christians took scripture and other books and preached. Mr. Pak compared their deliverance from oppression to that of the Israelites' deliverance from Egypt, and stated, "It is the same God who has now delivered us and there is not one cash worth of help to be looked for anywhere else." By 1898 there were 132 Christians among the butchers in Kyonggi province alone.

With the freedom to do so, butchers began leaving their despised work and their number decreased dramatically—from 400,000 in 1900 to about 33,000 in the 1920s. Many butchers concentrated on the education of their children to improve their lot and by the 1920s, 40 percent of the butchers' children were in school, compared with 5 percent of the children of the general population.[17]

There were scattered examples of discrimination and oppression, and a few bloody riots for decades, but being a butcher in Korea would never again be what it had meant for 500 years. Samuel Moore may not always have been wise, but when he died, the butchers of Korea having heard of the custom from the Catholics, wanted to canonize him.[18]

A Little Light

Nansa Hahn Kim came one night to call on Lulu Frey, a Methodist schoolteacher. Setting the little lantern she carried in front of the missionary, Mrs. Kim blew out the candle. Then pointing to the dark lantern she said dramatically, "My life is like that—dark as midnight. Won't you give me an opportunity to find light?"[19]

The missionaries were appalled when they discovered just how black that darkness was. One Korean woman summed up the collective anguish of her sisters with the remark, "There are two times of regret in a woman's life: when she is born and when she is married."[20]

In the prologue to her book, *My 40 Year Fight for Korea,* in which she describes torture, flight and other hazards of aggressive patriotism, Louise Yim recalls "my father and my 40 year fight to gain his respect and acknowledgement that a woman could succeed in a man's world, and that a girl child was not thought to be less than a boy child."[21] Her opening, titled "My Father Wanted a Son," could be the first chapter of most Korean women's autobiographies.

Subjugation of women was based primarily on Confucian teaching. The Confucian classic *Mencius* states, "There are three ways that a man can be unfilial to his parents and ancestors. The most serious of these is not having an heir." In the Confucian ethos, of the seven wifely offenses considered serious enough to merit divorce, not producing a son was at the top of the list. Because only males could perform Confucian ceremonies honoring the ancestors that must be carried out, the only posterity that counted were sons. The wife had a strong, personal vested interest in producing male children—she could be cast aside for failing to do so. Her marriage, value to her in-laws, standing in the community, her entire reason for being was dependent upon having at least one son.

Confucius based his teaching about human society on the patriarchal family, ancestor worship and filial piety, and each of these depended on having sons. The function of a woman within this system was simply to obey; the woman was to obey her father, her husband and her son in turn, and the quality of that obedience was to be unquestioning and absolute.

George Heber Jones wrote that "woman's sphere in Korea means seclusion to the point where outsiders have no entrance, and women no exit."[22] The Yi dynasty custom of seclusion was a reaction to the supposedly dissolute last decades of the preceding dynasty, and also an attempt to protect women from being carried off by all-powerful local officials. The custom of separating the sexes from the age of seven precluded the idea of simple friendship or any association for purposes other than sexual intercourse. Any contact between a man and a woman married to someone else would be construed as adulturous; missionaries Sherwood Hall and Robert Moose wrote of having seen a number of Korean women whose noses had been cut off as punishment for infidelity.[23]

Since men did not choose or court their wives, there was little emotional investment in their matches. Isabella Bishop noted that while it was correct for a man to treat his wife with external marks of respect, "he would be an object for scorn and ridicule if he showed her affection or treated her as a companion. Among the upper classes a bridegroom, after passing three or four days with his wife, leaves her for a considerable time to show his indifference."[24] Marriage in Yi dynasty Korea was for most brides a lonely ordeal, and their wedding day a time to weep.

A Korean novelist, Yonghill Kang, described a wedding in his family. He told of the special bridal palanquin—red and green, with characters painted upon it meaning longevity, wealth, male children—kept by the village and used to fetch the new brides. "It was a long journey for a frightened girl with only men attendants. In every village the carriers stopped and the people ran out of their houses to peer at the bride and to say, 'Oh, how beautiful she is!' . . . . And you could tell that she had been crying all the way when she got to our house. The brides always cried very much, and for some reason everybody wanted to see them doing it.

"Sometimes the bridegrooms cried, if they were very young. I could not help noticing in those days that nobody *liked* getting married . . .

"One intimate receptacle a bride always had, bringing it like a hat box: a small basin, delicately decorated and given her by some very near relative. It was a practical article for she might become nauseated on the way, which was very likely to happen if the carriers had taken too much wine; or if they considered that they had not been given enough, for then they shook the sedan purposely.

"After the feast was over all the young girls of the village went with my new aunt and her little maid into my junior uncle's new room, where the bride's chests, sent the day before, were neatly fitted into the wall . . . .Everybody examined my new aunt's trousseau and exclaimed and admired. They sat with her laughing and talking until midnight.

"Out in another room, my childless aunt was giving her brother, my junior uncle, certain instructions. I got behind the door and listened and the next day was able to tell my friends how to kiss the bride. 'When you go in, you must put out the light,' said my aunt. 'She will be sitting with her face to the wall, at the screen of the mandarin ducks, beside the pillow-of-two. Grasp her and put her under the comfort when you undress her, because if you don't she will be cold.' Then my childless aunt told him how to undress the bride, a rather important piece of information, for she was mysteriously wrapped up, like a great parcel, with long silk gloves on and even her sleeves tied down. The last layer, according to my childless aunt, was not to be taken off, for it was the wedding pajama, which the bride had put on underneath everything before she left home.

"My junior uncle was embarrassed and kept saying, 'Don't talk, I know all about that. That's easy.'

"At midnight my new aunt's relations and her little maid said goodbye and left for home. My new aunt wept and wept at the parting and used up all the long silk kerchiefs which were laid out. Two dozen—for a bride is supposed to cry hard at this time, whether it is sincere or not."[25]

The wedding night was depicted by one historian who said, "The bride never saw her husband, nor indeed any man outside the circle of the family, before her wedding day. Even then etiquette did not permit her, throughout all of the wedding festivities and ceremonial, to exchange a single word with him, not even when both had retired to the nuptial chamber. There, let the young husband be as gallant and amorous as he might, even heap compliments or questions on her, etiquette demanded that, seated in a corner of the room, she should remain dumb and immovable as a statue. The husband might disrobe her of her voluminous wedding garments; she could neither utter a word nor make a gesture. The female servants were likely all the time spying from the windows and straining their ears at the doors, and the least violation on her part was quickly reported and made her a laughing stock."[26]

The first Korean Protestant wedding ceremony took place in 1888. The bridegroom was Han Yong-Kyeng, Henry Appenzeller's convert whose first wife had died four months earlier. Appenzeller officiated in his parlor and wrote of the couple that "nothing could be more brave than to see these people coming to the front and in a Christian way be made man and wife."[27]

Gradually Christian practices began to be included in Korean weddings. But officiating missionaries sometimes encountered unexpected snags. J.L. Gerdine was to perform a wedding ceremony at "Kang Puin's" (Mrs. Josephine Campbell's). He had arrived late and only when it was time for the bride to repeat her vows did he realize that not only did he not know her name, but the likelihood was that she didn't have one. So he said as though reading from the ritual, "Will Kang Puin please name the bride." Without hesitation Mrs. Campbell replied, "I name her Elizabeth," and the ceremony proceeded.[28]

Charles Bernheisel recalled "how conscience-stricken I was once when performing a wedding. As the bride and groom came before me, I noticed the bride covertly lift her eyes to glance at her groom. It was the first time she had ever seen him. I determined then and there I would never marry another couple until they had seen and approved each other."[29]

As Christianity began to take root, Korean men began questioning some of the traditional practices. In 1901 Samuel Moore recorded some of the man-talk that was going on in the villages: "I was stopping at a little country town, when the evening conversation turned upon the position of women in the home. A young man from a neighboring village remarked that some of the Christian women had forgotten their names. Another suggested that when their names were called in heaven and they did not recognize them it would be rather embarrassing. The subject of women's names, or rather the lack of them, came up. Someone asked if girls in America had names given them just the same as boys . . . .

"When this had been explained the question was broached: What term should a Korean husband use in addressing his wife, or in speaking of her to others? One man answered that if there was a child in the family the wife would be called *'So-and So's* mother but if there were no children it would be decidedly embarrassing . . . . It was remarked that foreign husbands in addressing their wives often make use of the term 'My Dear,' but the Korean agreed that this would not do for if a man should use such a term to his wife all his relatives would think he was crazy.

"Mr. Chun said that after adopting Christianity he came to dislike his former habit of using 'half talk' to his wife (addressing her as an inferior) while she had to use high language to him . . . . He mentioned the matter to his mother and said he had determined to use the forms of equality to his wife but his mother objected so strongly that he was obliged to refrain from following what he felt to be a good impulse, which he believed came from a new life within him and not from specific instruction from the [missionary] on the subject. He said that after moving to his present home where he lived alone with his wife, he had been using the form of equality to her and that she was delighted, and her treatment of him had undergone a marked improvement. And he finished by remarking pointedly: 'The rest of you fellows had better try it.' "[30]

All over Korea similar conversations were taking place; "the new life within" mentioned by Moore's parishioner, rapidly multiplying, was affecting community life. In some cases the women were more conservative than the men, and would hold to the old ways until they saw a striking change in their menfolk. A husband who quit drinking, gambling, whoring and wifebeating was a strong argument for the attractiveness of this new Christian doctrine.[31]

In other instances, the women were the first to accept Christianity. Whereas they had been forbidden to take part in the all-important rituals of ancestor worship, they were welcomed by the churches where they could participate in worship services. Many found the doctrine of heaven a great consolation after their hard, drab lives. The church and Bible study groups gave a newfound sense of community to women, enabling them to meet together socially with a common purpose. It also gave them something in common with men.

The concept of equality among human beings, with women as well as men being recognized as the children of a loving heavenly Father, had great appeal. The church not only encouraged them to read but taught them how and provided their first reading materials, the Bible, catechisms and tracts. The women went on to teach their neighbors and to take up other responsibilities in the church and in their villages and then in other villages, as evangelists and teachers.

In the Bible they read of women who were friends and helpers of Jesus, and women like Lydia who were active in founding and leading new churches (Acts 16: 11–15). This was a more aggressive and positive role than any previously open to them. The coming of Christianity revised their image of who they were, what they were capable of, what their worth was. Figuratively and literally, thousands of Korean women received new names and new identities through the church. Certainly they received new hope.

The Methodists had begun a Sunday school at Ewha in 1888, and started an evening service for women the following month. This was in spite of their misgiving that the small missionary force was inadequate for such expansion. Mary Scranton wrote: "This step would not have been taken quite so early had it not been for the repeated requests of the Korean Christian men. They said, 'We are being taught, why should not our wives learn the doctrine also?' "[32]

The meetings for women, held at night, were interrupted for a while by the American legation's prohibition on religious activities, but when they resumed in September there were 35 women in attendance, taught by the Seoul colporteur from behind a screen. The same month William Scranton baptized three of these women, through a curtain to shield them from his veiw. The Methodist mission hired two Bible women to organize study groups and bought a house, placing it under the care of one of them so women could hold their own separate classes and services.

Samuel Moffett's letters provide a glimpse of the early village churches in the north and how women were included in the worship services. "Before the death of our Evangelist Paik, his wife had begun to gather the women together every Sunday night and since my arrival on this trip she has continued, so that some 20 women meet to hear of Christ and his message of love. Arrangements for the services are peculiar. We meet in a double room separated by sliding doors. In one of these, where a light is placed, I seat myself with Mrs. Paik's son and two or three of the old women. In the dark room the women are gathered, so while they can see me they remain unseen."

On this same trip, in a village two days' journey from Uiju, Moffett led a service on Sunday night and suggested that the women assemble the next night "but my helper spoke up and said, 'No, let us do as we did last night, for while we were holding services almost all the women of the village gathered in the adjoining kitchen and listened to all that was said.' I accepted his advice and that night preached to both a visible audience of men and to another of unseen women."[33]

In 1902, Moffett wrote from Pyongyang, "examination of some 20 or more women today—little girls and old women all just as eager to be baptized as can be. One young woman who was not called last year and was not called again this year was so disappointed she cried and cried. When I heard of it I sent word to her to come. Examined her today and she is all right and so went off happy knowing she is to be baptized. Her husband has taken a concubine, and poor girl she has been just as brave and patient as can be. She has learned to suffer in silence when her mother-in-law upbraids her. Such testimonies as these women give!"[34]

The same month, Moffett wrote that he "had a long talk today with a poor young widow and her mother—both Christians, and assured them that the church people would see to it that the plans of some wicked men for carrying off the 23-year-old widow would be frustrated. I laid down the law pretty plainly to the officers telling them of their duty to protect the women in such cases."[35]

The first Bible training classes for men began in Seoul before 1890; the first of such classes for women was held in the spring of 1898 in Pyongyang, and was described as "one of the happiest successes ever permitted to us." Only about six women had been expected from outside the city, but 25 came to join the 40 Pyongyang women. Two old women walked more than 200 miles; others came with babies in arms and on their backs and with older children they couldn't leave at home. Blanche Lee, who taught this first class with Annie Baird, reported, "Think of women walking 150 miles to study the gospel! . . . . The girls' school is flourishing and many mothers are learning to read with the little girls."

Attendance at the training class in 1902 was 302. A missionary wrote, "It was interesting to see the husbands and fathers accompanying the women into the city to find places for them to stay and provide for their entertainment, and then return to their houses. It is certainly a marked contrast to the way the men treated their womenfolk some years ago, or before they became Christians."[36]

Gradually the missionaries found themselves officiating at joyful ceremonies ushering in happy marriages. Charles Bernheisel described one in 1928: "The bride and groom had met each other once before and had mutually agreed to the arrangement . . . Both of them had reached maturity, the bride being 20 and the groom 22. This is unusual, even in the church, and unheard of outside the church. I have been gratified at the tremendous benefit that has come upon the young womanhood of the church these last years by reason of the postponement of their nuptials until they have reached maturity. It has made a very great difference in the appearance of the young women, especially those in the church. Early marriage and early assumption of family duties prevented their full development. Now they are getting an education and getting physically and otherwise fit for marriage before entering on it."[37]

As striking as such differences were to the outsider, they were more impressive to the women undergoing them. There is little reading more touching than the testimonies of the Christian women of Korea. One such autobiography is that of Dorcas Kim Kang, born in 1848 and married at age 17. "I first heard of Jesus in 1898 when I was over 50. Our family became probationers in the church on Christmas that year. Next month I began attending women's prayer meetings. I studied the Bible and I learned to read and write. I also attended the Bible Institutes held every spring and fall and was baptized by Methodist Missionary W. Arthur Noble in 1899. It was the happiest day of my life. I rejoiced most that I was acknowledging the Lord as my Saviour, but I also rejoiced that freedom had come to me—a woman."[38]

Dorcas Kang emphasized, "The day that Jesus Christ was preached in Korea began the emancipation of women from the bondage of thousands of years."

She continued, "Since my babyhood name had, according to custom, been discontinued when I was eight years old, I had never had a name. Think of it—for nearly 50 years without a name. On my baptismal day I received a name all my own, 'Dorcas.' Women in North Korea at this time still wore white turbans or kerchiefs covering their hair. That day the women to be baptized were kneeling at the altar in great reverence, and none thought of removing her turban. As the ritual began, Dr. Noble carrying the baptismal bowl in one hand, kept the other free ready to place on our heads in baptism. As he came to each one he would call out our new names. Beside him came Mrs. Noble, who with one hand would remove the turban and place it beside its owner, and with the other would slip into the hand of the woman a card with her new name written on it. Can't you feel the joy we experienced? God's daughters called by our own names!"[39]

CHAPTER IV

Education as Mission

How Shall We Educate Our Girls?

Schools for girls were such an innovation that one Korean remarked to George Heber Jones that he expected the next thing from the missionaries would be schools for cattle.[1] Of the 25 schools founded by the Protestant missions from 1886 to 1908, half were girls' schools.[2] Previously, Korean education had meant studying Chinese classics to prepare for civil examinations in order to enter the ranks of officialdom, and there was no place in this scheme for women's education. The traditional attitude toward education for women was reflected in the words of an ancient sage, "Woman's virtue is her ignorance."

Since their role was limited to domestic routine, systematic learning was not considered necessary. Yet women were socialized into the Confucian ideals by education in the home. In the upper classes this included some book learning. In a 1902 study Homer Hulbert reported that girls in *yangban* families were taught by their fathers, brothers or female tutors. Although 40 percent of them studied at least the primer, *The Thousand Character Classic,* perhaps only one percent gained enough knowledge of Chinese ideographs to be able to read Chinese freely. Korean script or *hangul,* however, was read by almost all upper-class women.

"If one of them is lacking in this, " said Hulbert, "she will be looked upon much as a western lady who should speak of George Eliot as a gentleman."[3] He claimed about 30 percent of middle class women and none of the lower class could read *hangul.*

One work every literate Korean woman was expected to master was the *Samgang Haengil-do* (The Three Principles of Proper Conduct), compiled by the scholars of King Sejong's court in 1432. It dealt with treatment of parents, rearing of children, and housekeeping. Loyalty, filial piety and chastity were considered the foundation stones of women's conduct, and of these chastity was the most important. A modern writer said traditional "education for women was indoctrination."[4]

Mary Scranton came to Korea "firmly believing that for the most speedy advancement of the country the women and girls must be educated."[5] Although she offered free food, lodging, clothing and tuition, there were no takers because Confucian culture did not permit respectable girls to venture from their own homes.

The first students came from homes of abject poverty; desperate parents sent the girls rather than let them starve to death. The students' mothers were accused of being negligent or evil to entrust their daughters to the "Old Lady Foreigner," and were warned that their girls were being fattened for slavery or worse and would probably be carried out of the country. Mrs. Scranton had to give written pledges that the girls would not be taken to America, and her school was watched very closely.

At the time of the 1888 baby riots, Ewha hired guards to protect its 18 students. None of the girls or missionaries were injured by the inflamed mobs, but there were several casualties among the guards. During times of upheaval such as the Tonghak rebellion and the Sino-Japanese War, parents would reclaim their daughters saying, "We cannot offer them more security, but at least the family will be able to die together.[6] On several occasions the entire student body was withdrawn from the school.

At first, the average age of the girls at Ewha was 12, with pupils ranging from 8 to 17 years old. Because many girls were married at age 12, it was difficult to continue the girls' education into their teen years. Parents were prone to force their daughters into early marriages, often to non-Christians. The mission schools therefore began matchmaking students with suitable Christian candidates. When Ewha held its first high school graduation in 1908, the school had arranged marriages for the graduates and the commencement exercises included a wedding ceremony.[7]

For years mission schools were plagued by the problem of students being abruptly withdrawn. As late as 1920 a newspaper carried an item that a 15-year-old student at Toksong Mission School had to be taken out after her grandfather had suddenly become very ill: a fortune-teller had warned the family that his illness was a supernatural punishment for allowing his granddaughter to attend school, and he would die unless the girl quit.[8]

Another problem was lack of teachers. Since there were almost no educated Korean women, one solution was to have the more advanced students teach the younger ones. In 1892 when Ewha started a class in Chinese classics, no suitable woman teacher could be found, so a male teacher was hired. When teaching, however, he was required to sit in a chair facing the blackboard, keeping his back to the students.

The Seoul Presbyterian girls' school encountered more difficulties than did the Methodist. For one thing, they didn't have Mrs. Scranton. For another, they were chronically understaffed and underfunded. Annie Ellers began the school with one waif in March, 1888. The next fall she passed the school, which then had seven students, on to Mary Hayden. After Miss Hayden's marriage to Daniel Gifford in 1890, the school was taken by Susan Doty, who suffered several breakdowns during her early years on the field. The Presbyterians made the mistake of taking very young girls, hardly more than toddlers, into their school. Susan Doty was a self-sacrificing woman who worked night and day. Few of her colleagues could match her standards, and they found her difficult to work with,[9] so the turnover in school personnel was rapid. The school was further handicapped by a lack of sympathy—at least as expressed in financial support—on the part of the Presbyterian board.

One of the mission doctors wrote Ellinwood in May 1892: "Miss Doty's health is being gradually undermined, her strength is continually overtaxed. She is a person of decidedly nervous temperament who besides trying to learn the language is endeavoring to fill a work which would occupy the whole time of three women if done properly . . . She has the actual daily routine of teaching the little girls and also the large work among the women who are drawn naturally to the school, being relatives or friends of the children. . . . It is the abiding sense of her inability to *begin* to perform these large duties that weighs so heavily upon her. . . .

"There is much sickness among the little girls of Korea, partly I suppose because they are unwelcome in their homes and are not cared for. I find upon inquiry that the same is true of the Methodist school. Here we have from five to nine children requiring medical care constantly . . . some cases in which all-night watching is necessary. And the last case is one in which the child died after a severe illness which demanded constant personal attention night and day for three weeks.

"Miss Doty says there has been some such difficult case nearly all the time she has been at the school . . . at least three cases have already had to be sent to the Methodist hospital for proper care. For this reason we need a trained nurse even more than a teacher."[10] Ewha school found it necessary to include both a nurse and a woman doctor on its staff.

The overwhelming problem facing the girl's schools in Korea

was to what purpose should girls be educated at all? One of the government schoolteachers, G.W. Gilmore, wrote that Ewha's aim was "to develop the school girls in such ways as to make them model housewives and to make them missionaries of the cross among their relatives and associates."[11] Mary Scranton emphasized that her school did not intend to westernize its girls—"We want Korea to be proud of Korean things, and more, a perfect Korea through Christ and his teachings."[12]

If the missionaries were naive not to foresee the improbability of westerners teaching Koreans to be more Korean, Japanese reformer Fukuzawa clearly perceived the difficulty. He wrote of woman's education that "Marriage will at one blow make all her learning vain;" and that if woman's position in society were not improved and Confucian notions dispelled, the education of girls was useless. The subjects he recommended that Asian girls study—he called them the "civilized girl's dagger"—were physics, economics, law, hygiene and physiology.[13]

The missionary schoolteachers were at first unaware that educating girls would topple women's traditional seclusion. They thought they were teaching girls to be "helpmeets in building up and maintaining *true* homes, teachers of day schools, assistants in our boarding schools, nurses or assistants in medical work."[14]

Louisa Rothweiler, a Methodist teacher, posed the question, "How can we best do this, or: What shall we teach in our Girls' Schools?" It was the question facing Ewha and all the other girls' schools. Answering it in 1892 Miss Rothweiler said: "Whatever may be the private opinion concerning women's sphere and proper occupation we must, for the present at least, act under the supposition that in Korea domestic life is her sphere and her destiny. Whatever else we may want our girls to do or be, it must be secondary to this first calling."[15]

An early Ewha graduate has left an account of how Korean domesticity taught by American schoolmarms worked out. "There were no classes on Saturday, so we spent the day washing, ironing and sewing. This latter chore was no simple one. In the winter we wore padded blouses made from 10-12 pieces of cotton or silk for the outer part and seven pieces for the lining. When a blouse became soiled we had to rip it apart, remove the cotton, wash the cloth, redye it if necessary, starch it, partially dry it, then fold the pieces and lay them on a polished granite slab and beat them rhythmically with two smooth, round sticks until a peculiar luster came to the cloth. Then we sewed all the pieces together, put the cotton back, and pressed the garment with an open charcoal iron. The teachers soon taught us to give up the old beating method and simply iron with a flat iron. We gladly followed their advice."[16]

In Methodist and Presbyterian classrooms, the courses taught—religious studies, Bible, simple arithmetic, geography and science—were a far cry from Fukuzawa's "civilized girl's dagger." *Hangul* was of first importance. Because most girls could not progress enough in Chinese during their few years in school, some felt it was useless to teach it at all. Miss Rothweiler disagreed: "While I would not urge it for all, I would neither entirely discard it and so with the English. If the study of dead languages is considered a good thing for the minds of students in Europe and America, why should the study of living ones not be good for Korean minds and even for girls?"[17] The girls appear to have agreed. In 1897 they asked that Chinese, which had been dropped from the curriculum four years earlier, be restored. This request is noteworthy on two counts; not only did it reveal the desire of the girls to pursue the same studies as their brothers, it also reflected a new spirit in that they would dare express what *they* wanted.

As to how the girls should be educated, Louisa Rothweiler advocated "giving them much practical and general knowledge, teaching them to observe, to draw conclusions, to make practical and useful application of what they learn, in a word to teach them to *think*, to solve questions for themselves."[18] That *was* revolutionary. The process of cultural transmission is the hidden curriculum in schools, and whatever traditional education in the home had accomplished, it certainly had not encouraged women to think for themselves. To free half of the Korean population, the female half, to think was one of the missionaries' most significant contributions in changing Korean culture.

Determination and strength of mind also was imparted by the doughty mission school teachers. Said one mission school graduate, "At that time we were not even aware of how much more we learned from what our teachers *were* than from what they *taught* . . . their hearts along with their disciplined minds made a deep impression on Korean young people in a period of transition."[19]

Just attending the new-fangled schools would take a certain amount of courage, and the early schoolgirls were a daring lot. One of them, Louise Yim, described how she came to attend school. At the age of seven, after meeting a woman missionary for the first time, she went to the neighborhood scholar and asked if it would be possible for her to learn to read and write. "He said nothing for awhile, and then replied, 'If the gods have given you courage to ask, we can hope they have given you the power to learn, little one. Come to school anytime and I will teach you.' She returned each afternoon with her older sister and two servant girls. She asked her mother for money to buy a Bible and hymnal and later her mother bought her books to read aloud at home. She attended the girls' school begun by the local church for a year at which time her father ordered her to stay home to prepare for marriage; instead she sneaked off to school.[20]

Sports were among the innovations missionaries brought to Korean education. By the turn of the century in Seoul, Pyongyang and other cities, school athletic meets were wildly popular events. In May, 1907, 15,000 people gathered for the Christian schools' field day in Pyongyang. Invitations had been sent out to country schools and many responded: one school of 25 boys marched a distance of 25 miles into the city with their teacher at their head. A girls' school shocked the conservatism of the crowd by demanding a place on the program. They were refused.[21]

The first school uniforms for boys were adopted in 1897, modeled after European military garb. Schoolgirls also wore uniforms, but in the Korean style. The first Korean woman recorded as wearing western clothing publicly was Yun Chi-Ho's wife Ko-Ra, in 1899, and the next was Emily Hwang, a teacher at Chinmyong Girls' School. Western clothes were not worn for many years, not only because they attracted staring crowds, but also because the western styles of the day were bulky and impractical.

The missionary schoolteachers by no means limited their teaching to young girls in schoolrooms. They tried to teach the mothers, sisters, cousins, church women—everyone they could. They began schools for the deaf and the blind, for widows and cast-off wives. Untold thousands of adult Korean women who had never had the opportunity to attend school learned to read and write so they could read the Bible; in every baptismal examination, reading knowledge was tested. Husbands were exhorted to give their wives time to read and to teach them to read.

Helen Kim, one of the great women of Korea, remarked of the change in Korean women's personality: "Middle-aged women who had been formerly about half asleep, suddenly transformed into Christian live wires, surprised their husbands with their new knowledge and determination. They claimed their rights and asserted with finality that their daughters were going to school too. And they went! My mother is a striking example of this point. Father could do no better than to let her have her way, for it was the right way. And the family did begin an upgrade climb."[22]

It was Helen Kim also who wrote of the lonely uphill struggle of the women missionaries: "When the school that became Ewha Women's University, the first in Korea and largest in the world, was begun with one pupil in 1886, only a few like Mrs. Scranton, then a little later Miss Frey and Dr. Rosetta Sherwood Hall believed in the possibility of Korean womanhood. The Korean women themselves could not look into their own future, neither could the men of the country nor could the other foreign missionaries on the field. The three strong women of vision went ahead against opposition and indifference."[23]

Mission and church schools preceded public schools. When a large woman's club in Seoul was lobbying for the establishment of a girls' public high school, they discovered that there wasn't one government-sponsored elementary school for girls in the whole country. The government tried to solve the problem by ordering boys' elementary schools to start separate classes for girls if possible. Four schools did so in 1908 and two more in 1909, bringing the total number of girls in public elementary schools to 423 in 1910. The same year the Methodists alone had 210 primary schools, with 6,500 students of whom about 3,000 were girls.[24]

In the spring of 1914, the first three women graduated from college in Korea. The ceremony was described by Helen Kim, who herself later graduated and became president of Ewha University: "I sat among the Ewha high school students watching breathlessly as the first three women college graduates marched in, wearing caps and gowns . . . . Everyone was proud of these potential leaders in the nation. The audience rose and stood in silence. It was a scene that had never before taken place in Korea. For girls to go to college, graduate and enter into professions was an unheard of thing . . . tears rolled down my cheeks. I looked around and saw that others were crying, too, even some men. They were tears of joy for the accomplishments of girls so long neglected and looked down upon."[25]

The First Aim

"The purpose of Confucian education," according to a Chinese scholar, "is to inculcate moral principles and to train young men in proper behavior. Such skills as reading and arithmetic are of secondary importance, even in primary education, and should be treated merely as a means to a higher ethical end."[26]

To the missionaries also, the ideological content of education was paramount. Their view was stated in the 1904 Methodist annual report: "All our teaching must aim at one goal—a saving knowledge of Jesus Christ. If the students experience the 'washing of regeneration and the renewing of the Holy Ghost,' all knowledge will be satisfied to their enlargement and usefulness. Otherwise all is failure. This experiential knowledge is the knowledge that the Korean needs. If he possesses it, and it posssesses him, it solves all questions of time and eternity."[27]

How these ideological goals worked out in practice is another story. The content of Confucian education did not appear very moral to foreigners. Daniel Gifford in an 1896 report on education in Seoul concluded that "two things the naturally bright people of Korea especially need, and which their present system of education certainly fails to give them, are a broader intellectual view and a deepened moral sense."[28]

Admittedly looking through chauvinistic eyes, the missionaries found it as difficult to recognize Korean schooling as education as to recognize its moral content. Robert Moose described how traditional schools appeared to him: "The teacher calls out the Chinese character, and the boys repeat in concert at the top of their voices. At first the meaning of the character is not considered, but the point to be gained is to be able to call it by name. You do not need to inquire if there is a school in the village, for if there is one you will hear it. School hours are from early morn to dark, seven days a week, 12 months a year with an occasional holiday thrown in . . . After two or three years of this meaningless study of the character, the pupil begins to learn its meaning, and advances into the study of Chinese history, philosophy and poetry as they have been handed down since the time of Confucius. There is no end to this line of study, so the boy who sets out to make a scholar of himself has the work of a lifetime before him. The saddest part of all is that he can never be a scholar in any true sense of the term."[29]

From the beginning, the missionaries taught. H.N. Allen, Horace Underwood and John Heron taught at the Government Medical School. As many other missionaries did, Henry Appenzeller began by teaching English because that was what was wanted. For him it was necessary to maintain a toehold in a land inhospitable to evangelists.

With the permission of King Kojong, however, he was able to open a school in June 1886. Within a month, his first six students dispersed—one had the proverbial business in the country, another found June a bad month for hard study, etc. But by October, there were 18 other students. And there were 67 by 1887 when the King bestowed his royal approval and the name Pae Jae Haktang, the Hall for Rearing Useful Men, on the school.

Horace Underwood's boys' school and orphanage, begun in 1886, was described by his wife a few years later: "There are about 25 boys in the orphanage, and they do a great deal of the work necessary for running the school, taking care of their rooms and preparing most of their food. They rise at 3:30 a.m. and after putting themselves and their rooms in good order for the day, study Chinese until eight, when they have morning prayers with one of the foreign teachers, after which they have breakfast. . . .

"After breakfast follow a few English lessons and a Bible lesson. These recitations are interspersed with short recesses and the afternoons are given to play, study hours, and Chinese, which is the most important factor in the education of Koreans. The mission board have been obliged to cut down so largely in the appropriations for this school that the possibility of carrying it on at all has become a very serious question."[30]

Indeed the problem of support for the school was critical. The Presbyterians, seeing growing opportunities for evangelistic work and committed to the goal of first building up a Korean Protestant church, simply did not choose to put funds or personnel into schools. Overworked Underwood passed the responsibility for the boys' school to James Gale and Sam Moffett, who tried to get the school on a self-supporting basis. A missionary wrote from Seoul in 1892 that "Mr. Moffett has been cutting the boys' school right down to starvation."[31]

F.S. Miller, who was put in charge of the school in 1893, wrote of his experiences, "We did not teach English as we found out that when they learned a little English they would go off to the ports or the mines and become interpreters, and those were bad places for the young folks in those days. For another reason—we found we could learn Korean better if they knew no English! I used to put pictures up on the wall and ask them 'What is this?' so I learned.

"Equipping and feeding the orphans bothered me the first summer but by the next summer I had some logs of wood and a saw. I learned how to mark the logs and then put the boys to work sawing them into boards. Three days later I found one of the boys had gone. . . . Next day another disappeared. I think I should have framed that saw for it changed our orphanage into a school."[32] This account, besides indicating that the Protestant work ethic had come to Korea, illuminates both the frustrations of the misionary teachers and the limitations of the education they were able to offer their students.

Little wonder there were so many drop-outs. At Pae Jae, too, in 1894 only 21 of 104 registered students remained for the full year. But even so, some persevered and in 1896 the Presbyterian boys' school graduated its first class: four of those graduates eventually became physicians, one a colporteur, another an assistant to a Methodist missionary, and still another minister of the interior.

In 1891 Henry Appenzeller reported that "the educational work of the (Methodist) mission continues to hold a chief place." That was not true of the Presbyterian mission, and the assessment of Korean educator and historian George Paik that Pae Jae was "the only school worthy of the name in spite of many wants,"[33] during this period was valid.

In 1895, Pae Jae entered into an agreement with the Korean government, accepting 200 students to be supported by the state. The initial three-year contract proved so successful that in 1898, the king personally directed its renewal.[34] In 1899 Pae Jae Haktang had grown enough for the Methodist mission to ask the board for $35,000 to start a college and seminary, but the request was denied.

The guiding principle of the Presbyterian mission was "the gospel for the heathen and education for the Christians." Educational work stressed Christian education for the church rather than secular education for the public.[35] The selectiveness of Presbyterian educational policy was explicitly stated in the mission's 1896 *By-Laws:* "As pupils, the children of Christian parents are to be preferred to heathen children, because they are more likely to fulfill their engagements to remain in the school and more likely to make good and reliable men and women in the end."

The 13th annual meeting of the Presbyterian mission in August 1897, was an unusually important one. Dr. Robert E. Speer of the mission board was an honored guest. After three days' discussion, the mission, with Speer's approval, adopted William Baird's paper, "Our Educational Policy," a decision which was to dominate the history of the mission and relations with its home board for the next 25 years.

Baird's paper began by quoting from the mission by-laws, that "the religious and spiritual influence brought to bear on the pupils is the most important thing in the school." He would add, he said, that "the main purpose of a mission school should be to develop the native church and its leaders for aggressive Christian work among their own people." The missionary teacher should be primarily a manufacturer of evangelists, and in so far as he fails to do this he has failed as a missionary teacher, however successful he may be as an educator."[36]

There were two reasons why Baird spoke so strongly. One was the phenomenal growth of the Korean Christian community. No longer were the foreign evangelists spurned. There was great clamor for them to preach, teach, baptize and organize. Statistics given at this meeting were eloquent testimony to the growth of the Presbyterian work: 101 meeting places; 982 communicants; 2,344 catechumens; 347 added by confession of faith that year; 38 church buildings. The church and its constituency needed educated leaders.

The second reason that Baird stressed so strongly that education should be provided primarily for the children of the church was that this was perceived to be part of the Nevius method. John Nevius was a missionary in China where his ideas on planting and developing churches had largely been rejected. But from the beginning, even before Nevius' visit to the Korea mission in June, 1890, the young Presbyterian missionaries in Korea had enthusiastically accepted and implemented his methods. These have been abbreviated to: self-support, self-propagation and self-government. There is no doubt as to the effectiveness of this method in the evangelization of Korea.

After adopting William Baird's educational policy, the 1897 annual meeting tried to solve one immediate problem by doing away altogether with the boys' school. "To continue the present unsatisfactory system was felt to be a waste of money and of valuable missionary time," wrote C.C. Vinton. Instead, "the mission took action distinctly approving the establishment of primary schools in connection with and supported by individual churches, such schools to be for the children of Christians, taught only by Christians, and conveying largely Christian instruction."

Underwood, Baird and Avison voted not to close the school, but in October 1897, it was turned over to West Gate Church's primary school, one of the six schools already founded by Seoul churches. By this time there were between 20 and 30 church-sponsored elementary schools in the country, and the missionaries believed the churches were capable of taking up the task of primary education.

The Presbyterian girls' school continued, as there were yet no church primary schools for girls. Within a few years, the Presbyterians began a secondary-level boys' academy in Seoul.

The missionaries now faced the need for training Koreans to teach in the many new church schools. In June of 1897 Baird organized a small normal school. A very primitive affair, he said, but the most congenial work he had done. Twenty-five men, 10 from Seoul and the rest from the provinces, met in the capital. "Dr. Underwood gave lectures on the art of teaching. Dr. Avison lectured on general hygiene. I gave a course on the Book of Acts, and some lessons in pedagogy suitable for Korean Christian schools. The expense of the school was $12, being chiefly that of rice at 12¢ a day per pupil."[37]

A major problem was textbooks—or the lack of them. In the autumn of 1896 the government educational department published the first school books reflecting western influence. Typical in this series was the *Kukmin Sohak Tokpon* or *A Reader of Little Learning for the People,* a 142-page book with 41 chapters in Chinese and *hangul.* The first five chapters were representative: "The Land of Great Chosen," "The Extension of Learning," "Hanyang" (the capital), "Our Home," and "The Story of His Majesty Sejong."

In 1898 a book on human physiology was translated and a book of elementary Korean was written for Ewha, one of the first schools to have regular textbooks. In 1901, the first in a series of Chinese readers for Korean schools, written by James Gale, was published.

Lesson material for each semester was broken down into what had to be covered daily; the missionaries with the invaluable aid of Korean secretaries would put the day's lesson into Korean. This was mimeographed and handed out to the students in class. The following day the students recited and were quizzed on the first sheet and handed sheets for the next day. By saving his sheets and binding them at the end of the term, the student had a textbook in that subject, and by mimeographing extra copies, the teacher had texts for the next semester's class. Avison followed a similar procedure in developing medical text books.[38]

The first volume of "Hulbert's Educational Series," a 60-page geography book in Korean, written by Mrs. E.H. Miller, was published in 1906. It was banned from government schools by the Japanese, but was used in church and mission schools until 1909 when it was forbidden by the residency-general on the grounds that it was "too stimulating to the people's processes of thought.[39]

By the turn of the century, education along western lines had gotten underway in Korea. Progress was not all in a forward direction, however. In 1901 Pae Jae school dropped its inappropriate title of "College." The following year the Korean government's subsidy ceased and the missionaries began charging tuition for the first time, approximately a dollar a semester. Enrollment was halved but the missionaries claimed that "our best men, nearly all Christians, remained."[40]

In the summer of 1904 all schools received a boost by a new Korean policy of nominating only graduates for government office. As the *Korea Review* noted, "The knowledge that graduation will put them in line for the civil service will fill the schools as nothing else could do."[41]

Presbyterian missionary Charles Bernheisel recorded in 1905 that "The Methodists feel that the time has come for them to begin educational work in Pyongyang, and so to avoid having two institutions doing the same work it is proposed to have a union school. Should this be done it would mean a great step forward. We are expecting to put two men in the academy and should they do so too, it would be possible to raise the rank of the school to a college grade."

Within four months "The Academy opened with about 75 or 80 new applicants. About 60 have been accepted so that the total will be between 130 and 140. This is a great increase. . . . As a result of the union movement, Methodist Missionary Arthur Becker commenced work in the Academy." In 1906 Pyongyang academy began a college class. Becker wrote in 1907, "We have already the only college in Korea."[42]

One feature of that first college class which became a perennial aspect of Korean education was a student boycott. Hardly had school begun in 1907 before the students decided to strike. Becker reported, "They drew up their list of grievances and demands, and petitioned the heads of the school and mission as well as Bishop Harris. The American and Korean faculty agreed on a course of action about curriculum and schedule grievances and they held firmly to their decisions. So the students soon decided to give up their demands and go back to study."[43]

This was not, however, the first student "demo" in Korea. Pae Jae had its first student strike in 1903. Twenty students sent a letter of protest to the principal saying they found the religious teaching in the school distasteful and would leave if it were not discontinued. The school made no attempt to negotiate and allowed the students to withdraw. Most soon returned.[44]

From 1905 there was an increasing demand for education. Bernheisel described a community meeting in June 1906 "in the interest of the college which we plan to open next fall. . . .The first gift received was a deed for a field valued at $100. Then followed one for a field worth $65, then one for $400. . . .Many women gave the rings off their fingers and the ornaments off their hair and clothing." Gifts of cash and real estate totalled $2,000, an exorbitant sum in Korea in 1906.[45]

There were several reasons behind this dramatic increase in the desire of Koreans for education. The Sino-Japanese War had shattered the myth of the invincibility and superiority of Chinese culture and learning; seeds planted by Philip Jaisohn and the Independents, a group of Korean liberals, had taken root; efforts of the missionary teachers were showing results, students from the many little country church schools were ready for more advanced study; and anxiety over the political situation spurred many to arm themselves against Japanese encroachment with the one weapon at hand: education.

The increase in schools and students during these years is noteworthy. In 1907, there were 6,294 students in government schools, and more than twice as many, 14,189, in Christian schools; in 1910, there were 15,774 in government schools and 22,963 in Christian schools. The only college and the only medical school in the country were mission-related. In 1909, Bernheisel wrote, "Pyongyang is getting to be quite a large Christian educational center with its lower schools, academies, college and theological seminary. By 1912 there were 47 boys in the Pyongyang College, 200 in the Boys' Academy and 150 in the Girls' Academy. The same year it was estimated that there were 245,000 Christians in Korea or about one person in 60 was a Christian, compared to one in 600 in both China and Japan.[46] In 1916, there were 900 students in three Japanese-sponsored secondary schools as compared to 1800 students in 18 mission-related high schools.

The increasing Japanese control of the educational system in Korea was ominous to Koreans and missionaries alike. As early as September 1906, according to the *Korea Review*, "The government has adopted the policy of putting a Japanese at the head of every common school or other school in Korea. A beginning is made by employing 20 Japanese. These men cannot speak Korean and Japanese text-books will be used. It is not difficult to imagine the degree of enthusiasm with which Korean boys will attend such schools. There are plenty of Koreans capable of teaching these schools and willing to do so at a fraction of what a Japanese would require."[47]

Japanese regulations were the beginning of a long series of ordinances which were to vex mission educators for years to come. All denominations fearing that Bible study, a mainstay in their schools, might be curtailed or forbidden, went about their educational work with more urgency. In the long run, these stiff regulations had a beneficial effect on the educational undertakings of the missionaries. "Too many of their institutions," wrote Methodist historian Charles Stokes, "like Topsy, had 'just growed,' with insufficient attention being given to such matters as equipment, curriculum, textbooks and divisions of classes into grades. The desire, or later necessity, to meet government standards stimulated much improvement along these lines."[48]

Such improvement was at a cost, however, and the cost was to the Koreans. With Japanese control of the Korean budget in 1916, one third of the budget for education went to schools for Japanese children; the Japanese population that year numbered 320,938 compared to 16,309,179 Koreans.[49] During this same year the Japanese demanded that all lessons except English and Chinese literature be taught in Japanese, a regulation that enraged the Koreans.

Of all the countries with interests in Korea, Japan alone had one consistent policy—colonization. Even before the Japanese annexation of Korea in 1910, that overriding policy had influenced the educational system. The first aim of the Japanese in regard to education was stated explicitly by T. Sekiya, director of education, before a meeting of the Christian Education Association of Korea in June, 1917: "The fundamental principle of Korean education, stated in a word, is to bring up the Koreans as citizens or subjects of the Japanese empire; to foster a loyal and patriotic spirit in the minds of the Korean pupils. . . .The language, customs, and manners of Chosen are now somewhat different from those of Japan proper, but we believe that in time they will become the same."[50]

Of course Koreans vehemently rejected that goal. The missionaries, too, were opposed to Japanese attempts to assimilate the Korean people. For all their cultural myopia, the missionaries had learned the language in varying degrees of fluency and appreciated and admired many aspects of Korean people and their culture. They stood with the Koreans in opposition to cultural and spiritual assimilation by the Japanese.

As elsewhere, there were many critics of mission education, including some Korean Christians and missionaries. George Paik, a leading Christian educator and a product of mission education, criticized the Presbyterians' early efforts with their boys' school: "The school was not satisfactory. The name itself (Yesu Kyo Hak Tang—Jesus Doctrine School) marked it as so distinctively sectarian that people of the higher classes would not send their children to it. The curriculum consisted almost entirely of propagandist literature which the boys could not understand. The teaching force was inadequate. They not only failed to employ respectable Korean teachers, but used their own students as instructors. The teaching of English was entirely done away with. Undue emphasis was placed on religion. No adequate building was provided, as in the Methodist school. The industrial feature of the school was of such a nature that it could not win the respect of the people. As the [Presbyterian] board frankly admitted, 'It is a matter of regret that the resources of the board are wholly inadequate to meet this manifest need.'"[51]

These charges could be made, in general, of all mission education in Korea at first. Certainly too few people with too few resources were able to do too little when so much was needed. But the attempt was made, and the amazing thing is that the influence exerted by the missionaries in education was as positive and far-reaching as it was.

It was not until 1903 that the first full-time educational missionary, Arthur Becker, a Methodist, arrived in Korea. For almost 20 years there had not been a single Protestant missionary appointed wholly for educational work. Although Horace Underwood, Henry Appenzeller, Mary Scranton, Susan Doty, the Bairds, Homer Hulbert and a number of others did educational work, they all did other kinds of work as well. It has been said that the mission field is the paradise of amateurs, and this has been especially true in the field of education.

In *Democracy and Mission Education in Korea,* Earnest Fisher, a later Methodist teacher, pointed out a number of weaknesses in mission education. He maintained that education with a predetermined goal did not fully respect the student's personality and was little more than indoctrination; that Christian schools used as "bait" to attract non-Christians for the purpose of conversion were neither Christian nor educational; that intellectual and scientific findings were sometimes suppressed; that Korean art and literature were underrated and the term "heathen" was especially damaging in its ramifications; that the schools had poor architecture; that translation was poor; and that the missionary schools did not pay adequate attention to the economic and technical aspects of society or to bettering their students' present life.[52]

Granted the justice of these criticisms, what did the mission schools accomplish?

One Korean analyst has said that "by stressing the spirit of national independence and the dignity of the human being, these schools laid the foundation for the growth of a democratic spirit in the country. . . . These schools paved the way for modern Korea."[53]

The comparative liberality of spirit of the mission schools was one reason Koreans wanted to attend. George Paik wrote that "In spite of their handicaps, the Christian schools were popular and those who did go to school flocked to the Christian institutions. This at once commanded the attention of the Japanese. They built fine-looking schoolhouses and provided Japanese teachers, but very few went to their schools. In my town during 1910–1911 the public school under Japanese control had thirty to forty students, while there were enrolled about four hundred boys and girls in the two Christian public schools. .".[54] Inadvertently the mission schools aided Korean opposition to Japanese colonialism. Political enlightenment was a by-product of mission education, and a spirit of nationalism was fostered by the Christian schools.

The missionary schools pioneered in education for girls and women, and freed them from centuries-long seclusion and intellectual bondage. Education for the handicapped was also first attempted by the missionaries. Mission schools introduced the concept of education for all, rather than just the elite, providing the groundwork for an entire modern educational system, from primary schools, secondary schools and colleges to medical, technical and theological schools. They were the first to use modern teaching methods and a scientific approach. Open discussion and debate were introduced by the mission educators and textbooks were another significant contribution. Yet another important feature of mission schools was sports for boys and girls.

The missionaries even achieved their own first aim by inculcating Christian idealism and values in some, if not all, of their students, and by training leaders for the vigorous young Korean church.

CHAPTER V

A Ministry to the Sick

Shelter for the Ill

Before the arrival of Christian missionaries there were no hospitals in Korea, only *Han Yak* apothecary shops. One of these was described by Dr. J.B. Busteed in 1895:

"On the floor sits the old doctor surrounded by his assistants who prepare the medicine, grind the powders, and fill the prescriptions. The doctor himself is a jolly old man and enters into conversation heartily. Above us are many paper bags filled with dried herbs, barks and powders some of which have been brought from China, the rest from his own heath. Each bag is labelled on the bottom with the name of the drug in Chinese."[1]

Dr. Busteed concluded his article on the Korean doctor with the prophecy that after many centuries, "the time is near when native medicine will be confined to a few drug shops. The more enlightened, seeing the advantage of foreign medicine, will adapt it to their country better than we have done or perhaps ever will do."

It didn't happen overnight. Certainly the government hospital established by Horace Allen could hardly be called "modern" and even the term "hospital" seems exaggerated. Yet, during its first year, Horace Allen and John Heron treated 265 inpatients, 10,460 outpatients, and performed 394 minor operations and 150 operations requiring anesthesia.[2]

In 1887 the government hospital moved to a better, more commodious site and its name was changed from *Kwanghyewon* or House of Extended Grace to *Chejungwon*, House of Universal Helpfulness.

William Scranton began Methodist medical work in his home in September 1885. He saw more than 500 patients there while renovating a Korean house for a hospital building. The hospital received its first patient in June 1886. The Methodist annual report described it as having "five clean, wholesome wards" and as being "much better than the government hospital." Scranton's language teacher posted a sign in Chinese and Korean, "American Doctor's Dispensary — Old or young, male or female, everybody with whatever disease, come at 10 o'clock any day, bring an empty bottle, and see the American doctor."[3] The following year the government bestowed a name, *Si Pyungwun*, which was somewhat freely translated as Universal Relief Hospital. With the name came invaluable official recognition and by the summer of 1888, attendance at the Methodist hospital nearly equalled that at the Presbyterian government hospital.

The Methodists began medical work especially for women with the arrival of Dr. Meta Howard in October 1887. After her health broke two years later, she was succeeded by Dr. Rosetta Sherwood, who began work the day after her arrival, seeing four patients. In three years Dr. Sherwood treated 14,000, many of them in house calls. Among her first 500 patients, she counted more than 50 different diseases. Swollen glands, goiters, syphilis, parasites, eye, ear and skin troubles predominated. "The majority of my patients are from the lower class, as the others must not be seen in the daytime. Sometimes the better class women come in closed chairs, or they send for me to come to their house. . . .I would like to have a night clinic so that it would be proper for any woman to come."[4]

Methodist medical work was intentionally directed toward the poorest classes. Dr. Scranton's 1886 report requested his board for funds and personnel to start a hospital for patients suffering from infectious diseases, who were often driven away from their homes and left without shelter. Scranton noted that the Presbyterians were not involved in this kind of work, or any medical work outside the government hospital.[5] Funds were granted and in December 1888, the Methodists opened a relief house and dispensary for people abandoned outside the city wall.

During 1888, Scranton's third year in Korea, he treated 5,500 patients. He urged that the Methodists adopt a policy of expansion, suggesting four projects: medical-evangelistic trips into the country; a dispensary at East Gate; a general hospital with a modern building and equipment in the center of Seoul; and medical work in Chemulpo.[6] Gradually all these projects became reality, though not all under Methodist auspices. Scranton pioneered in medical-evangelistic itineration, but after 1892 he did more evangelism and less medicine.

Because of the checks placed upon evangelism by the American legation and the Korean government during this period, the Methodists saw the healing ministry as their best opportunity for Christian witness. They decided that half their missionary personnel should be medical. Dr. William McGill joined them in the summer of 1889, opening his own hospital near South Gate a year later. Dr. W.J. Hall arrived in 1891 and Dr. J.B. Busteed in 1893; Miss E.A. Lewis, a practical nurse, reached Seoul in January, 1892, and Dr. Mary Cutler in the spring of 1893.

The hospitals and dispensaries were centers of evangelism. At the Universal Relief Hospital, the staff began the day at 8 a.m. with a prayer service; at 9, a Korean evangelist conducted Bible study for ward patients and at noon preached to the dispensary patients. In mid-afternoon he instructed inpatients in the Methodist catechism. The hospital matron at the Woman's Hospital doubled as a Bible woman. Personal witnessing and distribution of Christian literature were accorded an important place at all the hospitals.[7]

The 1890s were a time of many small beginnings for mission medicine. In 1893, in Seoul there was Dr. Scranton's hospital in Chong-Dong; McGill's at Sang Dong; the government hospital. Dr. I. Wiles, an Anglican, built the Hospital of Saint Matthew in Naktong, the southern area of Seoul, in 1892. Presbyterian doctors Hugh and Fanny Brown were in Fusan from 1891 to 1894, followed by Dr. C.H. Irvin. Both Methodists and Presbyterians opened small hospitals in Pyongyang in the 1890s. The Northern Methodists had doctors in Wonsan and the Southern Methodists opened a dispensary in Songdo in 1899. W.O. Johnson, a Northern Presbyterian doctor, began work in Taegu in 1897, and the Southern Presbyterians had Dr. Damer Drew in Kunsan, Dr. Mattie Ingold in Chonju, and Dr. C.C. Owen in Kwangju.

In 1893, new hospitals were started in Seoul by the women doctors. Lillias Underwood opened the O'Neil Dispensary for Women and Children, a seven-room brick building. The Methodist Woman's Hospital outgrew its quarters. Work continued there, but construction began near the East Gate on the Baldwin Dispensary, which was completed in 1898 and became one of the capital's medical centers. Dr. Rosetta Hall was director until 1897 when Dr. Lillian Harris arrived. Dr. Harris' health collapsed, however, forcing her return to the United States where she died in 1902.

Although the Methodists closed their hospital for infectious diseases in 1890 because of a lack of patients, another area on the outskirts of Seoul continued to be crowded with the pitiful huts of the abandoned sick. Horace Underwood, who had been assigned evangelistic work in this neighborhood, was haunted by the misery. With gifts totalling $1,000, many of them memorials to his brother Frederick, the Underwoods purchased several Korean houses nestled among trees outside West Gate. These were made suitable for a hospital. A number of different doctors treated patients free at The Shelter. Ninety percent of fever patients, most of whom would surely have died as outcasts, pulled through, and the survival rate of cholera patients at The Shelter was the highest in the city. The Shelter was an example of a missionary institution that worked so well it was no longer needed; its existence shamed the government into passing laws against abandoning the ill. Eventually it was no longer needed.

By that time, medical work in Seoul was centralized in one truly modern hospital, Severance. Often described as the offspring of the government hospital begun by Horace Allen, it is really more a step child. Allen worked in the hospital as a government employee rather than as a missionary. John Heron had followed his lead. The next three missionaries to direct the hospital found it difficult to work there at all.

R.A. Hardie's tenure, the shortest, lasted less than a month. Within a month of trying it, C.C. Vinton was ready to give up, but continued on a part-time basis at the insistence of the mission board and urging of American Minister Augustine Heard. Vinton reported that during 1891 he had been at the hospital 119 days and had treated 1,633 patients, admitting 67 as inpatients. He had performed 74 minor and 19 major operations,[8] only a fraction of the work load of Drs. Allen and Heron six years earlier.

New missionary F.S. Miller wrote six weeks after his arrival in February 1893: "I found the government hospital to be only a dispensary, controlled by almost 20 superintendents who would do high honor to Tammany Hall and over whom the doctor is given almost no control. The accommodations for inpatients are practically nil. Two rooms 8 x 8—heating apparatus is useless. The bedding had all been stolen. Three thousand yen ($1,500) had been appropriated for the year, but Dr. Vinton sees only 600 yen and only 250 of that has been turned over. . .there is no money for drugs. If a patient comes to the gate he is asked how much money he has, is told give us half and we will get the doctor to treat you. Dr. Vinton knows this, but cannot help it. . . .The patient is charged three or four times for his food, bottles, etc. These superintendents and a large corps of hangers-on make their living this way. Dr. Vinton has had to quarrel with them to prevent drugs from being stolen and sold. . . .What Christian influence can go out from such an institution? What impression can the physician make on hearts hardened by such unmerciful extortion, even if he were permitted to preach the gospel, a thing forbidden?"

The board was unusually slow responding to repeated requests from 1890 to 1893 of the mission to withdraw from the hospital. This was largely due to Horace Allen who wrote many letters presenting the hospital in the most favorable light and stressing its strategic importance. It is remarkable that in this case and a few others, the Presbyterian Board of Foreign Missions took his word against that of every missionary they had on the field.

In October 1893, Ellinwood wrote assigning O.R. Avison to the government hospital, "leaving Dr. Vinton to devote himself to medical and evangelistic work in other portions of the city or country."

When Avison began work at the government hospital in November 1893, the hospital consisted of a one-story Korean style building, 16 by 28 feet. The front yard served as the waiting room. Patients entered at one door, were examined and treated, given their medicines and sent out by another door. There were almost no instruments or drugs. The 34 minor officials who were appointed to the hospital received no salary; all made their living by what they could extort from patients or embezzle from the yearly appropriation from the king.[9]

Avison began by posting a notice to the effect that the clinic would be open regardless of weather. Next, Avison had a kitchen and a laundry put in, and hired young men to take care of the male inpatients.

There were no nurses in Korea at this time. The palace again sent a group of *kisaeng* or dancing girls to the hospital. Avison ejected them at once, convinced of their medical inexperience and doubtful of their moral character. Instead, missionaries Mattie Tate and Victoria Arbuckle were recruited to help with the nursing of women patients; later widows and cast-off concubines were trained as nurses. It was quite a while before nursing was considered a suitable profession for respectable young women.

Six months after his arrival, Avison was summoned to go on a two-day journey into the country to see a *yangban*, an important gentleman who was sick enough to try the foreign doctor after all other efforts had failed. The mission doctors dreaded these calls because they inevitably meant the patient was near death. But Dr. Avison, accompanied by Horace Underwood to interpret, made the trip. The patient was already dead when they arrived, so the two men turned their attention to a large town nearby that was having a market day. They rented a small room in the marketplace where Avison examined cases and wrote prescriptions for medicines which Underwood dispensed.

"Empty beer bottles served as containers for liquids, dry drugs were given out in paper wrappers, and ointments were served out in large clam-shells. . . .I was often at my wit's end to diagnose and provide treatment for a great variety of ailments. I had with me a supply of antiseptics and plenty of cotton and bandages, together with scapels, forceps and probes, so I could perform minor operations without anesthetics. Of course there were some simple dental instruments and I extracted teeth, opened abscesses and scraped out diseased bone cavities with but few complaints from the sufferers."[10]

On his return to Seoul a week later, Avison had an unpleasant surprise. He found the space he had carefully selected and readied for an operating room had been rented by the hospital officials to a Japanese doctor. The following morning Avison told the chief official that he would see patients that day but then he was terminating his association with the hospital. This official and the others, fearful of the king's displeasure, begged him to stay on. Avison refused. Horace Allen was called to mediate.

Avison told Allen that he would return only if all the officials but one (to act as a liaison) were recalled; if Avison were allowed to select his own assistants; and if the entire hospital property were turned over to the Presbyterian mission which would pay for all future renovations and running expenses. After six months' negotiations, these terms were accepted.

This time the mission board backed their doctor and even sent him reinforcements, Georgiana Whiting M.D. and Anna Jacobson, a trained nurse, who arrived in April 1895.

In 1899 Dr. and Mrs. Avison, both in dangerously poor health, took an emergency furlough. In Canada, Avison requested an architect friend, H.B. Gordon, to draw up plans for a modern hospital. Gordon was somewhat taken aback to find there were no funds, but he drew up plans for a modern building to accommodate 40 patients, to be built at a cost of $10,000.

One of Avison's former patients gave him the first contribution toward the new hospital—$5. Board Secretary Ellinwood remarked to a missionary that he was afraid Dr. Avison would have great difficulty raising the money for a modern hospital since he was not acquainted with any monied men. The reply was, "Yes, but he is acquainted with a monied God."[11]

In the spring of 1900 the Ecumenical Conference on Foreign Missions met in New York City. A vast audience of 5,000 crowded Carnegie Hall every day. Avison made one of the major addresses, speaking on Unity in Medical Missions, a subject dear to his heart. Avison was a small man, and he was awed by the size of the audience. He was afraid he could not make himself heard so decided to himself to speak to a man sitting on the farthest back row of the second balcony—"if I can make him hear, all will be able to hear." That man was Louis Severance.[12]

Avison suggested that if the seven missionary doctors then assigned to Seoul would cooperate to establish one strong hospital, it could do more good than seven inadequate, small hospitals. Only three or four of the missionary doctors would be needed to work there and the others would be freed to scatter out and extend medical work more widely through the country.

After the speech, Louis Severance, a Standard Oil executive, was introduced to Avison, and told him how much he had enjoyed the speech and that the two best words were comity and unity. He made an appointment for another meeting, at which he closely questioned Avison. He was impressed to hear the doctor had already had a set of plans drawn up for a union hospital. The Presbyterian General Assembly met in May in St. Louis, and it was there that Avison first heard announced from the platform that Louis Severance would donate $10,000 for the construction of a modern hospital in Seoul.

A majority of the mission board members and the Presbyterians on the field had reservations about accepting so much money for a single hospital. Dr. Ellinwood wrote, "The board must have an eye to the symmetry and proportion of the work. In higher education we have as yet done almost nothing in Korea, and the need of an educational institution in Seoul is certainly far greater than that of a new hospital."[13]

The board and mission felt it would be better to divide the Severance gift rather than put it all into one hospital in Seoul. When this idea was broached to Avison, he replied with remarkable restraint, "I am very grateful to God for the contribution that Mr. Severance has been led to offer. I note what you say about the division of the amount and am prepared to weigh it very carefully and to adopt whatever course God may lead me into."[14]

Avison returned to Korea with the question of accepting the $10,000 still unsettled. In the fall of 1901, new board secretary Arthur J. Brown visited Korea. From Seoul he went to Pyongyang, overland by pony as there was no railroad yet. Dr. Avison, who accompanied him, had decided privately that he would not attempt to lobby for the hospital he still hoped to build, that he would not even mention the hospital. But, as always, the doctor took a supply of medicines, surgical instruments and dressings. The news of foreigners coming preceded them and all along the way people came out of their homes to greet them, bringing their sick to the side of the road or taking the doctor into their houses to see those who could not be moved.

One day, as they were walking along, Dr. Brown suddenly confessed, "Doctor, I was one of the board members who felt that a smaller hospital would be adequate. I thought I was doing the right thing, but I was ignorant of the actual conditions of these poor, sick people. Since we have started on this trip, I have seen the hope aroused in the patients and their friends when there was a doctor in the party. I have changed my mind. I shall urge the board to reconsider the question."[15]

At their annual meeting in Seoul in September 1901, most of the Presbyterian missionaries objected to putting $10,000 into one hospital. They felt that such a plant would go against their policy of subordinating medical work to evangelistic aims. They feared that with the construction of a large hospital, they would be embarked on a course of institutionalism. Also, the Nevius mission policy called for all institutions to be simple and inexpensive enough for the Koreans themselves to support. Pyongyang station, bastion of the Nevius method, was particularly opposed. The Northern Presbyterian mission recommended rejection of the $10,000 gift or accepting only part of it for the hospital.

This prompted editorial comment in the *Korea Review:* "It does not seem to be the general wish of the mission to have a large and thoroughly equipped institution even though the funds should be ample. It is feared that if prominence is given to this work it will give the impression that Christianity is a sort of eleemosynary institution bent on benevolence and philanthropic work. With this it is difficult to agree, for if medical work is valuable at all from an evangelistic standpoint, as an entering wedge, then there should be no fear that the work will be too large. . . . A large and thoroughly equipped hospital would be a grand object lesson showing the Korean Christian that the constant pressure in the direction of self-support is not because the church in America is not willing to give the money, but because it is necessary to building a strong self-reliant native church."[16]

Most of the missionaries remained unconvinced, but with the capitulation of board secretary Brown, their opposition was no longer heeded. Avison was allowed to accept the gift, which soon trebled to include funds for a suitable site and equipment. In 1902, with $500 from Severance and money from the sale of the government hospital, land just across from the new Seoul railway station was purchased and in early August, ground was broken for the hospital.

The cornerstone of the new building was laid on Thanksgiving Day 1902, by Horace Allen, who was then American minister. Avison's friend, architect H.B. Gordon, had become so interested in the project that he came to supervise the construction (and that of several missionary residences in Seoul and in China as well). With the Russo-Japanese War in 1904, prices went so high that the builder found it impossible to fulfill his contract. Work continued by day laborers. Since no one in Korea was experienced in installing heating and plumbing systems, Gordon and Avison did it themselves.

Severance Hospital was opened ceremoniously with a silver key by Mrs. Avison in November 1904, beginning as a 40-bed hospital, with each bed "endowed" by contributions of one hundred yen or $50 per patient-bed per year. Louis Severance provided the salary for another physician, J.W. Hirst, who remained in Korea until his retirement in 1934.

A report 17 months after the opening noted that besides "a large number" of house calls by the doctors, 490 inpatients had been admitted and 16,000 patients were seen in the dispensary. Operating expenses were close to what had been projected, just over $4,260 a year, not including salaries of the foreign staff which were provided by the missions. Of the hospital income, $1,250 had been received from patients; the rest was from contributions or "endowments," many from Koreans.[17]

In 1907, Louis Severance visited Korea with his own physician, A.I. Ludlow. He was so pleased with the hospital that he helped draw up plans for additions that were more extensive and more expensive than the original building. He also contributed handsomely to other phases of Presbyterian mission work. Not the least of his contributions was that of his doctor, Ludlow, who returned to Korea as a staff surgeon until retirement in 1938.[18]

The first nursing school in Korea was opened in 1903 by a Methodist, Margaret Edmunds. The first two nurses graduated in 1908. Esther Shields began a school for nurses at Severance in 1906 and its first graduate in 1910, was Kim Pae-Se, sister of Korea's first woman M.D., Esther Kim Pak.[19] At first Japanese nurses served as head nurses at Severance under Miss Shield's direction, with, as the hospital report put it, "a sufficiently large staff of Korean women under their guidance to ensure the thorough care of every patient."

There were many obstacles to nurses' training in Korea—the customs of seclusion and early marriage, unfamiliar housekeeping methods and differing ideas of cleanliness and popular disdain for the profession. Prerequisites for admission to the first nursing course indicate some of the difficulties; the student was required to "know how to read and write and tell time by the clock." Students were also expected to be Christians, give absolute obedience, comply with training rules and serve for two months or more on probation. The standard nursing course lasted six years, but a shorter three-year course also was offered.

After Severance Hospital opened, Dr. Avison continued to teach his medical class of seven young men, using textbooks and vocabulary he developed as he went along. These men passed demanding examinations and were graduated in 1908, after 15 years of training. More than a thousand people attended the graduation ceremony.[20]

The night before the ceremony, Dr. Avison met with his students for a farewell gathering. During the evening he told them, "I have a private hope that some of you will come back and be teachers in this medical college we want to build up." Without hesitation all the men pledged to help Dr. Avison in the college. Deeply moved, Avison said, "I thought I was graduating just doctors, but now I know I am graduating Christian medical men who will work for their own people."[21]

The Methodist and Anglican missions assigned doctors to teach in the medical school, while the Southern Presbyterians provided Dr. Oh Kyung-Son, a brilliant Korean educated in America. In 1902, Dr. A.J.A. Alexander had arrived in Korea to join the Southern Presbyterian mission. While he was enroute to Korea, however, his father died, and as the oldest son, Alexander felt compelled to resign from the mission and return to the States. In the brief time he was in Kunsan, he met Oh Kyung-Son, who was a missionary's language teacher. Dr. Alexander took the bright young man back with him, supported him through medical school and sent him back to Korea as his own replacement. Dr. Oh worked 50 years at Severance, becoming its first Korean president after O.R. Avison's retirement in 1934.

Gradually modern hospitals grew up in Korea, staffed by well-trained doctors and nurses. The development of these hospitals very much paralleled that hundreds of years earlier of hospitals in Europe. The first European hospitals had offered hardly more than shelter for the sick, a place for them to rest and be fed until they recuperated or died. These were run by the church, and medicine was first practiced by the clergy. In Korea, too, hospitals came with Christianity, and at first were little more than hospices or shelters. Until Severance, they were simple affairs, inadequate in many respects, but perhaps their worth can be assessed finally only by those who availed themselves of them, the weary ill.

Medical Missionaries

No one ever said mission work was going to be easy, but it proved especially difficult for the medical workers.

From the first they were caught up in a continuing controversy over the place medicine should hold in relation to evangelism in Korea.

The first Protestant missionary to Korea, physician Horace Allen, had hardly arrived when he wrote to his board, "Secure the confidence of the people by well-organized and officially-recognized medical work and everything else will follow without hindrance."[22]

William Scranton had reservations about Henry Appenzeller's school. The Methodist physician wrote his bishop in 1889: "I have heard nothing but school, school, school. . . . I endorse with my whole heart the school plans . . . but I do not believe school work is the best means now in Korea to reach people, nor that by which we can accomplish our ends most speedily." Naturally, in his view, the best means was medicine.[23]

Was a doctor-missionary primarily a doctor, or primarily a missionary? It was a question of identity and priorities, both for the individual medical worker and for the missions. Scranton himself spent most of his life in Korea and never resolved the issue. After some years as a missionary doctor, he became a full-time evangelistic worker and later resigned from the Methodist mission to serve as a doctor in the Japanese hospital in Seoul.

Presbyterian physician J. Hunter Wells wrote in 1896, the year after his arrival, "we are not here so much as medical missionaries as we are missionaries medical. No patient comes but that he or she gets a religious pamphlet and is spoken to as to the reason we are here."[24] But five years later he was refuting the view that missionary medicine had no value apart from its evangelistic usefulness: "This is not in accord with the spirit of aid given to the man who had fallen among thieves,"[25] he said.

Dr. David Seel has pointed out that "The mission hospital, some have said, is a sort of bait to allow fishers of men to hook patients into the Christian 'boat'. The problem in this concept is not in the evangelistic zeal of those who advocate it but in the abusing of the objects of that zeal. It is a delicate line between sharing our testimony to Christ's redemptive power with those whom God has sent to us for loving ministry, and utilizing our human ministry as a trap or a threat or a goad so that the afflicted might be captured during the crisis they face in the hospital. It is the love of Christ that should constrain us, and we dare not cheapen that love, even for evangelistic success."[26]

The demands put upon the medical workers were simply too many. Mission doctors often had to raise or supply their own funds and in most cases had to build their own hospitals. They had to be administrators. They were the only "medical school" faculty available and had to train their staffs and write their textbooks. In addition, each had numerous mission and station responsibilities, served on a number of boards and committees, attended innumerable meetings, wrote frequent reports. And they were also expected to do evangelistic work, to lead Bible and prayer services for foreigners and to witness as often as possible to Koreans.

When the Southern Presbyterian mission in 1911 started "Heathen Sunday Schools" for the children of non-Christian parents, the physicians were assigned the responsibility of setting up and overseeing the classes. Many of the mission doctors did country itineration, holding clinics in Korean houses and church buildings, and conducting worship services. Some, such as Scranton, R.A. Hardie, Georgiana Whiting, William McGill, C.C. Owen and Robert Grierson, did as much evangelistic work as they did medical work. In fact, Grierson and Owen were ordained Presbyterian ministers as well as doctors and the Methodist Scranton also had been ordained.

In 1909 Robert Grierson admitted that "medical work is but an incident in the life of Sungjin station" where he was assigned. Yet he pointed out that his was the only hospital between Wonsan and Vladivostock that did surgical work. He reported having performed 100 operations and having examined 1,743 patients that year.[27]

O.R. Avison claimed Presbyterian A.M. Sharrocks, who worked in the northern station of Sonchon, had the neatest native style hospital and dispensary Avison had seen either in Korea or China. "If Dr. Sharrocks could have devoted his whole time to his hospital and other medical work the results would no doubt have been multiplied, but no other member of the station has contributed as much as he to the business end of the mission work, to working out plans of finance, to erection of buildings, to organization, or even to evangelization."[28] In his first five years in Sonchon (1901–1906) he built a dispensary and hospital and trained a very efficient group of Korean assistants. Sharrocks was one of a number of missionary doctors—D. E. Sawdon, Hugh Brown and Wiley Forsythe—who, health worn and broken, was sent home to die.

In every mission the doctors carried a work load that was mind boggling. R.M. Wilson recounted a typical day: "Prayer with nurses at 8:00 a.m. Prayer in the wards with the staff at 8:30. Prayers for individual patients by some of the helpers. Morning rounds of inspection made, patients in bed examined, treated, etc. Inspection of the kitchen and electricity plant. Visit the new building under construction. . . . Instruct some men about trimming trees and fixing the fence. . . . Then clinic was held . . . special classes falling to me. . . . Lunch. . . . After lunch to the operating room. First operation a goiter infected by the native doctor's dirty needle, removed with much sweat and hard work. Second operation: a tumor of the tongue, which also had been pierced with the *chim* (acupuncture needle). . . . Third: a tumor of the neck . . . then two entropian or eye cases, and a circumcision. . . . At six o'clock a labor case. . . . Supper. . . . After supper I was called back to the hospital."[29]

Some of the doctors broke down under the strain and were lost to the field. One of these was Methodist Dr. Douglas Follwell, who arrived in Korea in 1895. In 1901 Follwell wrote his board, "This year's appropriation gave me nothing for support of hospital patients . . . and only $100 for drugs and instruments, this sum will buy but $60 worth in the United States. I ask you, how can I do satisfactory work?"[31] In 1905 he treated 9,000 people, indicating an abundance of patients if not of funds. He wrote, "Working under present conditions is most disheartening. It is not enough to tell the physician you are sorry, very sorry for him and that he must do the best he can."[32] In 1909 he lamented, "Our present plant is a blot upon our mission. We have a semi-native built dispensary, a small detached building used for in-patients consisting of two wards, each twelve feet by twelve . . . with living quarters for the hospital orderly, and an old barn used for isolation purposes."[33] According to a 1914 letter of Sallie Swallen, "The [gold] mines are trying to get Dr. Wells or Dr. Follwell. Dr. Follwell had accepted their offer and was just going to mail the letter when he got a letter from the [Methodist] board saying they would build his hospital, so he did not accept."[34] A modern brick building was finally constructed in 1915. But by then it was too late for Dr. Follwell, who left Korea.[35]

The women physicians worked under all these handicaps and more. Dr. Mattie Ingold in Chonju, for instance, headed an all-male staff because the people in that conservative area would not allow women to assist in medical work. But the men would often refuse to take instruction from a woman, so almost daily Dr. Ingold climbed the hill to call on W.M. Clark who would return with her to the dispensary, repeat her every word, and stand by while the staff carried out the directions. He did not have medical training, but he had male authority.[36]

The Methodist women doctors had the advantage of working under a separate woman's mission board. At the time the Methodist men's hospital in Seoul was closed for lack of funds and personnel, there were two Methodist women doctors in the capital and two in Pyongyang. But even so, with hospital construction, illness, vacations and furloughs, there was rarely more than one woman doctor available for full-time medical work at any given time. In November 1906, the woman's hospital in Pyongyang was completely destroyed by fire, and it was not rebuilt until 1909.

Medical education for women was begun in 1912 by Drs. Rosetta Hall and Mary Cutler at the Woman's Hospital of Extended

Grace in Pyongyang, and was later transferred to Seoul. This work was opposed by the male missionaries, who felt that male doctors and women nurses were urgently needed and should be trained before attempting training of any women doctors.[37] For this reason, when the Northern Presbyterian mission's medical committee set up guidelines for medical education in 1903, it expressly recommended "all the practicing *male* physicians of the mission be formed into a Medical Board to control the issuance of certificates of proficiency to student assistants."[38] This effectively eliminated any Korean women medical assistants from consideration for further training. The Presbyterian women physicians complied. Of course, married women doctors (like all the married women in the mission) were not allowed to vote on mission matters for many years, so had no voice in such decisions.

The married women physicians had so many pressing duties, not the least of which were maintaining their own families' health and supporting their husbands' work, that they had little time for medical practice. In at least one case, that of Dr. Alice Fish Moffett of Pyongyang, the woman physician though considered a better doctor, was discouraged from much medical work because the male physician in the station resented women M.D.s.[39]

But none of the medical workers, men or women, received a great deal of support from their other colleagues. The 1911 report of the medical committee of the Methodist mission remarked that "the medical workers on the field are in a very small minority and have to deal with problems and bear responsibilities which are generally recognized but not fully or adequately appreciated by non-medical members of the mission. . . . A comparative study of the different phases of our mission policy would seem to indicate a tendency on the side of our non-medical co-laborers to minimize the part played by medical work in the ingathering of a church for Christ out of a heathen people."[40]

Nor did the Presbyterians do better. Dr. Arthur Judson Brown of the Northern Presbyterian board wrote that, "the development of hospitals was retarded by the misgivings of the evangelistic missionaries, who while recognizing the physical woes caused by ignorance, filth and superstition, regarded hospitals merely as a means to open doors of opportunity for preaching the gospel, and when the receptiveness of the people made them unnecessary for this purpose, the majority of the mission favored their continuance on only a small scale."[41] Dr. Brown was referring to the initial gift for the construction Severance Hospital, but he neglected to mention that he himself had been among those opposed to using the money for a single hospital, until he visited Korea and actually saw Dr. Avison at work.

For mutual encouragement the missionary doctors formed the

Korea Medical Missionary Association, which held its first meeting in September 1907, with twelve doctors present. They elected Avison president.

Other responses to isolation, overwork and under support were not so positive. A number of doctors died on the field from disease brought on or intensified by fatigue. Among these were John Heron, William J. Hall, Eli Barr Landis and C.C. Owen. Dr. Owen, a Southern Presbyterian, opened Kwangju station in the southwest in 1904, and besides doing all the medical work there, itinerated over a vast territory. In the spring of 1909, after 10 days of country work 70 miles out of Kwangju, he was taken ill. There was no one to help him medically. As he became worse, Korean friends carried him in a chair over three mountain passes to the nearest town. The next day he was carried the last 33 miles into Kwangju. A colleague wrote, "What that terrible journey meant to him, without medicine or proper nourishment, sitting in a cramped position in a chair, facing a bitter north wind, and all the while suffering with the excruciating pain in his side, none will know. . . . The end came four days later. Among his last words were these, 'Oh, if they would only give me a little rest.' "[42]

Some doctors broke down and had to return to the States. Other turned their energies to other things. H.N. Allen went into diplomacy. C.C. Vinton and R.A. Hardie became full-time evangelists, as did William Scranton for a time. The first Northern Presbyterian trained nurse, Esther Shields, also became an evangelist because her health couldn't take the strain of medical work. Dr. Georgiana Whiting became an evangelist in 1897, only two years after her arrival. Annie Ellers Bunker gave up her dream of finishing medical school and put her efforts into working with her husband in education and evangelism; Lillias Horton Underwood did the same, and wrote three books as well. J.W. Nolen, according to a Southern Presbyterian colleague, "left us to take a fine salary at the gold mines."[43]

Of those who continued practice, there were other kinds of breakdowns. The personality and performance of some missionary doctors became warped under pressure. One doctor was said to scream at his staff and rant at patients, to throw things and kick the hospital equipment when things went badly. Two men fell in love with Korean women and left their families. These men probaby were no less dedicated or less spiritual-minded than their co-workers; it is likely that they simply burned out under stress.

In fact, very few of the medical personnel survived many years as missionaries with their emotional and physical health intact. Of the 23 medical doctors appointed as "regular service" (continuing terms) missionaries by the Southern Presbyterians during the past century, only one so far, R.M. Wilson, managed to serve in Korea until retirement. The percentage is similar in the other missions. Dr. Wilson explained that he was able to endure so long because he early learned to escape stress by going hunting.[44]

With all the obstacles that the medical workers had to overcome, they made magnificent contributions, medical, social and evangelistic. To them it was not surprising that the church of the Great Physician fostered medical care. The word "savior," after all comes from the Latin *salvare,* meaning to save or to heal, words in Korean as elsewhere that are very close in meaning.

CHAPTER VI

The Great Revival

A Live and Growing Church

One factor hindering Protestant medical work in the early 1900s was the spectacular growth of the church. All hands, all funds, all energy seemingly was called on to cope with the vast evangelistic success.

This growth, though unexpected, was not nearly so explosive as it appeared. Fifteen years of quiet, steady expansion radiating out from Seoul had preceded the tremendous increases in church membership at the turn of the century. West Gate or Saemunan Presbyterian Church was organized on the Underwood compound in September 1887 with 14 charter members; Chong Dong Methodist Church was organized in December 1889. By 1895, small congregations dotted the city and there were a number of "preaching points" as well.

From the first, the missionaries gave country work high priority and made every effort to branch out from Seoul. The Methodists in 1892 inaugurated the circuit system with nine circuits, although most of these were later dropped for lack of personnel. When George Heber Jones, the only Methodist then assigned wholly to evangelistic duties, was appointed to the Chemulpo circuit in 1892 there was only one Methodist probationer there; within the year membership grew to nine baptized members and 23 probationers. Three years later there were 22 full and 55 probationary members, and Chemulpo circuit was the second after Seoul to be organized into a Quarterly Conference.

In 1894 the first chapel to be built by Korean Christians was constructed; within two years, membership was 94 and by 1905 it had increased to 2,625, about the same rate of increase experienced in the fast-growing church of the north.[1]

In 1893 Dr. William McGill and his family moved to Wonsan. At the end of a year, McGill reported 15 probationers scattered over his circuit. In 1898 Henry Appenzeller accompanied the doctor to one of his preaching points 15 miles up the mountains. The missionaries turned off the road on the way to see three men who had reluctantly received scriptures from McGill the previous summer. One of them, the village teacher, had read the Gospel of Matthew with a friend. "They professed to believe and when invited to the service in Wonsan the next Sabbath they came five or six miles and enrolled themselves as adherents of the new faith.

"We continued our journey through rice fields bending under the rich harvest . . . across clear, sparkling streams of water, passed hamlets nestled in picturesque nooks at the foot of hills. By five o'clock we reached our destination—a small mountain village with the only recommendation of pure air and fresh water. Dr. McGill without any delay commenced the examination of candidates for baptism. They were fine men . . . . They first heard the story of the Savior at the dispensary in Wonsan; brought home books; the villagers all read them or more had them read, and thus they became interested in the salvation of their souls.

"For three hours, we were engaged in examining the applicants . . . most of whom had attended services for two or more years. Their testimony was clear and their knowledge of Scripture exact though not extensive."

The Presbyterians also were spreading out from Seoul. Samuel Moore, working with colporteurs along the Han River, founded churches in 25 places in three years. Daniel Gifford, until his death in 1900, often itinerated with C.C. Vinton just south of Seoul, while F.S. Miller was assigned to the area east of the capital. Horace Underwood had charge of the large west district along the Han River into Kanghwa and the Hwanghae province. Sorae was the farthest and oldest church in this district.

Samuel Moffett visited Sorae in the fall of 1890, writing his board, "Here we have the most promising and successful work which had been done in Korea. In this neighborhood where I stayed eight days, we have some 15 baptized Christians who meet regularly for the study of the Word—It is the only neighborhood in which I heard of no Roman Catholics. Under foreign supervision this might become a small but influential center of Protestantism, for there we reach the middle class of Koreans—those most free from the moral and political corruption of the country, the class which will certainly become the 'back-bone' of the new Korea."[2]

A name often associated with Sorae is that of William John McKenzie, a Canadian Presbyterian. As a seminarian he had served as a missionary to Labrador, where he read a book from the 1887 World Student Missionary Conference on Korea that impressed him so much that he applied to go to Korea. The Canadian Presbyterian Foreign Missions Committee, in debt for $9,000 and already committed to begin work elsewhere, could not see its way clear to begin a mission in Korea. McKenzie sailed anyway, as an independent missionary. His diary entry as he first saw the rugged hills of Korea from his steamer was: "It is with feelings of awe I approach this land as ambassador of no earthly nation. . . .How weighty is my responsibility! 'Except a corn of wheat fall into the ground and die, it abideth alone.'"[3]

The tall (6'3"), attractive Canadian was 32 years old when he arrived in Seoul the week before Christmas in 1893. Six weeks later he went to Sorae, from February 3 until April 23 when he walked back to Seoul for his mail. From Seoul he went with Sam Moffett as a relief party to aid the beseiged Christians and missionaries in Pyongyang. After their return, McKenzie lived in Chemulpo with George Heber Jones until September 27 when So Sang-Yun, leader of the Sorae Christians, sought him out to ask him to return there.

The eight months from his arrival back in Sorae in October 1894 until his death the next summer were a time of war and violence, the time of the Tonghak rebellion and the Sino-Japanese War. McKenzie met a number of the rebels, with whom he discussed Tonghak doctrine. He wrote that the group had "spread here among the ignorant and vicious, particularly the poor. The object seems to be to make an easy living. Every one of them have done very little farming, which means robbing in winter and plunder. I take it to mean simply a desperate attempt to live."[4]

He took his gun apart, leaving it that way to show he was neither an adversary nor afraid, and this seemed to impress them. Three times it was rumored that the Tonghaks would attack the village, and the third time the attacking force was reported to be 10,000 strong. After coming part way, they turned back and did not again threaten Sorae, the only place in the area to escape a raid.

In order to distinguish the Christian church from spirit shrines, McKenzie made a flag emblazoned with the red cross of St. George and hoisted it over the church building. He wrote Moffett, "All joined in . . . singing 'All Hail the Power of Jesus' Name.' All were glad to have the banner of peace waving over the village."[5] By this sign the Christian church later came to be known throughout northern Korea.

McKenzie was living Korean-style in his housing, clothing and diet. At Christmas the Underwoods sent him a box of homemade bread, plumcake, canned fruits and vegetables, tea, milk and sugar. He gave it all away, writing them that he dare not taste even a bite for fear that he could not revert to wholly Korean food. He did some medical work and a lot of tooth pulling. In February 1895 he opened a day school for a group of 10 children.

By this time there were 26 baptized Christians and more catechumens in Sorae. They chose a site near the village on which stood a neglected and partially destroyed spirit shrine for their church. The people gave $160 for the cost of the building and supplied the labor; it was the second chapel after Chemulpo to be put up by Koreans, the first Presbyterian church building and the first to be built entirely with Korean funds.

As Lillias Underwood described it, the church was not imposing or lofty, "but it was the best building in the place. The poor people put into it their best wood, stones and tiles, the loving labor of their own hands, with fervent prayer. When it was finished no debt hung over it, and God blessed and honored it by filling it to overflowing with sincere, earnest people."[6]

In one of his last letters, McKenzie wrote that he had been eight months in Sorae "without speaking a word of English or seeing a white face." On June 1, he planted a corn crop and on June 5 wrote his friend George Heber Jones, "Church roofed with tile. Pillars and beams of more than ordinary workmanship. A perfect beauty. In a grove where devils received homage for centuries. Eighty days labor given free. . . .I take no part in the business. I let them know it is their work. They attend to it far better than Americans could, or even Canadians. As for the women they will not keep silent in the church—bound to be Methodists."[7]

His next letter was to Horace Underwood requesting him to come dedicate the church, but before Underwood could set out for Sorae, a courier arrived with a disturbing message. Lillias Underwood said it was "a pitiful letter, written with his own trembling fingers showing in every sentence the evidence of terrible suffering and of a mind already unhinged."[8]

McKenzie's last diary entry was made on June 22: "Keep people from coming in today; will not go out, too weak. . . .Hope it is not death, for sake of Korea and the many who will say it was my manner of living like Koreans. It was imprudence on my part, traveling under hot sun and sitting out at night till cold."[9]

The next day, Sunday, he called in Mr. So and others. He said that he was going to die, and less than two years from the time he first saw Korea, he quoted John 12:24 again: "Except a corn of wheat fall into the ground and die, it abideth alone." He asked that they distribute his clothes and money on hand among the poor and bury him beside the church. He complained a great deal of pain in his head, but insisted the Koreans go on with their worship service; about 11 a.m. McKenzie took up his gun and shot himself through the head.

The Christians of Sorae and the missionaries were stunned. George Heber Jones wrote Appenzeller, "I am shocked. I am grieved. I cannot collect my thoughts at the news of McKenzie's death. Such a man! Such an end! Alone, sick, insane, a suicide! Oh, God, there is some mystery here."[10]

Lillias Underwood, just as McKenzie had feared someone would, wrote a "few words of warning": "There are men and women, who, being John the Baptist sort of people enter the work with such zeal and enthusiasm that they forget the just demands of the body. . . .They forget that a solitary life gradually unseats the intellect, and that a body which has reached maturity fed on plenty of nutritious food, cannot suddenly be shifted to a meagre diet of foreign concoction, and retain its power to resist disease and to accomplish the heavy work they mercilessly extract from it . . . and so they drop, one by one, our noblest and most needed laborers."[11]

Horace Underwood and Dr. Hunter Wells left for Sorae as soon as news was received of McKenzie's illness, immediately followed by word of his death. They found the Koreans had "held a funeral as best they knew, after our custom, with prayers and hymns," and had buried McKenzie as he had requested. Underwood and Wells stayed on long enough to dedicate the church, baptize 19 men and women and treat more than 100 patients. The Christians of Sorae petitioned the Canadian Presbyterian Church to send them another missionary, and McKenzie's estate of $2,000 was used to start the Canadian mission in Korea.

Although Sorae, Chemulpo and Uiju all had promising congregations at this time, it was unprepossessing Pyongyang that was to grow into the vibrant center of Korean Christianity.

No other city was more difficult or took so long to enter as ancient, wicked Pyongyang. Henry Appenzeller made his first visit there in April 1887. Horace Underwood visited the following fall and the two men went together in the spring of 1888. The Underwoods stopped in Pyongyang in March 1889, on their honeymoon trip and Appenzeller made his third trip with William Scranton in October. From 1890 to 1894 Appenzeller, Moffett and W.J. Hall made repeated trips, staying for weeks at a time. But the city remained closed to foreign residence and all efforts to buy property were effectively blocked.

Moffett wrote his board from Pyongyang in January 1894, that the mission had "finally relieved me of all work in Seoul that I might give my whole attention to the work of this new station. I came in November to take up a nomad's life until such time as a residence here seems advisable." He was gaining friends and preaching "all day every day." His room, the *sarang*, was open to anyone, with a run of visitors from early morn until midnight.

He hardly had time to eat or rest, and when he went walking for exercise, he talked to more people and distributed tracts. With Han Suk-Jin, his helper, he visited the surrounding villages and from these came a constant stream of inquirers. He wrote that Koreans "look upon the gospel as a harbinger of better times for the oppressed people." Although he heard of a good many who were secretly praying to the true God, "as usual the great mass of people look upon the truth with suspicion, ridicule and hatred."

The first eight men had been publicly baptized that month and the Lord's Supper was celebrated for the first time in Pyongyang. "A joyful day for Mr. Han and me to see souls gathered into a Church of Christ . . . With the baptism of the Spirit—for which I look and pray—there will certainly come a harvest of souls of which I believe we are reaping the first fruits."[12]

During these six months that Moffett worked alone in Pyongyang, the first boys' school was organized, the first women attended services, and the first church offering of 13 cash (1¼¢) was taken. Once Moffett was attacked by his next door neighbor, a scholar who decided in a drunken rage to kill "the foreign devil." Mr. Han and the cook subdued the would-be murderer, but such experiences convinced Moffett that it was not yet advisable to attempt a permanent residence.[13]

In April Moffett returned to Seoul to meet his colleague Graham Lee, just returned from his wedding in America. He was still in the capital in May when W.J. Hall's effort to settle with his wife and child in Pyongyang resulted in riots and the imprisonment of the missionaries' Korean associates. Moffett and McKenzie rushed to Pyongyang to lend aid and Moffett reported that underlings of the magistrate were agitating to make it unpleasant and dangerous for foreigners. "Our men witnessed a good confession and stood the persecution nobly . . . . Dr. Hall's house was stoned and Mr. McKenzie and I were stoned twice on the street in front of the mayor's office . . . . The telegraph was freely used and in time quiet secured."[14]

The Halls withdrew from the city in June as Japanese soldiers were entering. Moffett remained until mid-August and the arrival of Chinese forces. The decisive battle of the Sino-Japanese War fought on Korean soil took place in Pyongyang on September 15 and 16, 1894. Two weeks later, W.J. Hall, Homer

Hulbert, Sam Moffett and Graham Lee set out from Seoul for the stricken city. Hall died on November 24 from typhus. But no one gave up on Pyongyang. In January 1895, Moffett and Lee returned and were able at last to purchase property, and eventually secured 110 acres of land for the Presbyterians.

It was about this time that Isabella Bishop visited Pyongyang. She described the missionaries' quarters: "a very rough Korean room, about the length and width of a Railway carriage. It had three camp-beds, three chairs, a trunk for a table, a few books and writing materials, as well as a few articles of male apparel hanging on the mud walls. I waited . . . imagining the devotion which could sustain educated men year after year in such surroundings, and then they came in hilariously, and we had a most pleasant evening."

The next day Moffett guided her around the city and battlefield and she saw the once-proud "city of 80,000 inhabitants reduced to decay and 15,000—four-fifths of its houses destroyed, streets and alleys choked with ruins, hill slopes and vales once thick with Korean crowded homesteads covered with fragments of broken walls and roofs . . . walls standing, but doors and windows all gone, suggesting the horror of human faces with their eyes put out . . . When the Japanese entered and found that the larger part of the population had fled, the soldiers tore out the posts and woodwork, and often used the roofs also for fuel, or lighted fires on house floors, leaving them burning . . . They looted the property, taking even from Mr. Moffett's house $700 worth . . . Under these circunstances the prosperity of the most prosperous city in Korea was destroyed."[15]

Nevertheless, by October Moffett reported that "the work in Pyongyang has passed the initiatory stage and has become an established work, a church beginning to develop, to expand and to make itself felt as a factor in the life of the city and the surrounding country. It is becoming a self-propagating, self-supporting church. We are quite free as to the reception of catechumens but exceedingly careful and cautious about baptizing them."

Isabella Bishop visited Pyongyang again the next month and gave a detailed account of the church growing up almost literally on the ashes of the ravaged city. She described one of the first training sessions for the north Korean church leaders. "In the dilapidated missionary quarters 30 men were living for 21 days, two from each of 15 villages . . . studying for six hours daily with teachers, and for a far longer time among themselves, and had meetings for prayer, singing, and informal talk each evening. Mr. Moffett interpreted for me and I learned more of missions in their earlier stage than anywhere else.

"Besides the 30 men from the villages, the Christians and catechumens from the city crowded the room and doorways. Moffett and Lee sat on the floor at one end of the room with a kerosene lamp mounted in front of them. There were a few candles on the floor, centers of closely-packed groups. Hymns were howled in many keys to familiar tunes, several Koreans prayed, bowing their foreheads to the earth in reverence, after which some gave accounts of how the gospel reached their villages, chiefly through visits from the few Pyongyang Christians, who were 'scattered abroad.'

"A young man told how his father, nearly 80 years old, had met Mr. Moffett by the roadside, and hearing from him 'some good things,' had gone home saying he had heard 'good news, great news,' and had got 'the Books,' and that he had become a Christian and lived a good life, and had called his neighbors together to hear the news, and would not rest till his son had come to be taught in the 'good news,' and take back a teacher.

"An elderly man, who had made a good living by sorcery, came and gave Mr. Moffett the instruments of his trade, saying he had served devils all his life, but now he knew that they were wicked spirits, and he was serving the true God.

"There were groups in the dark, groups round the candles on the floor, groups in the doorways, and every face was aglow . . . . As I looked upon those lighted faces, wearing an expression strongly constrasting with the dull, dazed look of apathy which is characteristic of the Korean, it was impossible not to recognize that it was the teaching of the doctrine of sin, judgment to come, and divine love which had brought about such results."[16]

Obviously the ground was prepared for growth in the north. Now the need was for workers: "on a single afternoon four requests for Christian teaching came to the missionaries, each signed by from 15 to 40 men."[17] At the evening service, "One old man, with his forehead in the dust, prayed like a child that, as the letter bearing to New York an earnest request for more teachers was on its way; 'the wind and sea might waft it favorably,' and that when it was read the eyes of the foreigners (the Presbyterian Board of Foreign Missions) might be opened 'to see the sore need of people in a land where no one knows anything, and where all believe in devils, and are dying in the dark."[18]

After the death of William J. Hall, the Methodists assigned W. Arthur Noble to Pyongyang. From 1896 to 1901, when he was joined by Charles Morris, Noble was the only Methodist evangelistic missionary there. Yet between 1896 and 1898 in Noble's territory 11 chapels were built and church membership grew to 1,700.[19] In 1895, total church membership in Korea was just over 100 for the Methodists, slightly more than 200 for the Presbyterians. A decade later, there were 2,457 on Northern Methodist mission rolls and 9,756 under the care of the Northern Presbyterian mission.

During this 10-year period growth was so rapid that it was difficult even to keep records. Board Secretary Robert Speer in the Northern Presbyterian report for 1898 declared, "In the north, the church has spread and penetrated as we saw nothing to surpass anywhere else in the world. The churches are crowded: the opportunities are unlimited." Growth was most spectacular in the north. In Seoul, church membership increased 1000 percent in 10 years, but it grew that much in only three years in Pyongyang. By 1896, Presbyterian church membership there had tripled from the previous year, and it quadrupled in another two years, from 73 in 1895 to 1,058 in 1898! These figures are only for communicants, that is, for instructed baptized adult church members in good standing; the total Presbyterian Christian community—baptized children, church attenders, catechumens—numbered more than 3,000.[20]

Samuel Moffett wrote his board in 1898 to express what this kind of growth meant in terms of work facing the missionaries: "Think of two men within a month trying to visit over 60 churches, carefully examine over 400 candidates for baptism, hold services in one or more of these places, baptize 300 people and meet and receive nearly 1,000 catechumens besides discussing all the other various phases of church work."[21]

In 1900, when the Presbyterians reported a communicant membership of 2,500 and were increasing by 100 communicants and 230 catechumens a *month*, the entire Presbyterian missionary force in the north consisted of 16 adults.[22]

Obviously so few missionaries, dedicated and hard working though they were, were not responsible for such increases, nor could they themselves possibly nurture and train so many new Christians. The growth of the Christian church wa a spontaneous people-movement. The nature of the Korean Christians accounted for much of this growth; and it was into their hands, and God's, that the future of the vigorous young church was committed.

The Korean Christian: Convert and Disciple

Many studies have been made in attempts to find the key to the success of the church in Korea. Mission policy, historical, sociological, economic, geographical and psychological elements have been thoroughly examined. But it is the Koreans—the converts who so quickly became disciples and evangelists, reproducing themselves again and again—who are the real secret of church growth.

George Heber Jones wrote in 1904: "From the very first, the convert is more than a church member, he is a worker for Christ. He may be only an ignorant, untutored, uncouth farmer, but he knows and possesses something his neighbors have not, and he presses it home on them. There is an impulse in him to work for Christ. He would not keep silent if he could, and could not if he would."[23]

There were a number of elements contributing to the remarkable receptivity of the Koreans to Christianity, which James Gale called the special providences preparing the way for the Korean believer.[24] Among these were—and are—geographical location, political uncertainty, and change, which predisposed Koreans to look for answers to their questions and deliverance from their problems.

The strong literary bent of Koreans was another factor. Traditional values in Korea were neither commercial nor military, but literary—Korea was a nation of scholars and would-be scholars. The Confucian classics had shaped their culture. Now another Book was to reshape their lives. George Heber Jones wrote that a scholar burst into his study one day, exclaiming, "I have found it, I have found it, I have found it!" Jones asked him what he had found and was told, "I have found the difference between the Confucian Bible and the Christian Bible." Asked what the difference was, the man answered, "The Confucian scriptures are made up of printed pages and beautiful thoughts. The Christian Bible is made up of printed pages and beautiful thoughts, plus a voice. As I listen, something within my heart awakens and responds to it."[25]

Koreans readily identified with Biblical customs and people. An allusion in a letter of Sallie Swallen's indicates the intensity: "In our Bible classes for this fall and winter we are teaching Ruth. The lessons strike to the hearts of the mothers-in-law. Many weep and confess their sin after the study, because of the hatred in their hearts."[26]

The freshness of the Bible provoked a powerful response. Lewis Tate sold a Bible to a young *yangban* named Sin whose spotless white garments and long, tapering fingernails showed he scorned labor. The next year, Sin was a candidate for baptism and when he came for examination, Tate noticed that his hands were rough and his nails stubby and broken.

The missionary asked if there had been a change in family fortunes and Sin replied no, but that he had read the Bible and was so impressed by the commandment, "Six days shalt thou labor," that he had gone to work.[27] He had also already gathered 34 persons into a church, in a village not yet visited by a missionary.

The Korean believers were always pushing ahead of the missionaries. As early as 1895, Samuel Moffett wrote from Pyongyang that "More than a score of men have taken books and visited other cities and villages, preached Christ, gathered groups of inquirers and started them to assemble on the Sabbath and instructed them as far as they could."

The Koreans used every means at their disposal to spread the word. For example, they adopted the flag of St. George first hoisted by William McKenzie, as an emblem announcing the presence of a church. Sallie Swallen, who made Wonsan Church's flag on her sewing machine, wrote in January, 1898: "The little band of Christians here seem very happy. They want to put up a sign at the chapel gate so people will know it is a church. They also want to raise the country's flag at each of the Christians' houses on Sunday and the church's flag at the church. One man, the only Christian in a big village, puts up his flag every Sunday. All the villagers say, 'What's that? Why has Mr. Oh his flag up?' They will all soon know the reason and no doubt it will be one way of spreading the message."[28]

In a clockless society, church bells served not only to call the faithful but to advertise the place and hour of worship. Bells, however, were expensive and their use came later to Korea. For many years it was the flags that identified and advertised Christian presence. James Gale described what was happening in north Korea: "On every hand there were miracles; drunkards reformed, gamblers rescued; men and boys of unclean habits saved. A tourist might have gone by and seen nothing except here and there a flag."[29]

The Christian faith was undeniably changing attitudes, lives, and customs. One of the factors often cited for the Koreans' acceptance of the gospel is the transference of their belief in animism to belief in Christianity. As Helen Kim described it, her mother's conversion was a repudiation of spirits whom she feared in favor of a Spirit whom she trusted. Her mother had previously been very religious in her observance of animism but recognized herself the large part fear played in that devotion. One Sunday after church service the entire Kim family, with their church officers, pastor and Bible women, burned all their fetishes and household gods and even the tablets of the ancestors in the family shrine.[30]

The early Korean Christians were convinced they were grappling with evil spirits and that their God would prevail. Exorcisms were a common occurrence. "In the days when Christianity was in the 'cutting edge' stage of its penetration of Korean society," wrote Richard Baird, "exorcism was an important church activity. Instances almost identical with New Testament casting out of demons accompanied the starting of many—perhaps most—new churches in the early days."[31]

The missionaries certainly did not teach the Koreans to cast out demons. Coming from a culture that did not recognize demonic activity, they were less certain of the personalized reality of evil spirits. Yet they witnessed exorcisms in which the results were so striking that most were convinced that spiritual encounters of some kind had taken place. Richard Baird wrote that he knew "of no cases in which missionaries encouraged or took active part in demon exorcism. The Koreans started and carried it on because they were encouraged to read the Bible and found it there."[32] It is not quite accurate to say no missionaries ever participated in exorcism. They did, although their participation was more passive, cautious and infrequent than the Koreans'. Annie Laurie Baird recounted an experience that was not unusual. Two church members brought a young woman about 18, listlessly holding her six-month-old son, to the women's Sunday school class. "She sat looking down as if absorbed in some sort of inward contemplation, and after the service was over, the other women told me her story. Ever since the birth of her child she had been tempted by two devils, one a woman, and one a big boy, both demoniac characters well-known to Koreans. Every time she shut her eyes she could see them menacing her. All day and much of the night she sat with head bowed and eyes closed, unable to resist the terrible fascination which they exercised over her.

"When all the arts of the heathen exorcists had been tried without avail, someone suggested that she be taken down to the Christian village . . . . 'They say the devils don't stay where Jesus is,' they said to each other in whispers, for fear the devils might hear. So she was taken to the church sisters who met and prayed over her. Their efforts availed to the extent of banishing the boy demon, but the woman still remained . . . . To go a step further and take her to where the missionaries were was next. So here she was.

"I had never expected to play the role of exorcist of evil spirits, but my mind was made up in an instant that if I had any power, be it no more than mere animal magnetism, this poor creature should get the benefit of it. I drew her close to my side, stroked her shoulders and arms and held her hands in a close clasp. She looked up at me dully, without the least change of countenance. The next Sunday the little scene was enacted as before, but on the third Sunday when I put my arm around her, her face relaxed into a smile. On the fourth Sunday she failed to appear, and when I asked after her I was told she had gone home cured.

"A fine drawn psychological explanation as to what her complaint may have been was of little concern to her or me. All we really knew or cared much about was that, whereas she had been oppressed and ill, she was now free and well, and we united in giving the glory to God."[33]

When a person was delivered from evil spirits by Christian exorcism, his whole family was likely to embrace the new religion, impressed by its power and effectiveness. In fact, the Christian faith most often spread through family channels. This was important, because the family was the basic and strongest unit of society. When a multi-individual decision occurs so that a whole social unit changes with only slight dislocation, it is called a "people-movement." In Korea, the people-movement flowed along the web of family relationships.[34]

As early as 1895, the pattern of whole families coming into the church was noticable. That year, Presbyterian C.C. Vinton mentioned "50 baptized infants and 55 families enrolled entire upon church records."[35] *The Korean Repository* reported in its December issue that in the Song family, with which Mrs. Mary Scranton had worked, "a baby of 10 months and his great-great-grandmother were baptized. The three generations intervening are members of the Church."[36]

Although family orientation facilitated church growth, it was not the complete story. Most Eastern societies are family-oriented, but in no other Asian country could it be said that the church grew like wildfire. The Korean zeal for evangelism, which began in a heart and then in a home and radiated from there, made the difference. George Heber Jones called this phenomenon "the Korean passion for souls."

The passion was systematized by the church; all the Protestant denominations required—most still do—that a candidate for baptism show evidence of having brought another to Christ. As Jones decribed it, "The final question in a baptismal examination is always this: 'Have you led some soul to Jesus Christ? Can you point out among those in attendence . . . someone who has been led there by you?'

"If the candidate is able to answer in the affirmative he or she is immediately approved, but if not, they are talked to kindly, somewhat after this fashion: 'Brother, our nation as yet is outside of Christ in the darkness of heathenism. It never will be won unless we who are church members bring to our neighbors and our fellow countrymen the truth. Will you be willing to postpone entering this high and holy relation in the church until you have brought some soul to like precious faith with yourself?' Of course the candidate consents, and so it has become the universal rule of Korea that the ticket of admission to membership in the Christian church is another soul won to Jesus Christ."[37]

Helen Kim wrote of her mother, "Right from the time she was converted mother was out doing personal evangelism . . . She herself had met Christ, not through a Pauline type experience, but through the day-by-day personal witness of the Bible woman. And that was the way mother shared her faith with others. Each week for the remainder of her life she sought to lead one person to Christ."[38]

Colporteurs and Bible women were the advance guard of the church in Korea and played important roles in its growth. The Presbyterian by-laws of 1896, defined the Bible woman as "a Christian woman employed in the distribution of Christian literature, and in biblical instruction." But she was much more than that.

The Methodists began teaching a class of five, later reduced to three, as Bible women in 1892. The women first had to learn to read. All of them were older women since younger women were neither respected enough nor allowed the freedom of movement necessary. The four graduates of the Methodist Bible schools in 1912 were aged 40, 50, 51, and 52.

No wonder classes were so small considering the qualifications for the job. The Bible woman was required to "be without home responsibilities; widows are preferred. She must be able to give her whole time and service to the Lord's work; she must be a woman whose life has proven her to be a doer of the word and a follower of the Master, not for any earthly gain but because of her love for the salvation of souls. She must be a graduate of a Bible institute able to teach . . . . [39] In addition, she had to be an excellent walker.

The lives of these Bible women were a startling breakout from the seclusion experienced for centuries by Korean women. Dorcas Kim Kang, who was appointed a Methodist Bible woman in 1900 when she was 52 years old, was assigned a circuit of 17 churches and had to walk 195 miles to get around it once. The next year, Hwanghae province was added to her circuit, and she had to walk 1,450 miles to reach all the places under her care.

She was frequently slandered and attacked verbally. When she was refused food, even to purchase, she either carried her own or went without. When she had an encounter with a band of robbers, she succeeded in converting one of them who later became a minister. In Anju she and the Korean pastor were imprisoned for buying a house for a church, but were released when the magistrate could find no law against it.

Her circuit was in a very mountainous province and she frequently climbed high, steep mountains. From the summits, looking down on all the valleys and villages still unreached by the gospel, she was painfully aware of her inadequacy. She wrote, "My body would tremble with weakness. I would kneel on those mountain tops and pray for strength. God answered me through the Bible verses I had learned; 'My strength is made perfect in weakness,' and 'My God hath chosen the weak things of the world to confound the things that are mighty.' " . . .[40]

Sam-Tok Chun, the first woman to be baptized in north Korea (by William Scranton through a curtain) had a family, so was not free to be a Bible woman. But she studied the Bible with her daughters-in-law and worked closely with the Bible women, and was credited with having led 600 persons to Christ.[41]

The Bible women frequently led services for women as well as instructing them. Practically they were the pastors of many female and/or new congregations and their role evolved into that of women evangelists. Although Korean women did the same sort of work as men, with equal responsibilities [but not equal reimbursement], the Korean Presbyterian Church in 100 years has not yet seen fit to ordain women elders or pastors, and the Methodist Church has only a handful [13 at this writing] of ordained women ministers.

The zeal for evangelism which resulted in the self-propagation of the Korean church was matched by a generosity in giving, which resulted in self-support. The Nevius principles, of course, included self-support, but the environmental factors in Korea, more than philosophy, were responsible for its success. Koreans, though hardly affluent, were self-sufficient. Their poverty was chiefly in contrast to a modern cash economy. They had few needs and usually, an ample supply of rice or in the north, millet and potatoes. Starvation was unknown except during famines. Beggars were rare.

Just as Koreans were able to evangelize over a wide area because they had the leisure to travel, they were able to give because they had the neccessities of life. For all but the wealthiest, any show of luxury was avoided rather than to run the risk of attracting the notice of greedy officials. Unlike other poverty-stricken mission fields, the common people in Korea had something to give.

Because the church served as the social center and welfare society of many villages and neighborhoods, and sponsored the local school as well, a contribution to the church was a way of supporting the community, just as contributing to the local cathedral was in the Middle Ages or donating to United Way is today.

But it should be added that Koreans often gave beyond their means. It was a common occurrence, when appeals were made for causes such as a church building, for women to place the rings off their fingers or their treasured silver and gold hair pins in the offering plate or bag. Men sold their fields or cows, and in more recent times, at least one man tried to sell one of his eyes to raise money for the church.

Mattie Noble wrote that "The most amazing gift that we have known came in the Haiju District. Gifts were being piled on the altar to help in the building of a new church. A traveling merchant who carried all of his merchandise on his donkey, and walked by its side through the country, was at the service . . . . His wife was on the woman's side. Both were touched with a great desire to lay something on the altar, but they had no money. The husband raised his eyes toward his wife, and without words asked her a question, which she understanding, answered with a nod. They went out and home, returning soon—the man leading the donkey which the wife had garlanded with flowers. Right through the church door and up to the altar was the donkey led, and . . . the man for a long time afterwards carried his heavy pack upon his back as he trudged lightheartedly along the country roads."[42]

By 1908, out of 188 Presbyterian churches in Korea, 186 were entirely self-supporting.[43] The Methodists, unlike the Presbyterians, had not originally demanded self-support, and had fewer self-supported congregations. Yet in 1901 there were 20 wholly self-supporting Methodist congregations in north Korea, and in the Methodist churches, too, contributions were generous in proportion to the people's means.[44]

Self-support certainly accompanied church growth, if it did not cause it. In Pyongyang, for instance, the Presbyterians had 53 groups meeting regularly for worship in 1897; of these, 25 had built their own church buildings. The next year there were 126 congregations with 69 church buildings. Forty-four church buildings were erected in a single year; if the churches had depended on funds from the mission or from abroad, growth would have been stunted. The mission could not possibly finance such growth. Since self-support was practiced more rigorously by the Presbyterians, and the Presbyterian church radically outgrew the Methodist, self-support is believed to be one of the factors in the discrepancy in the growth of the two denominations.

Church Historian George Paik has written, "Self-support produced wholesome effects in the establishment of the Christian church in Korea. It taught the people the spirit of independence and the habit of systematic giving and made self-propagation of the faith possible. Above all, persistance in this policy avoided the westernization of Korean Christianity and prevented the impression from arising that the church was an exotic and foreign institution.

"Furthermore, self-support not only aided the rapid naturalization of Christianity but also hastened self-government . . . . As the people supported their work, they naturally wished their voices to be heard in mission councils. The Korean church therefore became a self-governing church, without passing through a stage of ecclesiastical tutelage. Thus 'religious imperialism' and 'devolution' in missionary control which are a prolific source of friction in India and China . . . are not an acute problem in Korea. It is very possible, indeed, that the principle of self-support is the main cause of the rapid growth of the Korean Church."[45]

The early intent of the missionaries was, of course, to organize a Korean church. That was the work they had come to start. When the Council of Missions Holding the Presbyterian Form of Government, comprised of all the male members of the four Presbyterian missions, convened in 1893, it gave itself advisory powers only and stated its first object was "to carry on all our native work with a view to the organization of but one native Presbyterian Church in Korea."

Korean converts were supporting church work and functioning as congregations and evangelists long before the church was formally organized. What delay there was in ecclesiastical organization was due not to the lack of committed and effective Korean leadership, but to the lack of trained and ordained men.

In 1893, William Scranton wrote, "We are especially short of capable native helpers because we have expected them to grow all armored and equipped . . . and have not systematically trained men up."[46] The Methodists began such training with the establishment of a theological department at Pai Chai, where 12 students met two or three afternoons a week for elementary instruction in Christian doctrine and the Bible. This class evolved into a Biblical Institute that was held in Seoul and Pyongyang for several years until the Union Methodist Theological Seminary was formally established in 1910 in the capital. In December 1911, the first graduating class of 39 men received their diplomas. This was a decade after the Methodists had ordained Kim Chang-Sik and Kim Ki-Pom as deacons, qualifying them to administer the rite of baptism and officiate at weddings.

On September 17, 1907, 33 missionaries and 36 Korean elders assembled at the Central Church in Pyongyang to constitute the first presbytery in Korea. Samuel Moffett was elected moderator. One of the first actions of the new presbytery was to ordain the seven men who had graduated from a five-year study course at Union Theological Seminary, which had been founded in Pyongyang in 1901.

Samuel Moffett wrote Horace Underwood who was on

furlough, that the most significant action of the meeting was to appoint a committee to make arrangements, including a church-wide offering, to send a missionary to the island of Cheju, 60 miles off the southern coast. The new presbytery assumed jurisdiction over seven ministers, 53 elders, 989 congregations including 38 fully-organized churches, 19,000 communicants and 70,000 believers.[47]

Five years later, on September 1, 1912, the first General Assembly of the Presbyterian Church of Korea, incorporating seven presbyteries, met. Horace Underwood was elected moderator and presented with a gavel made of seven different kinds of wood, one from each presbytery, held together by three silver rings representing the Trinity.

Commissioners at this General Assembly included 44 missionaries, 52 Korean pastors and 125 elders. Their first action was to organize a Board of Foreign Missions, and the decision was made to send three Korean pastors with their families as missionaries to Shantung, China. In just 25 years from the organization of its first congregation, the Korean church had moved from being a missionary-receiving church to being a missionary-sending one.

Each of the growth factors mentioned has been cited by someone as a chief cause of the success of the Korean church. It is evident that the growth of the Korean church was not caused by any of these factors alone, but in their combination, and especially in their interplay with the national and individual charactor of Koreans. It is not surprising that a people who "out-Chinesed the Chinese" and in recent years "out-Communist the Communists," should not also "out-Christian the Christians."

Christian faith, when it came to Korea, was not merely imported but internalized. And because faith does not exist in a vacuum but is directed toward or reposed in something, the nature of the object of faith must be taken into account as well as the nature of the believer. Thus, Roy E. Shearer, after extended research on Korean church growth, concluded, "God gave the growth to the church in Korea. I say this not only because it is part of our biblical faith, but also because during the study I became increasingly aware that this church in Korea . . . while using human instruments in the environment of human society . . . grew as no mere human institution could grow."[48]

In one sense, all the growth factors together accounted for church growth in Korea; yet the sum of them still does not equal the whole; none of them nor can all of them together wholly account for what is inexplicable aside from the purposes of God.

Pentecost

For all its growth and strength, the Korean church at the turn of the century still seemed to lack something.

Henry Appenzeller, early aware of the problem, said in 1890 that if anyone asked him what Korea needed most, his answer would be "a mighty baptism of convicting and converting power. I want to see Korean sinners alarmed because of their sins . . . . Nothing else can save the Hermit Nation."[49]

William Franklin Sands, who came to Korea in 1898 as secretary of the American legation, agreed with Appenzeller. He wrote of the pre-revival period that "It was never clear to me that Koreans really sought the Christianity of American missions. It seemed that what they saw was a humanitarian ethical life, political principles which appealed to many, and a simple access to knowledge of western life which they wanted and needed . . . but that did not mean to them religion. There is a mystical content in religion to the Oriental mind. I would have liked to have seen their reaction uncomplicated by nationalism, electric railroads, telephones and political theories."[50]

What was lacking was heart, or in today's parlance, "soul." The emphasis on rules and regulations could easily have caused the Korean church to harden into Pharisaism were it not for another element that entered the church in the early 1900s; recurring revivalism. The revivals in the Korean church have given it life, warmth (even heat) and impelling force, and none more so than the Great Revival of 1907.

The Great Revival originated not from doctrine, but from the same source as the Wesleyan revivals of the 18th century in England and America—the experience of an individual whose heart was "strangely warmed." Coming without any elaborate plans or organization, the movement essentially grew out of and was carried on as a prayer meeting.

In 1903 a member of the China mission of the Southern Methodist Church, Mary Culler White, visited Korea. During her stay in Wonsan she met with Canadian Presbyterian missionary Louise McCully each day to pray for a deepening in the spiritual lives of the missionaries. This led the Wonsan missionaries to set aside a week in August for Bible study and prayer. Dr. R.A. Hardie, who had joined the Southern Methodist mission in 1898, was asked to prepare three papers on the subject of prayer. The request came to Hardie just when he was in despair. Many of the churches under his care showed little numerical or spiritual growth, and he had had to expel several church members during the year. He felt his ministry was a total failure.

In his preparations for the Bible studies and in his prayers that the Koreans would be convicted of sin and repent, he himself was so convicted, and in deep repentance turned to God. Hardie confessed to his missionary colleagues his failures and the following Sunday stood before his Korean congregation and, in his words, "with shame and confusion of face confessed my pride, hardness of heart and lack of faith and also much that these had led to."[51] This sparked a period of daily meetings for prayer and Bible study by the Koreans and they too were soon publicly confessing. On some occasions it was impossible to preach, as people rose and interrupted the sermon to make confession of specific sins. Those present were deeply moved. "The testimony of all was that they had never before known anything of religion as a personal and living experience."[52]

In the ensuing months, Dr. Hardie and Korean Christians from Wonsan were invited to speak at evangelistic meetings in Songdo, Seoul, Chemulpo, Pyongyang and elsewhere. Everywhere the meetings spontaneously followed the precedent of confession of sin.

The missionaries were among the first to feel the effects. Like Hardie, they found that as they prayed for revival, it began in them. Revival swept through one of the Southern Presbyterian mission stations in the early summer of 1906. The missionaries were not initiators, but like the Koreans, were recipients of this Holy Spirit movement. It did not come from them so much as through them, and not through all; after all, there has never been a revival in which everyone has been renewed.

The majority of the missionaries were not revival oriented. They feared dramatic emotional displays; leery of emotionalism, they certainly did not envision a revival like the one ahead. They had more in mind what happened in the winter Bible classes in Pyongyang in 1905 when more than 800 persons expessed their desire to become Christians. Charles Bernheisel wrote that Pyongyang "has just passed through the most remarkable evangelistic services ever held here . . . . One of the most remarkable and pleasant things about these meetings has been the utter lack of undue excitement. The hundreds of conversions have not been under the impulse of excited emotions but deliberate decisions made after careful consideration."

Plainly, "something spiritual" was taking place, ground was being broken for the Great Revival. The *Korea Review* for February 1906 reported that from Pyongyang, Seoul, the south, Wonsan and Hamheung came "the same glad news, of people turning their attention to divine things." One indication of this was a hundred-fold increase in colporteurs' Bible and book sales.[53]

In the fall of 1906 Southern Methodist missionary J.L. Gerdine led services in the southern port city of Mokpo. J.F. Preston, a Southern Presbyterian missionary, called it the most powerful revival meeting he ever participated in. "As the Spirit through Mr. Gerdine took the Word . . . a deathlike hush fell on all, and it was as if the Word was a scalpel, cutting deep down into men's hearts and laying bare secret sins and hidden cancers of the soul. Then it was that confession of sin poured out of scores of burdened souls and strong men wept like children. Then, as the yearning love of the Savior was dwelt upon, it was as a healing balm poured in."[54]

This spiritual ferment occurred at a crucial time. In 1905, in the wake of their victory over Russia, the Japanese had proclaimed a protectorate over Korea. They were supported by western powers, including America. According to William Blair, "Great was the disappointment when the United States, following England's example, recognized Japan's control of Korea. A violent anti-foreign, especially anti-American storm swept the land."[55] There was also some bitterness between missionaries and Korean church leaders, as the Presbyterians, not without some anxiety, were about to convene the first presbytery, beginning the transfer of church authority.

It was in this atmosphere of crisis that Methodist and Presbyterian missionaries in Pyongyang united for a week of prayer and Bible study led by R.A. Hardie. Wrote one Presbyterian, "We went out of those August meetings realizing as never before that nothing but the baptism of God's spirit could fit us and our Korean brethren for the trying days ahead."[56] Missionaries and Koreans decided to join in a season of concerted prayer that continued through the fall and into the winter.

Christmas came, and William Blair wrote, "our scattered force assembled in Pyongyang to share the season's joy. Usually we spend the week between Christmas and New Years getting reacquainted with our families, resting in preparation for the busy days of the Bible class season. Frequently the whole community will meet for a social evening, having the best time imaginable. That winter we had no heart for social gatherings. Prayer meetings were held each evening.

"Methodists and Presbyterians again united praying definitely for the Presbyterian men's Bible study class about to assemble and for the Methodist general class to be held later. When the Presbyterian class began on January 2, our evening prayer meeting had to be discontinued, but so strong was our desire to pray that although most of the Methodist men had to go to the country, we decided to hold noon prayer meetings daily during the class for those who could attend."

These classes, with an attendance of 900, were for men from the country. The evening sessions were open to men from the city and drew more than 1,500. Blair said that at first nothing unusual happened. "We were not looking for anything unusual. Only a hushed, upturned sea of faces and eagerness to lead in prayer showed how the Spirit was working."[57] And then came the last two evening meetings, on January 14 and 15, 1907.

On Monday, after a short sermon, Graham Lee called for prayers. So many began praying that Lee said, "If you want to pray like that, all pray," and the whole audience began to pray aloud. "The effect was indescribable. Not confusion, but a vast harmony of sound and spirit, a mingling together of souls moved by an irresistable impulse to prayer . . . . God came to us in Pyongyang that night with the sound of weeping. As the prayer continued a spirit of heaviness and sorrow came down upon the audience. Over on one side someone began to weep and in a moment the whole congregation was weeping."[58]

Precise, unemotional Charles Bernheisel, who had rejoiced that the meetings of 1905 had not been marked by undue excitement, now wrote, "Hundreds of men were under the most terrible conviction of sin, and, in awful agony, would arise and confess and would just break all to pieces, throw themselves onto the floor and cry out for mercy. The spirit of prayer fell upon the whole company and every person in the building would be praying at the same time. There had been some ill-feeling between some of the leading men of the church and they were constrained by the Spirit to come forward and confess. At times the whole company simply wailed aloud for 10 minutes . . . Every sin in the decalogue was confessed . . . The last two nights the meetings continued until 2 o'clock in the morning."[59]

Those who were present never forgot the scene. Ruth Noble Appenzeller Knight, a child at the time, vividly recounted her impressions more than 70 years later. "I saw a great agony of crying and calling out to God for forgiveness. More than that I saw them beating their heads down on the floor and striking themselves . . . . My mother told me that some of them confessed to throwing their infants against a stone wall in order to kill them."[60]

Graham Lee, in a letter to his parents written on January 16, said, "I noticed that Elder Chu was standing beside me on the platform asking for an opportunity to confess. Then began a scene the like of which I never saw and which I am not anxious to see again very soon. He was trembling from head to foot and he fairly shrieked in agony as he told of the sins that he had committed.

I have never seen a mortal in such agony of mind. He confessed to adultery and misappropriation of funds and at last he sank to the floor and fairly wilted and writhed in agony."

Many confessed to feelings of hatred. One such confession concerned William Blair, who wrote, "I never had a greater surprise in my life . . . . It seems that I had said something to [this pastor] one day in the hurry of a school field day exercise which had given offense and he had not been able to forgive me. Turning to me he said, 'Can you forgive me? Can you pray for me?' I stood up and began to pray, 'Aba-gi, Aba-gi,' 'Father, Father,' and got no further. It seemed as if the roof was lifted from the building and the Spirit of God came down in a mighty avalanche of power upon us. I fell at Kim's side and wept and prayed as I had never prayed before.

"My last glimpse of the audience is photographed indelibly on my brain. Some threw themselves full length on the floor, hundreds stood with arms outstretched towards heaven. Every man forgot every other. Each was face to face with God. I can hear yet that fearful sound of hundreds of men pleading with God for mercy . . . As soon as we were able, we missionaries gathered at the platform and consulted, 'What shall we do?' We dared not interfere. We had prayed to God for an outpouring of his Holy Spirit upon the people and it had come. Separating, we went down and tried to comfort the most distressed, pulling the agonized men to the floor and saying, 'Never mind, brother, if you have sinned God will forgive you.' . . . Finally Dr. Lee started a hymn and quiet was restored during the singing."[61]

The experiences of these meetings could not be contained. A period of confession and restitution settled upon the city of Pyongyang. Bernheisel wrote, "My own servant come to me the other day and with bitter weeping and tears confessed that he had been deceiving me by overcharging for things that he had bought and restored to me several dollars in cash. For the last two weeks there have been evangelistic services for unbelievers. Several hundred Christian men and women have been meeting in the mornings for Bible study, and preaching in the afternoons with hundreds professing belief in Christ. It is impossible to accommodate the crowds, seeking entrance to the churches . . . a fifth church will doubtless have to be organized soon."[62]

The movement spread to the schools where students were returning from their mid-winter break. The first two weeks of the new school term were given over—or taken over—by the revival. Annie Laurie Baird wrote, "meetings were held every afternoon at four o'clock. No attempt was made to lead these meetings. Indeed, any leadership would have been impossible."

It was decided to set aside the usual curriculum and devote

the first week to Bible study and prayer, reserving the evenings for devotional services. "The meeting of the first evening was a grateful change from the heart-rending scenes which we had been witnessing. One after another of the young men who up to this time had been agonizing for sin, sprang to his feet and in ringing tones testified to the sense of pardon, peace and joy into which he had been led . . . .While some were flaming up for God, very many sat cold and lumpish as ice . . .

"The students who had already received blessing spent hours of every day in prayer, and some passed whole nights on their faces before God. At the meeting of the second evening, before the leader took his place, the tide of prayer began rising . . . the building began to resound with groans and cries. When something like a semblance of order could be restored, an opportunity was given to all who had any ill feeling toward anyone present or who had wronged any of the others in any way, to make confession and ask forgiveness. In a very few moments the meeting was resolved into numberless groups of students weeping in each other's arms. Nor did the members of the faculty escape. It was interesting to see them, with perhaps two or three boys weeping at their knees and others hanging about their necks. Cribbing in examinations to thieving, and every sort of falsifying, spites and grudges were confessed."

While most of the Presbyterian students had been touched by revival, the majority of Methodist students were still unmoved. Annie Baird attributed this to the opposition of the leading Methodist pastor, a very able man who had resisted union and was "jealous and displeased," although this was not known at the time, that revival had come first to the Presbyterians. "On Friday evening he attended the meeting as a spectator, and that night the break in the Methodist ranks began . . . The 'slain of the Lord' were everywhere, and at midnight there were as many as 50 risen to their feet and awaiting their turn to confess their sins." A number of the young men threw themselves before the preacher, charging that he had led them astray and kept them from getting a blessing by his opposition to the revival. At the close of the meeting "this proud man was weeping in the arms of the missionaries and sobbing out penitent confessions of coldness, willfulness and jealousies . . .

"Then the Lord began pouring out blessings upon the Methodist congregations in the city, and the same wonderful manifestations were seen here that had been exhibited elsewhere.

"The night schools in the city, conducted entirely by Koreans, were also greatly shaken, and the spirit of prayer was poured out in great measure upon the girls' primary school, so that little girls spent hours in prayer apparently without any consciousness of the passage of time."[63]

Arthur Becker wrote that "About nine-tenths of the students were deeply stirred and born again at this time. A large number became evangelists burning with a zeal for the cross, carrying revival fires not only to the city and nearby country churches, but also as far as Chemulpo and Kongju."[64]

The storm overtook the Methodist mission's training class for preachers and church leaders in February, the Presbyterians' women's general Bible training class in March, and the students at the Presbyterian theological class when they gathered for their annual three months' training in May.

Reports of what happened in Pyongyang spread with the students to their home villages, and revival followed. As in Pyongyang, every sort of sin was confessed, and William Blair wrote that he witnessed "some strenuous scenes."

Although the missionaries unanimously acclaimed the results of the revival, its intensity frightened some of them. The revival brought not only blessing, but also stress. Arthur Becker confided to his diary a conversation with his Methodist colleague Charles Morris, a deeply spiritual-mined man.

Said Morris, "I have been to Pyongyang and passed through several sessions of prayer and confession. I can't say I enjoyed them but I believe in them. But when I'm back home again and with my wife and our baby and I am quietly enjoying our home, I feel a great relief. Am I lacking in consecration? Perhaps we should be praying right now. There are so many sinners who need our prayers."

"Well, Charlie," I said, "Maybe I'm not so sensitive as you are to my duties, but I sort of enjoyed your happy peaceful congregation this morning after the tensions of the Pyongyang meetings, and I thought of Ecclesiastes—'To everything there is a season and a time, to every purpose under this heaven; a time to weep, a time to laugh, a time to mourn and a time to dance' . . .God gave us capacity for many things, and too much of any one at one season may unbalance our judgment."[65]

One of the results of the revival was to bring the missionaries and Korean church leaders into deeper mutual understanding and better relations. William Blair wrote of the convening of the first Presbytery of the Korean Church in the fall of 1907, "The whole church was washed and made sweet and new. When we met to organize our independent Korean church, not a word was heard about fighting, only a great desire to pray and to preach the gospel as soon as possible to all Korea, and if God willed, to China and Japan."[66]

The perception that religious experience somehow differed for Westerners and Asians was dispelled. One missionary, J.Z. Moore, wrote, "Until this year I was more or less bound by that contemptible notion that East is East and West, West . . . With others I had said the Korean would never have a religious experience such as the West has. These revivals have taught me two things: First, that though there may be a thousand things on the surface that are the direct opposite of the West, the Korean is at heart . . . at one with his brother of the West . . . In the second place these revivals have taught me, that in the matter of making all life religious,in prayer, and in a simple, childlike trust, the East not only has many things, but profound things, to teach the West, and until we learn these things we will not know the full-orbed Gospel of Christ."

There is no way the missionaries could have engineered as significant and impelling a movement as the Great Revival. For contrast, there is a perfect example of how the missionaries would, and indeed, did, go about organizing a religious movement; it is the so-called "Million Movement" of 1910. The revival renewed interest in evangelism which helped give an impetus to the Million Movement; it also enhanced co-operation between missions and between missionaries and Koreans, which strengthened unity and helped make the logistics of the Million Movement possible.

This movement, too, began as a prayer meeting, when three young Southern Methodist missionaries and a group of Koreans met on a mountainside for a week of prayer in 1909. One of the missionaries was M.B. Stokes, who was led during his church itineration following this retreat to ask his Korean congregations to pray for the conversion of 50,000 souls during the coming year. Soon afterward, when the annual meeting of the Southern Methodist Mission convened, it adopted the watchword, "Two Hundred Thousand Souls for Christ." When the General Council of the Evangelical Missions met in Seoul in the fall of 1909, the group decided to enlarge upon the idea and adopted the slogan, "A million souls for Christ."

At this time there were only about 200 Protestant missionaries and 8,000 Korean Protestants, including catechumens, and virtually all of them were mobilized for the movement. It became a national undertaking with every believer and missionary preaching, distributing tracts and going house to house to witness to the Christian faith. At the end of the year far fewer than a million persons had joined the ranks of the Christians, and a fair proportion of those later fell away. But at least a million people had been confronted with the gospel.

As well planned, highly organized and skillfully executed an endeavor as it was, the Million Movement lacked the supernatural power and fire of the Great Revival, which has been aptly called the Pentecost of the Korean Church. The revival left many lasting imprints on Korean Christianity, and not merely visible ones such as the still-prevalent sunrise prayer services.

Philosophically, the concept of sin took on deeper meaning. George Heber Jones wrote in 1914 that prior to the Great Revival the word "choi" or "sin" in Korea was a spiritually anemic word meaning an offence against statutory law; all mourners for a three-year period, for instance, would refer to themselves as "choi-in" or sinners. Jones' first language teacher was typical in his denunciation of the Christian idea of sin as unreasonable, impossible and absurd. Yet, after the Revival of 1907, wrote Jones, "There cannot be found anywhere a clearer conception of the exceeding sinfulness of sin or a quicker recognition of it than in the typical Korean Christian."[67]

It has been widely acknowledged that the Great Revival was a spiritual renewal of Christian believers rather than a movement to convert nonChristians. But beyond its influence on the church, the revival had a national impact that was made manifest later, during the Independence Movement of 1919. Canadian Missionary William Scott recognized the national implications of the revival when he wrote, "Scenes similar to those that accompanied the revival in Pyongyang were witnessed in churches everywhere. It is probable that much of the agony of confession came not only from a sense of individual unworthiness but from a deepseated conviction that every Korean bore a responsibility for the tragedy that had befallen the nation.

"The practice of prayer in union, though causing a babel of sound, was a means of expressing corporate guilt as well as an opportunity for sensitive souls to pour out pent up emotions which natural pride and personal reticence would otherwise keep bottled up within. The utter helplessness of the nation and the individual made it easy to throw (oneself) unreservedly upon a God whose supreme revelation came in the bearing of a cross for the sins of (all) . . . God broke through the disillusionment and despair of countless Korean individuals and led their minds from the uncertainties of human institutions to the eternal stabilities."[68]

CHAPTER VII
Korea Mansei

The Usurpers

"A nation's memory is not erasible," wrote a Korean historian of the troubled relations between Korea and Japan.[1]

Both nations recognize the tremendous influence of Korea on Japanese civilization from the 4th century A.D.; in fact, up to the end of the 7th century, the industrial and intellectual development of Japan was largely in Korean hands. But Japan hardly felt indebted to her neighbor.

Hideyoshi's ambition in the 16th century was to conquer China as well as Korea. In 1592 he sent an armada of nearly 4,000 and an army of 250,000 men to invade Korea. "I shall take Korea," he boasted, "as easily as a man rolls up a mat and puts it under his arm."[2]

But it wasn't that easy. Seven years of blood and trauma followed. Korean industries and arts were virtually wiped out. Cities and hamlets were burned to the ground and whole villages were deported to Japan. All movable products of Korean culture were carried off, along with hundreds of artists and artisans. Tens of thousands of Korean men, women and children were brutally slaughtered. In a single battle 10,000 Koreans, their bows and arrows helpless against Japanese muskets, lost their lives. Ears of some of the dead were preserved in saké and taken to Japan where, it was said, over 200,000 Korean ears cut off during the invasion were buried in Kyoto's Ear Mound.

On land Hideyoshi may have won all the battles, but he was routed at sea, thanks to Admiral Yi Sun-Sin's turtle boat, the first armored ship. Its iron deck resisted Japanese fire arrows. Six cannon on each of its sides, two in its tail and two more in its massive head, inflicted enough damage that Japan lost more than 70 boats in one engagement and with them, the command of the sea and their vital supply lanes. The Japanese finally withdrew—until three centuries later.

Fukuzawa Yukichi, a voice of the enlightenment in Japan, was saying in 1881 that the nations of Asia must resist the west, and that the only country capable of assuming leadership for that task was Japan. "For her own sake Japan should take it upon herself to try to strengthen the other Asiatic countries. . .She must use her armed forces to protect her neighbors in order to ensure her own safety."[3]

He wrote that Korea was obstinately set in xenophobia, was incompetent to look after herself, had no idea how to live decently and honorably, and that Koreans were maltreated by their own government. His argument that it was better to be colonized by a civilized country than to remain in backward independence would obviously never apply to Japan at any stage of her development. As applied to Korea, however, such thoughts made a convenient rationale for invasion. "We cannot wait for our neighbor countries to become so civilized that all may combine together to make Asia progress. We must rather break out of formation and behave in the same way as the civilized countries of the west are doing."[4]

Thus, Japan's adventure in Seoul at the post office banquet of December 4, 1884, her efforts in the Sino-Japanese War of 1894 and the murder of Queen Min, and her coup in defeating Russia in the Russo-Japanese War of 1904-05. It took a while, but the stage was being set for the colonization of Korea.

A Korean observer, Hugh Heung-Wu Cynn, analyzed Japanese activities on the Korean peninsula and divided them into three periods:

1. Up to the middle 1890's, Japan was interested in separating Korea from the Chinese, a first step toward a Japanese take-over.

2. After 1895, Japan was interested in preserving Korea's national integrity to provide a buffer state between China, Japan and Russia.

3. After 1905 and the ouster of Russia, Japan gained Russia's concession and the tacit agreement of the western powers of her "prepondering" interest in Korea.

Cynn's conclusion was that "the animating spirit of all the political actions in Japanese international relations in the Orient date back to the time of Hideyoshi. Japan's ultimate aim was to conquer China. Japan's object to be the dominant factor in Asia does not seem to have been relinquished, and because of her early contact with Western civilization she has acquired the modern method by which she can enforce her will upon her neighbors."[5] In the 1940s, his statement made more than 20 years earlier, that "the Japanese militarists seem to be imbued with the idea of pan-Asian empire, or a world empire, as all militarists are" was recognized as having been prophetic. Koreans, however, were conscious all along that "Korea lies in Japan's way now as she did over 300 years ago."[6]

America was not unaware of Japan's lust for Korea. As early as 1898 and 1899 American Minister Horace Allen had reported to the U.S. Secretary of State that "gradually Japan has been aggressive here until they now seem to regard Korea as their peculiar sphere of action and all others to be mere interlopers."[7] If Russia were out of the picture, it seemed to Allen that Japanese control of Korea was "inevitable."[8]

In 1904, Ito Hirobumi, then president of the Japanese Privy Council, was sent to Korea to pacify opposition of Korean leaders to the wartime protocol allying Korea with Japan. His visit was followed by a Japanese "request" that Korea employ financial and diplomatic advisers recommended by the Japanese government and to consult Japan in regard to foreign affairs, including grants of contracts to foreigners. Megata Tanetaro was given control of Korean finances and a pro-Japanese American, D.W. Stevens, was appointed adviser to the Korean Foreign Office. Japanese advisers were appointed to police and education departments while other foreign advisers to the Korean government were gradually eliminated. Step by step, the administration was Japanized.

Japanese military authorities decreed that Japanese time be used for all public work, and they changed the names of the towns from Korean to Japanese. Japanese police were brought in and established everywhere, assuming control of all political activities. Anyone who protested was summarily arrested and imprisoned.

There followed increasing pressure for more and more concessions. In May 1904 the Korean government at last acceded to Japan's demand that fishing privileges along the entire coast of Korea be granted to Japanese for a term of 25 years.

On June 17, Japanese authorities made the startling suggestion that all uncultivated land in Korea, an area comprising one third of the peninsula's arable land, be opened for Japanese cultivation. They also requested all unworked mines be turned over to Japan. The comprehensive nature of these demands stirred enough Korean and foreign opposition that the scheme was abandoned until later when the Japanese had more complete control. But Japanese military authorities had already staked out and acquired large portions of the finest sites in Korea at a nominal price, often less than one-twentieth of its actual value.[9]

Official Japanese cabinet records show that the decision to establish a protectorate over Korea was made in April, 1905, five months before the treaty ending the Russo-Japanese War. This decision was confirmed at another cabinet meeting in October, in which it was decided that the protectorate would be established in early November, that Marshal Hasegawa Yoshimichi, commander of the Japanese army in Korea, would be ordered to "render necessary assistance: and should Korea refuse to agree, Japan would unilaterally establish the protectorate and announce its necessity to the world. It was also stated that the plan was being carried out with the consent of the United States, Great Britain and other powers.

At this time more than 150 Japanese emigrants were entering Korea in each boat coming into Wonsan harbor,[10] and the *Korea Review* succinctly remarked, "Korea just now, in the good old diplomatic phrase, is 'available.' "[11]

All these developments had not gone unprotested. In March 1905, a memorial to the emperor denounced six Korean officials who had co-operated with the Japanese in various ways as traitors,[12] and the same month, Japanese gendarmes found it necessary to arrest three men "for endeavoring to rid Korea of Japanese influence." An agreement had been signed on April 1, by which Japan acquired the entire postal and telegraph system, but when Japanese officials took possession of the post office on May 17, the Korean clerks and officials refused to perform their assigned duties. They resigned, as did nearly all the officials of the Communication Department. The resignations were not accepted, however, and a number of Koreans were arrested.[13]

Distressed over conditions in Korea, the secretary of the Korean legation in London committed suicide.[14] On August 10 all of the Korean cabinet members turned in their resignations, stating that they "could not care for government affairs because the demands of the Japanese minister were so oppressive."[15]

In September, an entire new slate of cabinet ministers was presented to Emperor Kojong, but all the nominees declined to serve. It was obvious that no one wanted to be in office when the Japanese got around to imposing a protectorate.

The Russo-Japanese War was concluded with the signing of the Treaty of Portsmouth, New Hampshire, on September 5, 1905. On November 9, Ito Hirobumi arrived in Seoul as special envoy of the Emperor of Japan. At a formal audience on November 15, Ito presented a series of demands drawn up in treaty form—that the Japan Foreign Office in Tokyo would henceforth control the foreign relations of Korea; Japan diplomats and consular officials would represent Korean interests abroad and Korean envoys in foreign countries would be recalled; Japan would appoint a Resident General to be supreme administrator in Korea, working under the direction of the Emperor of Japan, not of Korea. Japanese residents in different districts would have the power of local governors.

The Korean emperor and his cabinet ministers were aghast to hear these demands, and met them with point blank refusal in a dramatic five-hour confrontation. The gist of the conversation between the Korean emperor and Ito was reported by F.A. McKenzie, special correspondent of the London *Daily Mail,* whose account came from one of the ministers who was present. Ito insisted that the demands of the Japanese emperor "will be to the benefit of both nations and peace in the east will be assured forever." Emperor Kojong's final reply was "Assent to your proposal would mean the ruin of my country and I will therefore sooner die than agree to it.[16]

Then followed diplomacy at bayonet point. The next day, November 16, all the cabinet members were summoned to Ito's hotel. A furious argument ensued, lasting from 3 p.m. until midnight. The Japanese offered immense bribes, cajoled and finally threatened the ministers with death if they did not yield. They refused. They had sworn to each other before going to the hotel that they would not give in under any circumstances. Ito, Japanese Minister Hayashi and the military commander Hasegawa, were unable to budge them.

On November 17 at 2 p.m. the ministers were recalled to the Japanese legation. This conference also ended in a stalemate. Meanwhile, the Japanese army was making a demonstration of military force. For days, fully armed, they paraded in front of the imperial residence, through the streets and around the government buildings. Machine guns were everywhere and even field guns were placed at strategic points.

Before the November 17 conference resumed that night, Japanese soldiers with fixed bayonets entered the palace grounds, standing near the royal apartments. Ito, Minister Hayashi, and Marshal Hasegawa arrived and demanded an audience with Kojong, who declined to see them, saying he was not well. Ito forced his way into the emperor's quarters, where Kojong politely told him to discuss the matter with the cabinet ministers.[17]

The conference with the ministers was coercive in the extreme. Hasegawa drew his sword and Prime Minister Han Kyu-Sol, one of the abler Korean statesmen, said, "Cut us down if you dare."

He either ran or was dragged from the room and tried to kill himself with a knife. When Hasegawa informed the other ministers that he was dead (which was not true), three of them, demoralized, gave their consent to the noxious treaty. Last to yield of those present was Pak Che-Sun, foreign minister. Neither Emperor Kojong nor Prime Minister Han ever consented to the protectorate.

At midnight this convention providing for control of Korean relations by the Japanese was signed by *tojang,* or seal. Special messengers with a group of Japanese soldiers forced the Seal of State from its custodian, who had been ordered not to relinquish it.

Symbolically and literally, America looked on. American Vice-Consul Willard Straight wrote that at half past one a.m. on November 18 he went out for a stroll around the American legation compound. "There was a rattling of rickshaws and looking over the wall, I saw the Japanese were going away. Hasegawa's carriage had already gone. It seemed impossible, as I stood there in the moonlight behind the hedge, that the fate of a nation had been sealed within 50 yards of where I stood, that an independent empire of 12 million people had subjected themselves to bullying and exploitation."[18]

Min Yong-Hwan, of the once powerful and proud Yohung Min clan, had been his country's representative at the coronation of Czar Nicholas II and at Queen Victoria's Jubilee. In the spring of 1905, he resigned as Prime Minister rather than serve as a tool of the Japanese. After the protectorate had been imposed, he sent 40 memorials to the Throne to protest the treaty, to call for the execution of the five men who had signed it, and to encourage Kojong to continue his refusal to ratify it. Min was arrested in a group of former cabinet members who publicly opposed the protectorate.

After his release from prison, he wrote a letter to the Korean people urging them to "exert yourselves to the utmost, redouble your natural power and strength, educate yourselves and restore our independence and liberty,"[19] and to various foreign envoys and American friends, saying, "You must know the aims and actions of the Japanese . . . I beseech you to use your good offices in making known to the world whatever injustice my people may suffer, and . . . to uphold our independence . . . even the dead shall know, and be thankful to you."[20] He then committed suicide.

In grieving for Min, Koreans were grieving for their country, and that grief was real. An immense procession of guilds, schools, political societies and friends followed the casket to his grave, and the walls and streets through which they passed were packed by a dense mass of silent people. For days after his death the shops of Seoul were closed, with placards of bereavement posted all about the capital.[21]

One mourner—who had been Min's lover—was a beautiful young palace woman. Seeing her weeping, a poet wrote:

In the blood you spilt
The woman is soaking her hair;
Could weeping regain what's lost
You might let her weep for a hundred years.

The poem was circulated and copies posted on the wall near the dead patriot's house. The Japanese, reacting typically, arrested both the woman and the poet.[22]

Of such events are legends made. After Min's death, the knife with which he killed himself and his blood-drenched clothing were laid in a room adjoining his sleeping quarters where they were not disturbed for several months. When the room was reopened during the rainy season of 1906, shoots of bamboo, taken to be the manifestation of Min's unconquerable spirit, were found to be growing through a crack in the floor.[23]

A wave of suicides and violence followed. Of the five ministers who had signed the protectorate, two, Yi Kun-Taek and Kwon Chung-Hyon, were murdered, and the homes of two more, Yi Wan-Yong and Pak Che-Sun, were burned by angry mobs.

Marquis Ito was appointed the first Resident General, assuming office on March 2, and all foreign legations were withdrawn from Korea, the Americans leaving first. Japanese rule in Korea from 1905 to 1910 was military, harsh, and grasping, but not without achievements. The Japanese built a handsome post office in Seoul which opened in September 1901. Efforts were made to improve sanitary conditions. Seoul streets and drains were repaired in May 1904; in February 1905, police were authorized to collect eight cents from each household in the capital to pay for the removal of refuse.[24] In May 1906, Japanese medical authorities made smallpox innoculation compulsory and announced they would begin the program by innoculating 5,000 children.[25]

What must be remembered when discussing development under the Japanese, as Gregory Henderson has pointed out in his essay "Japan's Chosen: Immigrants, Ruthlessness and Development Shock," is that "what was being developed was, at least after 1907–8, not Korea, or a nation expressing the will and sovereignty of the Korean people, but rather Chosen, a possession, finally a part of Japan, a development expressing the will and benefit of Japan and the Japanese."[26] The distinction is vital, but perhaps not always understood, especially by Japanese. Others have also observed that in all colonial experiences, certainly in Asia, development and exploitation were so intricately linked as to be impossible to disentangle.[27]

It should be kept in mind also that there were any number of conscientious Japanese individuals in Korea, people of integrity and good will, many of whom deplored the less admirable actions of their government.

The *Korea Review* publicized one good deed—there must have been many others—in its October 1906 issue: "At Cho-chi-won station on the Seoul-Fusan Railway some Japanese police and gendarmes did noble work in helping people at the time of the recent flood. Fearing that there would be a flood these Japanese prepared some boats and at the time of the catastrophe they saved many lives and much property. The Koreans praise them highly and desire to raise a monument in their honor. This is a light in a dark place and shows how willing the Koreans are to make friends with the Japanese when such a thing is possible.[28]

The Residency-General published an annual report in English called *Report of Reforms and Progress in Chosun,* which foreigners in Korea referred to as The Book of Fairy Tales.[29] Unquestionably material progress was made, but it was eclipsed by wholesale confiscation of land, the attendant mistreatment of Koreans, and the partiality of the Japanese-controlled courts. Whenever Resident General Ito tried to restrain Japanese individuals, he was accused of sacrificing their interests to Koreans.

Crooked land dealings, seizure of property and coercive loans, common-place occurrences, were among the most bitterly resented of Japanese abuses, impoverishing thousands of families.

Homer Hulbert's book *The Passing of Korea* describes many such injustices, including cases of Japanese brokers denying having received money from Koreans and refusing to return funds entrusted to them, and the conscription of Koreans to work on the railroads at a fraction of the wages paid to Japanese coolies. Gratuitous insults and assaults were common.

The billeting of Japanese was highly resented by the Koreans. The *Korea Review* of September 1906 reported that the military had quartered soldiers in some Korean houses and prostitutes in others. "In a number of instances Korean Christians were compelled to give up part of their houses to these prostitutes who carried on their nefarious business on the premises . . . Every Christian man whose house was thus invaded was told by the church authorities that if he could not get rid of the horror he must leave his house, desert it and seek a lodging somewhere else."[30]

Following British practice in China, Japan permitted if not encouraged the sale of opium in Korea, although its use was a capital crime by Japanese law. The Japanese freely distributed morphine in north Korea and opium sales were concentrated there. Medical missionaries in Pyongyang were alarmed to find their hospitals receiving 30 to 35 opium addicts a month.[31]

Vandalism took place on every level. Viscount Tanaka, minister of the Japanese imperial household, visited Korea in late 1906 as a special envoy of the Japanese emperor. The viscount, a great curio collector, became interested in a famous pagoda near Songdo, a national monument that had been presented by the Chinese court a thousand years earlier. He mentioned wanting the pagoda to the Korean minister of the royal household, thanked bewildered Kojong for it, and 80 Japanese workers, escorted by a number of gendarmes, dismantled it for shipping to Tokyo. The Japanese press heatedly denied the incident until it appeared, reassembled, in Japan.[32]

The Japanization of education proceeded rapidly after 1906. Koreans were incensed by Japanese efforts to stamp out their culture by laws forbidding the wearing of white clothing, topknots and use of their own language. Court officials were ordered to cut their hair and even the palace ladies were required to wear foreign dress. They retired entirely from public view due to embarrassment.[33]

The Japanese did not brook any opposition. Sim Sang-Hun, an official described by the *Korea Review* as "one of the strongest Koreans of the present time and a man who stands for the autonomy of Korea," was exiled. Most dissidents were arrested. The pro-Japanese Ilchinhoi (literally, The Progressive Society) was granted authority to arrest persons "inimical to Japanese interests" and arrested a number of people even in the palace.

In July 1906, charging that Kojong had encouraged an armed uprising in Hongju,[34] a large number of Japanese police were placed in the palace and the emperor was once again captive in his own apartments. Many of his faithful retainers—palace attendants, *kisaeng*, and enuchs—were carried off to prison, where some were tortured.

The emporor, though he has been depicted as a timid man, refused to buckle under to the Japanese. He would not co-operate with them and took every opportunity to publicize abroad the unsavory circumstances surrounding the protectorate.[35] In the early summer of 1907, amidst great secrecy, he managed to finance and dispatch a delegation of three Koreans—Yi Sang-Sol, who had been vice prime minister; Yi Chun, a former supreme court justice; and youthful Yi Wi-Jong, former secretary of the Korean legation in Russia—with Homer Hulbert, editor of the *Korea Review*, to the Second World Peace Conference held at The Hague in the Netherlands. The group were able to get a sum-mary of Korea's case published in the June 30 issue of the daily *Courrier de la Conference*, a nonofficial but influential journal, but they were denied a hearing before the Peace Conference itself.

All the powers, they were told, recognized that under the protectorate treaty of November 1905, Korea's foreign affairs were to be handled exclusively by Japan. Yi Wi-Jong was invited to address an unofficial group called the International Circle on July 8, but this was small consolation after their long and daring journey. Broken-hearted, Judge Yi Chun died in The Hague on July 15 after a hunger strike.[36]

Even though the secret mission to The Hague proved futile, it infuriated the Japanese, and they were determined to depose Emperor Kojong. All the cabinet members, who had been appointed by Resident General Ito, were called to the Residency and instructed to demand that the emperor abdicate. At first Kojong refused to acquiesce, but on July 19, 1907 at 6 a.m., after an all-night "conference" with his cabinet and the Japanese, he was compelled to pass the empty title of emperor on to his impotent son, Sunjong.

Sunjong's coronation was held in late August, 1907, at which time his topknot was again cut. The event was met with apathy and gloom by the Koreans rather than with traditional celebration. The ceremony itself was attended by few westerners, only five foreign consuls-general and Bishop Turner of the Anglican mission, but hundreds of smartly uniformed Japanese were present. Two men were conspicuous by their absence—the Russian Consul-General M. de Plancon and ex-Emperor Kojong.

The Righteous Army

Within a week of the abdication, Japan had pressed on the new emperor a treaty providing even firmer control, with Japanese government "advisers" being replaced by administrators. Then, on August 2, Sunjong was forced to dissolve the Korean army.

The Korean military was not much, admittedly, with its navy of one ship and 39 admirals[37] and an army that was disorganized at the best of times. But it was their own, and the shock of its dismemberment resulted in armed rebellion.

Col. Pak Sung-Hwan, battalion commander of the Seoul Guard regiment, committed suicide. His men, with those of another battalion, fought a fierce battle against the Japanese in the streets of Seoul between Little West Gate and South Gate. There were many casualties, 30 Japanese and 68 Korean dead. The disbanded soldiers, 8,000–10,000 men, scattered across the peninsula, taking to the hills, and became the nucleus of a resistance group called the *uibyong* or Righteous Army, which was joined by malcontented Confucian scholars and ordinary villagers. In a sense, the Righteous Army was carrying on the tradition of protest by guerilla fighting begun by the Tonghaks, an ironic development since the Tonghak's philosophical arm, the Chundogyo, joined forces with pro-Japanese Koreans in 1905 in a desperate hope that Japanese influence would bring about much-needed reforms.

At the time the army was disbanded, Japanese authorities took up all the weapons they could find. William Blair wrote, "Even the old flint-lock guns that the mountaineers used for tiger hunting were collected and burned in heaps."[38] The Japanese were wise in trying to disarm the tiger hunters, most of whom joined the Righteous Army. Though their weapons were antiquated, they were sure shots. F.A. McKenzie reported that "The tiger-hunters, sons of the hills, iron-nerved, and operating in their own country, are naturally awkward antagonists even for the best regular troops. They are probably among the boldest sportsmen in the world, and they formed the most picturesque and romantic section of the rebels. Their only weapon is an old-fashioned percussion gun, with long barrel and a brass trigger seven to eight inches long. Many of them fire not from the shoulder, but hold their guns low. They never miss. They can only fire one charge in an attack, owing to the time required to load. They are trained to stalk the tiger, to come quite close to it, and then to kill it at one shot. No tiger-hunter in the field today has ever failed to hit his prey. The man who fails once dies; the tiger attends to that."[39]

Many of the Japanese-trained local militia turned on their officers, and went over to the Righteous Army, taking their guns with them. The widespread "riots" reported by the Japanese after the disbandment of the army were in fact a nationwide rebellion, which the Japanese vigorously suppressed by burning villages and killing some 12,000 "rioters" in the first 12 months. The Japanese reported 1,405 violent confrontations in 1908, 900 in 1909, and 147 in 1910.[40] Disturbances were so widespread that the 1908–1909 *Report on Reforms and Progress in Korea* stated that insurrection had become almost general throughout the country except in two or three northern provinces.

A good portion of F.A. McKenzie's book, *The Tragedy of Korea,* describes the Righteous Army's activities and the Japanese effort to suppress it. Traveling from Seoul to Chongju, McKenzie found half the villages on his route had been destroyed by the Japanese, and between Chongju and Cheechong, a town that was totally destroyed, four-fifths of the villages and hamlets had been burned to the ground. Of Cheechong nothing was left, and the five persons who had been wounded there perished in the flames, while the other townspeople had fled to the hills. Those who lost their houses could rebuild, but they were desolated by the loss of their family registers. With the destruction of the family papers, it was believed the family itself had been wiped out, though there might still be living members.

McKenzie noted, "As the province of Chung-Chung Do prides itself on the large number of its substantial families, there could be no more effective way of striking at them than this," but he wondered at "the futility of the proceedings, from the Japanese point of view. In place of pacifying a people, they were turning hundreds of quiet families into rebels."[41]

In Wonju, McKenzie was told he could find some of the Righteous Army in the village of Yangun. Entering the village, which at first seemed deserted, he was startled to see a dozen red crosses waving over various houses and one pasted on almost every door. A week earlier some Japanese soldiers had arrived and burned a few houses. They spared one house that was flying a red cross. As soon as the Japanese left, nearly everyone had pasted a cross over their door.

Gradually a few men and boys crept out and began talking with McKenzie. At supper time half a dozen rebel soldiers made their appearance, formed a line in front of the foreign reporter, and saluted. They were all young, 18 to 26 years old, and one wore the old uniform of the regular Korean army. None had leather shoes or boots and they had tied bits of rag around their heads.

"The six men had five different weapons, and not one of them was any good. One proudly carried an old Korean sporting gun of the oldest type of muzzle-loaders known to man. Around his arm was the long piece of thin rope which he kept smouldering as touch-powder, and hanging in front of him were the powder horn and bullet bag for loading. This sporting gun was, I afterwards found, a common weapon. The ramrod, for pressing down the charge, was home-made and cut from a tree. The barrel was rust-eaten. There was only a strip of cotton as a carrying strap. The second man had an old Korean army rifle, antiquated, and a very bad specimen of its time. The third had the same. One had a tiny sporting gun, the kind of weapon, warranted harmless, that fond fathers give to their sons at the age of ten. Another had a horsepistol, taking a rifle cartridge. Three of the guns bore Chinese marks. They were all eaten up with ancient rust.

"These were the men—think of it—who for weeks had been bidding defiance of the Japanese Army! . . . The smart young soldier who stood at the right plainly acted as sergeant, and had done his best to drill his comrades into soldierly bearing. A seventh man now came in, a Korean of the better class, well dressed in the long robes of gentility, but thin, sun-stained and wearied like the others. A pitiful group they seemed—men already doomed to certain death, fighting in an absolutely hopeless cause. But as I looked, the sparkling eyes and smiles of the sergeant to the right seemed to rebuke me."[42]

Later, others joined the group, "two old men, one fully 80, an old tiger-hunter, with bent back, grizzled face, and patriarchal beard. The two newcomers carried the old Korean sporting rifles."[43]

As more soldiers arrived, McKenzie was able to talk to the officer in charge. He learned the Righteous Army had practically no organization at all, but was a number of separate bands held together by the loosest ties and financed by local families of comparative means. "We may have to die," the man said, "Well, let it be. It is much better to die as a free man than to live as the slave of Japan."[44]

The commander-in-chief for the entire district, "a middle aged gentleman of rank," came to plead with McKenzie for weapons. Though his own helpers begged him to leave the little party's arms behind, McKenzie carefully counted the guns they carried before leaving.

The soldiers had come to Yangun for shelter, which was given most begrudgingly since the villagers had good cause to fear Japanese reprisal. They were a company of 200 men who had been attacked that day by 20 Japanese soldiers. One Japanese and five Koreans had been wounded in the fray. Of the Korean casualties, three made it back to Yangun, where McKenzie cleaned their wounds and washed their ragged bandages in Listerine, although he decided not to attempt to cut out the bullets still lodged in their wounds.

The two wounded Koreans left unarmed on the field had been savagely bayoneted by Japanese soldiers; villagers who witnessed the scene buried them and reported the incident to McKenzie the next day. Japanese accounts for such encounters gave figures for the number of Koreans killed, but never mentioned wounded or prisoners. Nor was any difference made between those killed in battles and the people, including women and children, who were killed when their village was suspected of aiding the rebels.

The Righteous Army was, inevitably, crushed. What happened to the surviving soldiers? Some escaped to Manchuria and Russia, while others, according to George Paik "went back to the country and became drillmasters of the school boys. It was said at that time that although the Japanese had disbanded the Korean army to annihilate the military power of the nation, they had increased it through the dispersion of the old army among the private schools. I vividly recall these drills and the field meets in which I participated. What a company of little soldiers we were!"[45] The spirit of the Righteous Army in this way spread among the populace to resurface in the 1919 Movement.

The Christians faced a dilemma in the confrontations between the encroaching Japanese and the resistance groups. On the one hand, Protestant Christianity and mission education had fostered a strong sense of nationalism and a sensitivity to justice. On the other, the churches and the missionaries were adamantly opposed to violence and counseled the Christians to be subject to government authority. But the missionaries were double-minded. They preached neutrality and tried to practice non-involvement in politics, but they could not help but cheer when Koreans took a stand. The 1906 annual report of a missionary, for instance, stated "The word 'oppression' has been on every Korean tongue many times of late. It would take too long to enumerate all the evils that are carried on under the name of Japanese occupancy, but a few ought to be mentioned. The seizure of Korean property without compensation still goes on unabated. . . An example is the forestry concession, the object of which seems to be the cutting of every stick of standing timber larger than a walking cane and the entire monopoly of all the lumber produced in Korea. Small proprietors of wooded grave sites or other pieces of timber land have found themselves unable to protect their property. Many of these have resorted to the expedient of presenting their timber to the church in order to save it from the Japanese. As 18 new churches have been built and 27 old ones enlarged during the year, the lumber was very acceptable, but its protection has cost very heavily in worry and American bluff.

"Forced labor still continues in many places, but the stand made by the Christians has compelled the Japanese to pay wages in the greater part of the province. In the districts where the Christians are in the majority, the laborers organized and refused to work without pay. There were beatings and outrages galore but the Koreans gradually won the day."[46]

Sometimes the Christians would find themselves caught between the Righteous Army and the *Ilchinhoi* (pro-Japanese Koreans). Charles Bernheisel wrote of such an occasion in 1909: "The country has been in a very disturbed condition all year on account of the insurgents who continually roam the country shooting Japanese and all members of the *Ilchin-whoi,* a progressive party among the Koreans who are supposed to be favorable to Japan. These progressives have sacrificed their topknots and wear short hair. Hitherto the only short haired people in the country among the Koreans have been Christians. They read in the Bible it is a shame for a man to wear long hair, and in order to obey the Pauline instruction and also to show their break with the old life of paganism most Christians cut their hair. It has not been forced on them by the missionaries, but spontaneously grew up among the Christians as a good custom.

"The short hair of the members of the Ilchin-whoi make them an easy mark for the insurgents. In one of my country districts recently I came to a place where there had been great excitement a few days before. The insurgents are not opposed to the Christians but they are opposed to the Ilchin-whoi and shoot them at sight.

"When they entered this village they caught a lot of short haired people and were going to shoot them. The short haired ones, fearing death, declared that they were Christians and not members of the Ilchin-whoi. There was great consternation. The insurgents asked these men to prove that they were not progressives, but Christians. They asked them who Christ and Paul were; they told them to sing a Christian hymn; they required them to pray. There were among them some who could meet these requirements. Still dissatisfied, the insurgents led the men to an old Christian whom they knew and asked him if the men were Christians. If he said they were Christians they would be released; if he said they were not Christians they would be taken off and shot.

" 'What was I to do?' said the old man, telling me of it a few days later. 'I sent a prayer up to God and then told the insurgents that the men were Christians. These men are all my neighbors and I could not take the responsibility for having them killed when it was in my power to save their lives.' The insurgents believed the old man, released the prisoners and left. That event raised a difficult ethical question. Was the lie justified? Is a lie ever justified?"[47]

Missionaries and other foreigners had their own small clashes with Japanese. Westerners in Korea were so used to being treated deferentially that the "incidents" which began to occur, although comparatively mild, were considered shocking.

Henry Appenzeller was the victim of one of the earliest of these attacks. The Methodist missionary had returned to Korea alone in September 1901 from his second furlough in 17 years, his wife Ella remaining behind with their sick daughter Alice and three other children in school. On June 1, Appenzeller and W.C. Swearer were accompanying visiting Bishop David Hastings Moore to a church near Seoul. Swearer and Appenzeller were on bicycles, the others in a jinricksha.

When the group approached an embankment of the Seoul-Fusan railroad line then under construction, they were halted by a Japanese workman. The bishop was wearing a pith helmet, headgear that had been favored by the Russians in Korea. The workman may have thought he was a Russian, possibly a spy; at any rate, the man grabbed the ricksha handle to stop its progress. The bishop impatiently—and very unwisely—rapped the man's knuckles with his cane. This enraged the Japanese, who threw a large stone at the bishop, which glanced off the helmet.

A group of workers wielding sticks and clubs ran up. Appenzeller, Swearer and Mr. Mun, the Korean evangelist, rushed over and threw themselves between the Japanese and the ricksha, absorbing the blows. When the Japanese saw blood streaming from their faces, they disappeared and the missionary group turned back to Seoul to seek medical treatment.

The matter was reported to the American legation and Minister H.N. Allen acted immediately. The Japanese arrested and tried three of the workers, who were sentenced to several weeks imprisonment at hard labor. Because Appenzeller was forced to remain in Seoul to recover and to attend the trial, he could not leave with Horace Underwood and James Gale for a Bible translation committee meeting in Mokpo. Instead he sailed later, on the steamer *Kumagawa:* that night the steamer was rammed by the 675-ton *Kisogawa* of the same steamship line, and sank, with the loss of 24 lives, including Appenzeller's.

Although the missionaries may have tried to be neutral, they felt as William Scranton, "As foreigners living in Korea, we are nearly all pro-Japanese to the extent of wishing well for Japan in Korea, if she will do well by Korea. We are Korea sympathizers first and look at Korea from the local standpoint."[48]

Scranton made this statement in a letter to the Methodist mission board concerning the visit of Bishop M.C. Harris. Harris, who had been a missionary in Japan for many years, was elected Bishop of Japan and Korea in 1904, but never established a residence in Korea. Scranton described him as "pro and ultra Japanese;" a Presbyterian missionary put it more strongly, writing that Harris was "quite generally considered an agent of the Japanese government rather than a bishop in the Christian church."[49]

This perception of their bishop could only hinder the Methodist church in Korea and may be one of the reasons that its growth lagged behind that of the Presbyterian church during this period.

There were very few places where Koreans could gather and speak with any freedom. The church provided meeting places, unified groups of people and a certain amount of cover. Some Koreans were quick to realize the potential of the church as a communication network and resistance organization. The missionaries were anxious to prevent the church's moving in a political direction. For that reason, the Methodist youth group, the

Epworth League, was disbanded. In November, 1905 Methodist Superintendent William Scranton wrote Secretary A.B. Leonard, "Today I have been obliged to do a very unprecedented thing and have circulated an order that the Epworth League may not meet again. With the universal unrest, our Epworth League has become filled up with undigested new members. It is being used for political purposes entirely obscuring its purpose. Unfortunately the League is strongly patriotic and that means it is used for anti-Japanese sentiment. We cannot allow any chances of political compliance with either government, and as yet we stand in the *best* of favor with *both* governments."

Scranton was highly optimistic in thinking the church was in the best of favor with anyone. Rather, both camps were suspicious. As historian Charles Stokes pointed out, a neutral stand is still a stand, and although it was not intended to do so, "there is no doubt that the policy advocated by the missionaries aided the Japanese."[50] Yet the Japanese were afraid of the church, because it was one area of Korean life they could not entirely control, and they distrusted missionaries. Midoru Komatsu, Japanese director of the Bureau of Foreign Affairs, wrote, "They are propagating Christianity in Korea, but pay no attention to the interests of Japan, the sovereign of Korea. While engaged in Christian propaganda work, the American missionaries run schools and diffuse foreign political and social ideas among the half-civilized people. The principle of liberty is recklessly advocated among them."[51]

Part of the reason the Japanese were unhappy with the missionaries is that through them, Korea, especially the Christians, had overseas ties, communication, and a broad base of sympathy. The Japanese, sensitive of their image, were carefully cultivating good will abroad. They did not want the seamy underside of their occupation of Korea to be publicized.

Nor is it difficult to see why the Japanese became almost paranoid about the possibility of a relationship between the church and armed resistance, after the assassination in 1908 of Durham White Stevens by a Korean patriot, Chang In-Hwan, a Protestant.

On June 14, 1909, Ito resigned as resident-general and was re-appointed president of the Japanese Privy Council. The Japanese government made the decision to annex Korea on July 6, and although the concluding agreement with Yi Wan-Yong, prime minister of Korea, bore the name of the new resident-general Sone Arasuki, it was negotiated by Ito before he left Korea on July 14. A little more than two months later, on October 26, 1909, at the Harbin railroad station in Manchuria, Ito was assassinated by An Chung-Gun, a Catholic.

These assassinations created, as is so often the case, an adverse effect on the cause they were meant to forward. Ito had been among the more moderate and fair-minded Japanese leaders; now the military party in Japan clamored for a harsher policy. Terauchi Masatake, a general who had served as minister of war, moved quickly toward the formal annexation of Korea.

This was hardly the time, from the Japanese point of view, for the Koreans to undertake a highly organized nationwide evangelistic campaign for the express purpose of adding to the numbers and strength of the church. Yet the Million Souls movement of 1910 was just that, and inevitably it was misunderstood and opposed by the Japanese. Spies and uniformed gendarmes attended all special church services. Pastors were required to report the names of converts at police headquarters and intimidation of Christians by police was common.[52]

The Australian mission station in Chinju reported that "the Japanese police are following the Million Souls Movement in each place, and went from door to door demanding whether any had decided to become Christians. The people were so intimidated that they were afraid to follow up their decisions. In some cases school children were forcibly prevented from attending church . . . all gatherings of people were suspect of being politically motivated.[53]

With annexation, the Japanese settled in. Government regulations dealing with every phase of life were promulgated in the name of reform and progress. Christians found themselves in more difficulty than non-Christians. There were numerous regulations to which the churches and missions had to submit—permission had to be obtained in advance to build a church, religious publications' contents reported in outline, qualifications of all teachers given. Religious instruction and chapel services in schools were restricted. Students of church schools wishing to enroll in advanced educational institutions were at a severe disadvantage. All printed matter was censored.

Pastors and missionaries had to be careful of what they said in sermons. A missionary who spoke on David and Goliath in a chapel program was promptly reported as having given a treasonable talk since David could only symbolize Korea, and Goliath, Japan! One Korean minister was arrested for preaching on the kingdom of heaven; "he was told that there was only one kingdom out here and it was the kingdom of Japan."[54]

Incidents such as these prompted Charles Bernheisel to write in 1916 that "There is a good deal of religious persecution in this country. Of course the Japanese deny that it is persecution or that it has anything to do with religion. But the Japanese have about as much regard for truth as for justice. . . . It is to the interest of the military power in this country to make it appear that Korea is full of anarchy and treason and that the church is mixed up in it."[55]

Korea became Japan's logistical supply base. Every year, millions of liters of rice were collected from Korea and shipped to Japan, leaving the Koreans to eat other grains or to go hungry. The main purpose of annexation was to exploit the Korean economy for the benefit of Japan. One of the chief instruments for doing so was a land survey. A date was set by which all landowners had to report the location of their land, its precise size and its quality. Korea had never had such a survey before, and as a result, many farmers failed to report to the government before the deadline and the land they and their ancestors had farmed for centuries was confiscated. The government general eventually owned a 20th of all arable land, besides the land owned individually by Japanese firms and families. The government general then proceeded to dispose of the land it had acquired to Japanese at bargain prices. By the end of the land survey the number of Korean-owned family farms had declined by nearly 40,000.[56]

These conditions encouraged Koreans to trudge north into Manchuria and Russia, as far as Siberia, especially after emigration to other countries was cut off by the residency general in 1905. Conditions in the Russian Usuri province were good, with available land, fair administration and justice; and the Koreans flourished there.[57] They also set up expatriate resistance groups, learning much from Russian revolutionaries. So the seeds for a Communist north Korea were sown, an unintended side-effect of Japanese oppression, just as the Russo-Japanese War had unintentionally provided one of the sparks to set off the raging flames of revolution in Russia.

The military party's hand in Japan was strengthened, and Japan was free to make Korea a bridge for their later invasion of the Asian continent. These long range byproducts of the annexation of Korea were mostly unknown and unsuspected at the time, but in 1907 one farsighted reporter warned, "If the military party in Japan gains the upper hand we shall have harsher rule in Korea, steadily increasing aggression in Manchuria, growing interference with China, and in the end, a Titanic conflict, the end of which none can see."[58]

March 1, 1919

It was the Japanese mindset that was defeated in Korea.

As one scholar of Japanese character wrote, "Japan, having attained unification and peace in her homeland, having put down banditry and built up roads and electric power and steel industries, having, according to official figures, educated 99.5 percent of her rising generation in her public schools should, according to Japanese premises of hierarchy, raise her backward younger brother. . . It was an appropriate fantasy for Japan to create. Unfortunately for her, the countries she occupied did not see it in the same light."[59]

At first Korean resistance was no more than a nuisance to be flicked aside like a buzzing fly. After the 1905 Protectorate, for instance, Ewha students stopped studying at 3 p.m. daily to pray for national independence. The prayers of school girls were hardly threatening to Japan. But then some of the students organized an underground society grandly named Yosong Aeguk Tongji-hoe, the Patriotic Women's League. The group was comprised of fewer than a dozen girls, including Marcella Cynn, the first graduate of the college program, Pak In-Duk, Shin Chul-lyo, Helen Kim and Hwang Ae-Duk. They met secretly in the school attic at midnight. Their plan to send a representative to the Paris Peace Conference of January 1919 to disclose Japanese oppression and appeal for Korean independence ended with the imprisonment of Pak In-Duk and Shin Chul-lyo.[60]

Students in other mission schools carried out their own small rebellions. In Chonju, in 1915 Louise (Young-Shin) Yim and her classmates each night by candlelight copied forbidden Korean history books by hand for young people to study. When a rule was passed that the Japanese national anthem was to be sung daily, the group who called itself the Suicide Squad, flatly refused and the order was rescinded. Next, the girls slipped into their classrooms early one morning and with sharpened pencils stabbed out the eyes of all the portraits of the Japanese emperor.[61]

The students became bolder. In 1917 students at Soongsil with other Pyongyang Christians founded the *Kukminhoe,* People's Assembly, and made contact with exile independence groups. Most of the members of the *Kukminhoe* were arrested.[62] Such student activism hardly went unnoticed. The Japanese were sufficiently antagonized that the number of private schools was reduced from 1,973 in 1910 to 690 in 1919.[63]

With the signing of the World War I armistice, as one Korean put it, "Hope leaped and faith in a righteous cause mounted its wings."[64] More than 200,000 people thronged the streets of Seoul in joyous celebration. Indeed, inspiration for the March 1 movement came primarily from U.S. President Woodrow Wilson's Fourteen Points, especially Point Five which spoke of the right of small nations to self-determination. His words were translated in the most hopeful terms by the Korean underground and circulated in the following message: "President Wilson of the United States has proclaimed a 14-point program for world peace. One of these points is the self-determination of peoples. You must make the most of this situation. Your voice must be heard. President Wilson will certainly help you."[65]

Christian and Chundogyo leaders had been meeting very quietly to discuss some sort of resistance movement. The Chundogyo were for revolution. They wanted to issue a Declaration of Independence and to achieve autonomy, by force if necessary, whereas the Christian leaders wanted to petition for the redress of abuses and for government reforms, and insisted that there be no violence. The compromise finally adopted was to call for a nationwide non-violent demonstration to declare Korea's independence.

Couriers traveled secretly, taking messages to groups in every locality, instructing them to make small Korean flags to take to an appointed place at an appointed time to hear the reading of the Declaration of Independence, shout *Chosun Tongnip Mansei*, Long Live Korean Independence, and to march peacefully through their city, town or village.

The Declaration of Independence was drawn up and 78 people volunteered to sign it. Ham Tae-Yong warned those who signed would surely be arrested and were likely to be executed. He suggested the group divide into thirds; if the first group of signers were all killed, then the proclamation could be reissued over the names of the second group, and should they be killed, there would still be a group of survivors to lead the movement. But 33 people –15 Christians, 15 Chundogyo and three Buddhists—insisted on signing.[67] The next move was to get copies to scattered Chundogyo groups to be mimeographed and distributed throughout the country. This had to be done with the utmost secrecy.

The youngest of the declaration signers, Lee Kap-Song, was in charge of student and youth activities in North and South Kyongsang provinces. He was carrying incriminating documents, perhaps the declaration itself, to Taegu when he was stopped by a Japanese police officer at the train station. The officer told Lee to wait while he went to call other police. Lee tried to pass the documents on to an elderly Korean gentleman standing nearby, but the man refused to take them. Just then a young school girl came up and said, "I will take them, hurry." Lee passed them to her and she immediately disappeared into the crowd, just as the police returned. Stripped, searched and questioned at length, Lee was finally released. He went on to Taegu, where the girl approached him on the street and silently handed him the papers. Lee wrote, "She was a true patriot; in those days anyone who could catch a person with this kind of document would receive a [large cash] reward and a two-rank promotion. The police were very eager to catch rebels."[68]

In such ways the Declaration of Independence was passed from hand to hand, duplicated and distributed all over Korea. In Choong Nam province, Louise Yim was working as a teacher. One day a messenger from Seoul, instead of meeting her in their prearranged location, rushed into her classroom, thrust copies of the declaration into her hands and raced out the door again. A moment later a Japanese officer entered the room demanding, "What did that man want?"

"Just a beggar," replied the school teacher.

The policeman stared hard at her as she stood, papers in hand. She asked permission to continue the class and as calmly as possible handed a student one of the precious sheets, asking him to read the Ten Commandments. The student understood instantly and pretending to read, repeated the commandments from memory. The officer grunted and left; only after he had gone did Louise Yim realize that he couldn't read Korean.[69]

On January 21, Kojong died a tired and disappointed man, under mysterious circumstances. It was decided that the day of his funeral, March 3, would be the day for the national nonviolent demonstration. The date was pushed up to March 1 when it was feared the Japanese were becoming suspicious.

Before dawn on Saturday, March 1, handbills were posted and passed out through the busiest section of Seoul saying that the former emperor had been poisoned because he refused to sign a paper declaring Korea was content under the Japanese regime.

Like the 1884 progressives who began their rebellion with a dinner, 32 of the signers of the Declaration of Independence (one, Kil Son-Chu, was delayed coming from Pyongyang) met over a meal, at the Tai-Wha Kwan, Bright Moon Restaurant. They invited all the top-ranking Japanese officials to this luncheon, but the Japanese, not too interested in a meeting of religious leaders and preoccupied with suspicion that a large demonstration was about to take place, sent only one of their number. In due time, the Declaration was read and the signers drank to the success of the movement they had thus launched. They must have been amused at the consternation of their lone Japanese guest. Then the signers notified the police of what they had done.

The police at the time were a block away, busily seraching the YMCA building, where they had expected some sort of uprising to occur. Rushing to the Bright Moon, they surrounded the restaurant and arrested the rebels. A convoy of motor cars was hurriedly commandeered to take the prisoners to the Central Police Headquarters.

At 2 p.m., the same time as the reading of the declaration at the Bright Moon Restaurant, under a Korean flag flying openly for the first time in 10 years, a young man mounted the pavilion in Pagoda Park and read the same declaration in ringing tones. He finished by lifting his arms high and giving a rousing cheer—"Mansei! Ten thousand years! Long live Korea!"—which was taken up by the surging mass of flag-waving people in the park and carried through the main streets of Seoul. By the time the cars with the arrested patriots were pulling away from the Bright Moon Restaurant, the street was dense with people who were cheering so energetically and enthusiastically that the police escorts thought it prudent to cheer along with them.

Meanwhile, the arrested signers were leaning from the car windows, handing out copies of the declaration right and left. Kil Son-Chu, arriving late, hastened to the police station to take his place with his comrades. The signers knew very well what they could expect in prison; not only had two of them, Yang Chun-Paik and Yi Seung-Hun, been held during the 1912 conspiracy trials, pastor Kil's son had died from the effects of Japanese torture.[70] Yet Kil's name was the second on the declaration, after Chundogyo leader Son Pyung-Hi's.

The declaration itself was read perhaps in 1,000 different places in Korea on March 1, and copies of it were mailed to the Paris Peace Conference, President Woodrow Wilson and the Japanese government. It was a document written by religious men, voicing the aspirations of the Korean people; it was the cry of a nation trying with dignity to find its way into a new age.

"We herewith proclaim the independence of Korea and the liberty of the Korean people," it said. "We make this proclamation, having back of us 5,000 years of history, and 20 million of a united, loyal people. We take this step to insure to our children for all time to come, personal liberty in accord with the awakening consciousness of this new era. This is the clear leading of God, the moving principle of the present age, the whole human race's just claim. It is something that cannot be stamped out, or stifled, or gagged, or suppressed by any means."

The amazing thing is that with the issuance of the declaration, Korea was indeed for the first time a "united, loyal people." The Japanese had succeeded in doing something no one else had managed; they had united the Koreans into a nation of one heart and one mind—dead set against the Japanese.

One of the signers, YMCA director Yi Sang-Chae, was roughly interrogated by Japanese police who demanded, "Who is the head of this movement? Do you know?" He answered, "Yes." They pounced on him like tigers. "Who? Tell us. Who is the head of the movement?" "God," he replied. "God is at the head, and 20 million Koreans behind."[71]

The declaration expressed Korea's grievances: ". . . after these long thousands of years to experience the agony of 10 years of foreign oppression, with every loss to the right to live, every restriction of the freedom of thought, every damage done to the dignity of life, every opportunity lost for a share in the intelligent advance of the age in which we live"—and unambiguously called for what was most wanted—"the first of all necessary things is the clearcut independence of our people."

The declaration affirmed that Korean independence could be a force for shaping not only a better Japan, but a better future for everyone: "Today Korean independence will mean not only daily life and happiness for us, but also it will mean Japan's departure from an evil way and exaltation to the place of true protector of the east, so that China, too, even in her dreams, would put all fear of Japan aside. This thought comes from no minor resentment, but from a large hope for the future welfare and blessing of mankind."[72]

Nonviolence was insisted upon. Placards signed by the Korean Independence Band were posted everywhere on Monday, March 3, reminding the people, "Whatever you do, do not insult the Japanese, do not throw stones, do not hit with your fists for these are the acts of barbarians. Whoever performs such acts injures the cause of independence and therefore is a danger. So let everyone without exception take great care."[73]

Ewha students served as a forward guard in the demonstration in Seoul, marching in the very front of the procession. Their first hurdle had been to leave the school grounds; Lulu Frey stood by the bolted gate, facing the girls with her arms outspread to make sure that none would pass. "Well, girls, you will go out over my dead body," she said.[74]

Miss Frey wasn't the only one having trouble restraining students on March 1. In South Kyongsang province, when two Australian missionaries, Misses M.S. Davis and D. Hocking, went out on the streets to gather their school girls back in, they were arrested and detained two days for having demonstrated.[75]

At Ewha, when the girls saw how determined Miss Frey was, some of them returned to their rooms in the dormitory, but a few climbed the walls at points not easily visible and went out to join the independence march. In spite of Miss Frey's protest, more and more of the students left to participate in the demonstrations.[77] Some were wounded and killed and a number were arrested and served three years in prison. When the school was recessed a few days later the other girls went home, but not to sit idly. They became leaders of the independence movement up and down the country.

One of them was Yu Kwan-Sun of Chung-chong province. She and her brother decided to organize a rally on the first of March by the lunar calendar. On the given day, Miss Yu addressed a crowd assembled in the marketplace, who waved the Korean flag and shouted *mansei* for independence. The Japanese police arrived and shot down many. Yu Kwan-Sun's parents were among the first killed. She was arrested and after a long period of torture and suffering died in 1920 at the age of 16.[78]

In Chonju, Louise Yim was one of 10 young Korean women aged 16 to 22 who were jailed; three girls under 12 were arrested but released. They were stripped, beaten, tortured and starved for some months before their trial, at which they received sentences of three and a half years' house arrest. Louise Yim's friend's sister, Cho Wha-Pok, carrying a Korean flag, was in the front ranks of the Kongju demonstrations. Caught by the Japanese, she refused to relinquish the flag. A Japanese officer on horseback rode up and slashed off her hands with his saber. When her parents rushed forward to catch the girl who was reeling with shock, they were killed, and she was left to bleed to death.[79]

The police used their swords freely. A little gathering of men started shouting *Mansei* in a street in Seoul. The police came after them and they vanished, but one man was pushed into a ditch by the road. As he was getting up, the police grabbed him, cut off his ears and fingers, hacked at his body, and left; horrified spectators carried him away and he died a few hours later.[80]

Three Christian women—O Hyon-Gwan, a school teacher in Chaeryong, O Hyon-Ju, a teacher in Kunsan, and Yi Chong-suk, a nurse at Severance Hospital—were leading members of the Hyolsong-dan, a patriotic group founded in April 1919 to collect funds for the families of the imprisoned. Later, their activity widened to help the exiled government in Shanghai and they renamed their society the Korean Women's Patriotic Society, the *Taehan Minguk Aeguk Puin-hoe.* In early November, some of the active members in North Kyongsang province were arrested and executed.[81]

In Pyongyang, Presbyterian and Methodist women united to form the Patriotic Women's Society, the *Taehan Aeguk Puin-hoe,* which collected money for the resistance movement and sent funds to the Shanghai government-in-exile. Several of their members were killed.[82] James Gale's long-time coworker Yi Chang-Sik's daughter, a school teacher, was vice-chairman of the society and for this was imprisoned at hard labor in Taegu for three years. Her sister fled the country, and a brother died under torture in prison.[83]

The women most prominent in the 1919 movement—Maria Kim, Esther Hwang, Yu Kwan-Sun, Kwon Ae-Ra and O Yun-Hui—were all Christians. A report showed that of the 2,656 Presbyterian church members known to have been arrested in 1919, 531 were women.[84] Since there were five times more girls in Christian schools than in other schools, the presence of school girls in the demonstrations was interpreted by the Japanese to mean that missionaries had instigated the movement.

Mission schools were closed after March 1, not by the government but because so many students and teachers had been arrested and those who had not, refused to study until independence was attained. At least two mission schools were warned that they would be closed permanently if they did not get their students back in class. Government schools were in much the same circumstances, but officially remained open with the teachers going through the motions in empty classrooms.[85]

The Japanese had problems even with the primary school children. At one elementary school in Seoul, the children were enticed to return for their graduation ceremony, but just as the principal began his congratulatory address, out from the inside of each youngster's coat came a Korean flag, with the cry of *Mansei!* The principal was left speechless on the podium as the children filed out into the yard, formed a line and marched away to the palace, shouting "Ten thousand years for Korea!"[86]

Some aspects of the independence movement were irrepressible, for instance a mimeographed newspaper called *The Independence News*. It first appeared on March 1, and its first editor was Yun Ikaun, president of Posung College of Law and Commerce. He was promptly arrested, but the paper continued to appear daily for many months, though the Japanese searched everywhere and confiscated all the mimeograph machines and materials they could find.[87]

All the stores in Seoul were closed from March 5 until April 1, when they were forced to reopen. A Korean writer explained the significance of the shuttered shops: "Even though Korea has always maintained a monarchical form of government, there were many checks upon the extravagant use of the king's prerogatives. One of the last resorts, in case the king is obdurate, is the merchant guild's strike, the closing of all business concerns on Bell Street (Chongno), the nerve center of Korea's commercial life. According to tradition, when the stores are closed for three days consecutively, the king must descend from the throne."[88]

The Japanese, who had been taken by surprise, reacted swiftly and brutally. Though no demonstrator was armed, many were killed, and within days the jails were jammed. On April 15, the government general decreed that any Korean participating in the independence movement in or outside of Korea would be sentenced to 10 years' imprisonment;[89] contributing funds to the resistance movement became an offense punishable by death.[90]

In Suwon, 25 miles south of Seoul, Japanese gendarmes attacked a group of villagers assembled to read the Declaration of

Independence. The following night, Koreans responded with a *Mansei* charge, setting fire to the Japanese police station. In retaliation, on March 17, gendarmes drove 30 hand-picked villagers into a church building, locked it, set the building on fire and shot down the screaming men, women and children who tried to escape. The police action spread to 15 neighboring villages. Word of atrocities reached Seoul and some school girls went to Suwon to render medical aid. They were bayoneted by the police.[91]

The worst massacre took place in the village of Che-Am-Ri, 17 miles south of Suwon. On the afternoon of April 15, some soldiers entered the village and gave orders that all adult males who were Christians or members of Chundogyo were to assemble in the church for a lecture. Some 23 men filed into the church; when they had sat down, soldiers surrounded the building and shot into it through the paper windows. Then they set fire to the thatch roof; men who tried to rush out were bayoneted or shot. Two Christian women, aged 19 and 40, trying to reach their husbands, were killed, the younger woman bayoneted, the older one shot. The soldiers set the whole village afire and left.[92] Horace H. Underwood, who visited the village the following day, was one of the first to report the atrocity.

Presbyterian missionaries wrote their board that "Undoubtedly the government regards Christianity as the chief factor of the disturbance. The leaders went into it with their eyes open. They said they had prayed the matter through and felt it was God's will for them to make this attempt to secure not merely civil but religious liberty at this particular time in the world's history when so many small peoples are apparently to secure these blessings. We learned this from the Rev. Kim Sun-Du, moderator of the Korean General Assembly, after the demonstrations began and before he and other leaders were arrested."[93]

So many Christians were arrested that in many places churches stood almost empty, like the two churches described by A.A. Pieters in Chaeryong. "Almost all the men of these two churches took part in the demonstration. Those who were not arrested fled so that now the congregation consists only of women."[94] In South Chulla, 63 church leaders were imprisoned and in North Chulla three pastors had been killed and more than 100 church leaders were in prison.[95]

In Pyongyang when missionary J.Z. Moore called the Methodists of the area together he found that seven ordained ministers, 15 local preachers, 19 exhorters, 20 class leaders, one district steward, 13 men and three women school teachers, three students and 60 church members, 140 people in all, were in jail for having participated in the independence movement. One had been killed and three were hospitalized. Moore wrote of those remaining, "Such a spirit of unity, of unselfishness, of willingness to give up for the good of the whole work I never have experienced among the Korean workers. One of the country circuits willingly gave up its pastor for Pyeng Yang City, and he was given the work six men formerly did."[96]

In Kunsan, the mission school and hospital staffs were imprisoned in *toto*. Southern Presbyterian missionary William Bull wrote, "The school boys and teachers had been working for some days making Korean national flags and hundreds of copies of the Declaration of Independence for a big demonstration on Market Day. . . . Japanese agents had gotten one of the weaker hospital helpers and had put such pressure on him that he had given the whole thing away. . . The day before the demonstration was to come off 10 police officers came out and arrested the school teachers, searching the building, and took possession of all the revolutionary literature they could find. As they were handcuffing the teachers to take them off to jail the school boys all crowded around saying . . . 'you will have to take us, too'. The police had not bargained for such a large contract. They had their hands more than full with only 10. They started off to Kunsan with the teachers, and the whole student body fell in behind waving Korean flags and shouting 'Hurray for the Independence of Korea' all the way to Kunsan.

"The afternoon clinic was in session and when word came that the teachers had been arrested the hospital helpers all threw off their gowns and caps and rushed out and said 'If you take them you will have to take us, too'. . . As they were tying up the teachers and school boys, all crowded around, the police pulled their pistols and threatened to shoot, some of the boys thrust out their chests saying, 'Shoot, shoot!' "[97]

The festive air that turned going to prision into a joyous demonstration was dissipated by the grim conditions there. Those released told terrible tales of being "crowded into prison like cattle in a cattle car, suffering agonies for lack of air . . . intense torture by active aggressive methods such as burning with hot irons, holding their heads back and pouring hot water down their nostrils."[98]

Although in jail, the Koreans were not idle. J.Z. Moore wrote that "One pastor reports that he is in a room with 19. At first there were but three Christians. Now they are all Christains and have services in their cell. One boy, a student, said it meant more to him than a year of study."[99]

Presbyterians in Pyongyang in 1920 reported that "Many of the converts have come out of prison with the joy of the Lord in their hearts and have gone back to their homes to bear witness to the gospel. They tell of catechumens received and baptisms administered behind prison walls. One of the pastors reports having received many letters since his return, asking for letters of transfer from the prison church to the ones in their home towns. This same pastor was moved about seven times from prison to prison during his 14 months. Each time he found himself with a larger company of men." This pastor could hardly have managed on his own to reach so many places and people; the Japanese government by moving him from prison to prison unwittingly gave him vast opportunities for Christian witness. Letters of transfer to many churches were issued from the Presbyterian Church, Westgate Prison, Seoul. For the Presbyterians, church membership rose from 69,025 to 72,138, an increase of 4.5 percent during the year.[100]

As the Koreans celebrated their faith in prison, they celebrated their hope, and independence demonstrations took place even behind bars. Lee Kap-Song described one: "While we were in prison, we decided to have a 'long live ceremony.' At this time there were about 1,000 people in prison, 600 of these were in there for different crimes, nothing to do with the Sam Il Movement. One night at 12 o'clock midnight we shouted 'long live Korea.' Soon after that they took us into the investigation rooms and beat us. I still have a scar. They found out that this activity was organized by a Mr. Oh and me, so they lengthened our sentences from three years to four years."[101]

It has been estimated that two million people, one out of every 10 Koreans, participated in the 1919 movement in 1,500 demonstrations throughout the country. About 7,000 people were killed; 15,000 wounded; 715 private homes, 47 churches and two school buildings were destroyed by fire. Close to 46,000 people were arrested, and 10,000, of whom 186 were women, were tried and convicted. The majority of these, including the signers of the declaration, were sentenced to three years in prison.

The Japanese were not moved to grant Korea freedom, although some reforms were made. In August 1919, Baron Saito Makoto, a moderate, was sent to replace General Hasegawa as governor general. Saito survived an attempt made on his life in September 1919, and became prime minister of Japan in 1932, after many years in Korea. Ironically, he was assassinated in 1933 by Japanese militarists.

Under Saito's administration, civil officials were no longer uniformed and were not permitted to wear swords, the military was placed under civilian authority, flogging of prisoners was abolished, at least in principle, and there was less censorship. Police oppression continued, however, and economic exploitation worsened. Korean land continued to pass into Japanese hands, and

Korean rice into Japanese stomachs. While rice production steadily increased, Koreans ate less and less of it. The per capita consumption of rice by Koreans dropped nearly 50 percent between 1915 and 1938.[102] After the Sam-Il movement, international opinion could no longer easily believe the fictions of the benevolence of the Japanese presence in Korea and the acquiescence of the Korean people in the annexation of their country.

The more Japan tried to assimilate Korea, the more the Koreans resisted. The spirit of the independence movement defeated the Japanese idea of assimilation. James Gale wrote in his 1927 history of Korea that "The end of the 19th century marks the end of Korea,"[103] and Homer Hulbert entitled one of his books *The Passing of Korea.* But they were wrong. Korea survived the encroachments of the Japanese with a sense of unity and national consciousness never previously attained. *Mansei* was stamped on the hearts of a nation.

March First and the Missionaries

The Sam-II movement came as great a surprise to the missionaries as to the Japanese. In all Korea, apparently only one foreigner had advance knowledge. That was Frank W. Schofield, who was visited on February 28 by one of his students, who requested to speak with him in private. Schofield wrote, "We went into my bedroom. I was surprised when he asked that the blinds be drawn. Unbuttoning his shirt he pulled out a piece of paper. Handing it to me, he said: 'This is our Declaration of Independence. Tomorrow this will be read in many places, followed by demonstrations. We must be free from Japan.' I was greatly surprised and said, 'Do you really believe that Japan will give you independence just because you ask for it and make demonstrations? The Japanese soldiers and police will simply shoot you as rebels.' He replied, 'This we know, but the United States and other democratic countries will help us.' "

When Schofield tried to persuade the student of the plan's futility, he replied, "You are an Englishman, so think like an imperialist, but we trust you. Please see that this copy reaches the White House as soon as possible." Schofield sent the declaration to the United States with a friend who was leaving the next day.

On the morning of March 1, the missionary was visited again, this time by his friend Lee Kap-Sung. "With smiling face and voice full of emotion, he said, 'This is the happiest day of my life. I am one of the men who will declare the independence of Korea today. There will be a big student demonstration this afternoon at Pagoda Park. Be there about 2 p.m. and please take some photographs for us. I will be in prison so may not see you again."[104]

At the park, Schofield watched a steady stream of students pass directly in front of four or five Japanese police officers. Suddenly shouts of *Mansei!* filled the air and students rushed from the park into the Chongno thoroughfare leading toward City Hall. Some leaped in the air, others threw copies of the Declaration of Independence to people attracted by the uproar who had come running from all directions. Schofield snapped away with his camera, but feared he was getting mostly blurs since the students were running straight toward him. He followed them on a bicycle to the plaza in front of Duksu Palace, but was too immersed in the crowd to be able to indicate its size in a photograph. Noticing a small Japanese shop with an upstairs balcony, he entered and asked a little girl to show him the stairs. Rushing upstairs and out onto the verandah he had a wonderful view of the milling throngs below and took several photographs, which he quickly developed and smuggled out of the country.

There had been enough anticipation in the air before March 1 for a few missionaries to have a hint of things to come. Robert Grierson wrote that in Sungjin, "On Thursday, February 27, as wife Lena and I sat reading after supper, a knock came at the door, and a group of our elder church people were ushered into our reception room. They said that they wished to hold a private meeting to discuss a certain matter, and might they have the use of a room in the hospital. I hesitated to have the hospital implicated in any secret matter, and suggested that in our home, as our guests, there was no subject that they might not discuss together. Considering it my duty as host to remain, I sat at one side and heard their conference. It seems that word had come from the capital that some movement was at hand, but so vaguely that they did not know what action, if any, was expected. Finally they decided to send two of their number to leave immediately for Seoul to get instructions."[105]

Grierson heard no more of the matter until Monday, March 3. "I went to the hospital as usual, but not a single member of the staff was there. Oh yes, there was one young fellow who did lab work for me, who with his back to me, was working at the lab table. When he heard my footsteps, he turned, and when he saw who it was, slipped something beneath his coat. I lifted his coat up and found that he had been making a Korean flag with paper and colored crayons.

"Then I heard from outside the sound of marching feet and cries of *Mansei! Mansei!* and looking out of the window saw a great crowd coming up from the town and turning into the hospital grounds. I went out to meet them. The leaders told me that they would use the hospital portico as a platform to address the people."[106]

So that he would not appear to be participating in the demonstration, Grierson withdrew and with his three daughters went up to the hospital attic. Looking down on the crowd, they could hear the orators and the cheering responses. After several speeches, the whole conclave moved off in an orderly manner, each person waving a flag similar to the one made by the laboratory helper. The Grierson family followed the crowd which went and stood before the post office, the mayor's office and the police station, peacefully shouting "*Tai Han* (Korea) *Mansei!*' " at each stop. "Then the crowd broke up and went home as we did also, and that was all. All quiet."

But next morning was another story. "Quite early, a squad of Japanese firefighters armed with fire axes and police armed with rifles paraded up from their settlement to the quietly resting Korean village street, beating, hacking, shooting. Soon casualties began to come into the hospital." One, who was beyond medical help, had been coming into town to visit his brother, a Presbyterian elder, when a Japanese soldier seized him, dragged him into a field and shot him pointblank in the heart.

Grierson was questioned that night at the police station about the meeting in his home. He said that since the meeting had been inconclusive he had been very much surprised by the demonstrations. The police apparently believed that he had no prior knowledge or involvement in the movement, served him tea and cakes and sent him home at midnight.

All his church elders and many of the older members had been arrested. On the following Sunday when Grierson went to church, he was almost alone. To encourage those in prison, he went out to the bell tower, and rang the big bell long and loud, "so that they in the prison across the river might know that we were signaling our sympathy and greetings."[107] Most of the Sungjin church members were sentenced to several years' imprisonment, many of them in Westgate prison in Seoul. Women of the church took turns going to the capital to cook food for the prisoners to supplement their meager prison fare.

In Pyongyang, too, the missionaries were caught off guard by the March First Movement, although there had been considerable suppressed excitement for several days. A memorial service for the late emperor had long been scheduled to be held in three places—Chundogyo headquarters, the Methodist Church and the Christian boys' school—on March 1. Presbyterian missionaries Samuel Moffett, Charles Bernheisel and J.G. Holdcroft were among the crowd of 3,000 at the boys' school. At the close of the service, it was announced that the people were to remain seated. Kim Sun-Du, moderator of the Presbyterian Church, read two Scripture passages, I Peter 3:13-17 and Romans 9:3. Charles Bernheisel recalled, "It was evident from his intonation as he read that something serious was on the docket. Then Chong Il-Sun, a graduate of the college, took the platform and said he had an important communication to read. He said it was the happiest and proudest day of his life. A great cheer went up from the audience. He then proceeded to read what was virtually a declaration of independence of the Korean people."[108]

A speaker instructed the crowd that they were to do nothing of an unlawful or violent nature and were to offer no resistance, whatever the provocation, to any Japanese. Then Kang Kyu-Chang spoke on national independence, after which men came out from the school carrying armloads of small Korean flags which were distributed to the people. A large Korean flag was fastened to the wall back of the speakers' stand and the crowd burst into cries of *Mansei!*

Japanese soldiers who were attempting to clear the school grounds began taking down the forbidden flag. Samuel Moffett intervened, and claimed the flag as foreign property. He told the excited crowd, "I will keep this flag until the day when Korea is free to fly it again."[109] Moffett's son, James, smuggled the flag out of Korea the next year when he went to the United States to study. In 1974 he brought it back to fulfill his father's promise and the flag was unfurled over the Seoul campus of Soongjun University.[110]

The Moffetts' son Samuel Hugh was three years old in 1919. Many years later he wrote, "My earliest memory as a child is of Japanese soldiers or police, with fixed bayonets, breaking into the room in our home in Pyongyang where my younger brother and I were supposed to be taking an afternoon nap. They were looking for incriminating documents and demonstrators hiding from the law. But to my brother and me the shouts of *Mansei!* and the excitement in the streets seemed like some gigantic happy game, so when the soldiers threw open the door we greeted them with the glad cry we had been hearing so much: *Mansei!*" His parents went pale but the soldiers broke the brief moment of tension with a laugh and left.[111]

Meanwhile, back at the boys' school grounds, Charles Bernheisel, J.G. Holdcroft and George McCune who had joined them after arriving late from Sonchon were standing and talking by the main gate of the campus. They decided to walk down the hill to see how things were going. Bernheisel wrote that "After walking for some distance down the main street of the city I happened to look behind us and found that we were leading a long procession. As soon as we had quit the school grounds the crowd, unknown to us, had fallen in behind us and we were thus in the position of leading the procession down the main street of the city. I told the brethren that we must not continue in this position, and they agreed, so we scooted off into an alley and allowed the crowd to follow other leaders."[112]

This incident vividly points up the position of the Protestant missionaries, who had no leadership roles in the movement. Instead, they were literally caught in the middle; their sympathies were with the Koreans, but they were not and did not want to be involved in a crusade for independence. They were, both by mission policy and personal inclination, basically apolitical. They were committed to the biblical injunction to obey government authority. For one thing, they had to work under those powers. And, if they forgot that they were not supposed to be in any way politically active, their mission boards and foreign legations were quick to remind them. Also, like Frank Schofield, they believed that the Koreans had no chance of obtaining independence from the Japanese either peacefully or by violence, which they certainly couldn't condone.

But the majority of those who fervently wished to remain uninvolved found that neutrality was not only unrealistic, it was a luxury their consciences could not afford. Actually the missionary response—outrage—was an appropriate one.

In Pyongyang as elsewhere, the nonviolent demonstrations of the Koreans were met with violent overreaction by the Japanese. Samuel Moffett was one of the first to report and protest Japanese atrocities. On March 4, he invited school inspector Yamada to accompany him on a fact-finding tour to verify his charges. Moffett wrote of having witnessed beatings, stabbings, clubbings and kickings, some involving 12- and 13-year-old girls. He reported the March 4 detainment and torture of five seminary students just returned from winter vacation who had taken no part in the demonstrations. These men had been dragged from their dormitory to the police station where they were tied face down to wooden crosses and given 29 blows, considered the maximum a person could survive in one day, on the bare buttocks with sharp sticks.

On March 5, Moffett sent his mission board an account of the brutality he had witnessed in Pyongyang, asking that the information be disseminated and giving permission for his name to be used. He ended a similar account compiled for the Japanese government with, "The above I saw myself and testify to the truthfulness of my statements. In all my contact with the Koreans these five days (March 1–5) and in all my observation of the crowds inside and outside the city, I have witnessed no act of violence on the part of any Korean."[113]

John Thomas, a Britisher with the Oriental Missionary Society, not only saw people set upon by police, but was himself attacked. On Thursday, March 20, according to his statement for government authorities, he went to Kokei to look at some mission property. While he and two Korean co-workers were standing outside the Korean pastor's house, "we saw about five young lads running down the hill, yelling *Mansei*! They ran past us waving flags and disappeared."

A few moments later four soldiers carrying rifles, followed by several police, rushed up. "They took hold of us and beat us and kicked us mercilessly, refusing to hear our explanation and started to take us to the police station. On the way I showed the officer who was dragging us about, my passport and police certificate issued by the Seoul police on the 17th, but instead of examining it, he threw it on the ground. I endeavored to pick it up but was struck and beaten on the head and kicked, and one Japanese man from the crowd of many Japanese and Korean onlookers hit me with a long stick as thick as a man's arm. My two Korean helpers were beaten cruelly. Police cuffed and kicked them."

The three men were released after several hours when the captured boys denied any association with them, or even knowledge that a foreigner was in town.[114]

Japanese officials called missionary representatives in for a series of meetings. The first of these was in Seoul on March 9 at the request of Usami Katsuo, chief of the Internal Affairs Bureau. Usami assured the missionaries that he was confident they were not involved in the movement, conceded certain short-comings in the governor general and asked their opinion as to the causes of the uprising. The missionaries recited a list of reasons for Korean discontent and appealed for more humane policies. The Presbyterian missionaries reported to their board that "Very frank statements were made, notably by Dr. Gale—who after many years of consistent pro-Japanese effort is now plainly outspoken in condemnation—who told Mr. Usami that the Koreans had been living under a reign of terror for the past nine years."[115]

Another meeting was held on March 22 at the Chosen Hotel in Seoul at the invitation of Judge Watanabe, a Presbyterian elder, and a Mr. Katayama to discuss "these regrettable disturbances." Ten Protestant missionaries were present—five Methodists, D.A. Bunker, J.L. Gerdine, R.A. Hardie, W.A. Noble, and Bishop Herbert Welch; four Presbyterians, O.R. Avison, James Gale, Samuel Moffett and N.C. Whittemore, and YMCA Secretary Fletcher Brockman. The confrontation, as it can be reconstructed from missionary notes, was extraordinarily revealing of both missionary and Japanese attitudes.[115]

Judge Watanabe chaired the meeting and began by insisting that the Japanese, like the missionaries, had but one object, "the welfare of the Korean people." He cited the "very deplorable" conditions in Korea at the time of annexation, saying that no legal records could be found. They had been intentionally destroyed to cover up the injustice, bribery and exactions of corrupt Korean officials. He claimed that forest lands had been denuded until half the country had been deforested and the mountains were bare, and noted that there had been practically no schools. The Japanese, he claimed, had in comparison developed the country and benefitted the people. "All we have done has been done with good intentions for the sake of the Koreans. There had been nothing like oppression on the part of the government."

James Gale replied that he had been a sincere well-wisher of both Japan and Korea "all my life here. The Korean has doubtless been greatly benefitted materially by Japanese rule. There is, however, his world of the mind. For 30 years I have tried to enter into it, but even today am only an onlooker. His is a world of ancient civilization that I have learned to respect the more I know of it . . . . Any methods adopted to govern him must sympathetically take account of his civilization and build on that rather than force something foreign. The body may be comfortable but if there is no comfort in the mind the comfort of the body does not count for anything with the Korean."

Moffett spoke next, saying the Koreans "place a higher value on moral and spiritual things than upon material. The thing which appeals to the Koreans is justice, and justice has a greater appeal to them than anything of a material nature. Koreans appreciate being treated like men and manhood and worth appeal to them much more than material comforts."

Dr. Hardie said, "While Koreans admit the existence of these material improvements, the feeling among them in general is that they are not wholly for their benefit. These benefits give no satisfaction as long as they are treated as inferiors with arrogance and overbearing repression. What we now see is the expression of their pent-up feelings of distrust, dissatisfaction and rebellion against a deliberate and forced form of race discrimination as they regard it. Koreans cannot be made loyal subjects of the empire by force." Dr. Whittemore added that the Koreans felt they did not have religious liberty and the multiplicity of laws grated on them.

Minister of Education Sekiya noted that although the students were not entirely responsible, many had taken part in the demonstrations. He felt this was because the education department had put its main emphasis on industrial education. "The Koreans have a weakness for laying too much stress on the spiritual as compared with their material life. They despise labor, we recognize this and have been endeavoring to make them see their mistake. They must be taught to work. We respect the character of the Korean people but it is expedient to root out their bad points."

W.A. Noble said that he had personally taught the Koreans to be subject to the powers that be, but that under present conditions the Koreans felt they had no hope, and D.A. Bunker suggested that a sense of injustice rankled in the hearts of the Koreans and that it would be wise to give them more to do in the line of governing themselves.

Mr. Katayama said, "The way in which the Koreans have acted is very wrong, because Korea is a part of the empire. The annexation was carried out in accordance with the rules of international law; there was no violation of international law. The annexation is a fact. It is therefore justified by fact and by law. If the Koreans express views of independence that is high treason, and perpetrators of treasonable acts must be brought to justice."

Minister of Justice Kokubo said he had heard that the missionaries had instigated the trouble but he had investigated and denied through the press that they had had anything to do with it. Yet the trouble was spreading. "Are you going to take the attitude of mere onlookers, or of co-operating with the government in putting down the demonstrations?" he asked. He acknowledged the missionaries had much influence, and said, "If you put forth your effort to quiet the people, you will do much service and in this way you will do much for humanity and for peace."

And, of course, this was the real purpose of the meetings—to enlist the aid of the missionaries in ending the Sam-I1 movement as quickly and as quietly as possible.

The Presbyterians wrote their board that "The Japanese plainly stated they wanted the missionaries to co-operate with the government in suppressing the uprising. Bishop Welch by previous agreement . . . replied, stating that anything other than absolute neutrality was impossible for three reasons:

1. It would be useless.
2. It would be resented and destroy our influence.
3. It was forbidden by our home government."[117]

When the question of "the actuality" of atrocities was raised, Samuel Moffett enumerated the incidents he had himself seen. In later private conversation, Mr. Yamagata, editor of the Japanese-sponsored *Seoul Press*, cheerfully admitted that although he was convinced of the truth of the atrocities, he had to publish denials as they were "official."[118]

Because the Japanese had said that they would welcome any reports the missionaries would care to make concerning cruelties, Dr. Avison and Bishop Welch compiled a list of these and met again with Minister of Education Sekiya at his home on March 29. Sekiya, after hearing of a number of atrocities witnessed by various missionaries, including doctors and nurses who had treated the victims, replied that he had no doubt such things had been done in certain places yet felt sure that "in most cases the Korean demonstrators had been the first to offer violence and that their actions in attacking gendarmes and police in country places where they were few in number had compelled the latter to use arms for their protection."

Mr. Sekiya then asked the missionaries what they would advise the government to do. Dr. Avison replied that he could not give any advice but if he were in the government's position he would be able to see that the Koreans, having no rights of free speech, publication or assembly, were entirely unable to consult with one another as to what they ought to ask of the government. The only course left to them was to make an outcry to attract the attention of the government and of the outside world and to unite Koreans. Avison said he would therefore lift the ban against free speech, consultation and meeting; he knew if he were in the Koreans' place he would at once stop demonstrating and take advantage of the permission to meet and discuss and then lay a petition before the government which represented the majority view of the people. Mr. Sekiya seemed to be intrigued by this proposal and asked that they meet again the next day at the Chosen Hotel.

At the March 30 meeting, Sekiya began by saying that Japan by putting an emphasis on farmers, had possibly neglected the small group of highly educated Korean men who perhaps should have been used in greater numbers in government service

Avison replied that might be a good thing to do, but it did not touch on the heart of the difficulty. Sekiya replied at once, "I know what you mean. You are thinking of free speech and other matters pertaining to human liberty." "Yes," said Avison.

Further conversation was all downhill. Mr. Sekiya introduced the missionaries to Col. Mayeda, second in command of the police department, who defended the action of the Japanese, denying the use of violence in all but 38 cases and in those, he claimed, Koreans had been the first to attack and that in each case the police had been vastly outnumbered, with only three to five Japanese on duty.

When asked about the case of John Thomas, the British missionary with the Oriental Missionary Society who had been beaten by Japanese police in Kokai, Mayeda replied that it was not police but Japanese "civilians, inflamed by reports that a foreigner had instigated the demonstrations," who had attacked him, "overwhelming the police who tried to protect him."

When asked about the brutal beatings of the five Pyongyang seminary students who could easily prove they had taken no part in the demonstrations, Mayeda explained that it was quite within the province of local authorities "to summarily administer justice." The colonel closed the meeting by saying the Koreans were becoming "more and more violent" and he would welcome reports from the missionaries at any time.[119] Seeing that further discussions were futile and could perhaps be used to compromise them with their Korean flocks, the missionaries refused to attend any additional meetings.

Some of the earliest reports of the March 1st Movement to get out of Korea were those of missionaries. A visiting foreigner, E.W. Thwing, returned to China with first-hand missionary accounts which appeared in the *Peking and Tientsin Times* of March 15. A Presbyterian missionary from Sunchon was quoted as saying the cause of the movement "lies in the 10 years of oppression and cruel treatment which these people have suffered;" that its character "is most wonderful . . . the peaceful manifestation of the thoughts of the people" and its aim "is by peaceful means to let the world know that they are unhappy under the Japanese rule. What do they hope for? First, that this awful military rule in Korea, which is like that of the Huns in Belgium, may be removed." This article and others printed in the *China Press* and *The Peking Leader* on March 21 and 29, described in harrowing detail Japanese treatment of Korean demonstrators.

The Presbyterian mission appointed a committee of two, Walter C. Erdman and Gordon Holdcroft, to go to Japan to consult with the American ambassador there, to inform missionaries and Japanese Christians of the true situation in Korea and to send their mission board reliable information.

Their seven-page report from Tokyo to the board, dated April 7, began with the warning, "Your correspondence will without doubt be examined in Japan before it reaches the mission, so please do not refer to the work of this committee as such but to Executive Committee Letter A." The men reported they had had two lengthy interviews with Ambassador Morris, who "practically forbade" them to meet with Japanese Christians, assured them that the information sent to the State Department would be accessible to mission boards, and cautioned them "to maintain strict neutrality." The missionaries wrote, "We have not the remotest thought of meddling in politics . . . but it is maddening to have to stand by and see unarmed and unresisting people treated with brutality and violence and even shot down indiscriminately."[120]

Although the committee had been very disappointed not to be able to meet with Japanese Christian leaders, the Japanese church sent a delegation of three to Korea in late May, who met and consulted with missionaries, Korean Christians and Japanese officials. This group issued a report that condemned Japanese actions in Korea. Protestant missionaries in Japan at their annual summer conference at Karuizawa issued a lengthy statement critical of the government-general, and they sent representatives to Seoul in September to the Federal Council of Protestant Evangelical Missions meeting. A number of missionaries in Japan also made direct, individual appeals to Prime Minister Hara and other officials there.

The missionaries in Korea tried to alert the outside world through the press as to what was happening, forcibly brought to the attention of government representatives the fact of Japanese infringement on human rights in Korea, and collected statistics of injustices and brutality. In Seoul, a number of missionaries including H.H. Underwood, E.W. Koons, W.G. Cram and Frank Schofield formed an investigation committee to document and verify violent incidents. S.A. Beck, a Methodist missionary with the American Bible Society, placed photographs of atrocities in the hands of Senator Norris of Nebraska who protested Japanese outrages in a fiery speech on the floor of the Senate on July 15.

Horace H. Underwood's account of the Che-am-ni massacre was read into the *Congressional Record* of July 17. Even Sallie Swallen, definitely a political mossback, was upset enough by such instances as the Korean pastor's daughter-in-law who was stripped and tied up and hung by the arms for five hours "because she hollered 'Hurrah for Korea: *Mansei*!' " to send statistics and hundreds of case histories to her brother-in-law, William Ashbrook, a prominent Republican in Congress. These were not only published in Ohio newspapers, but were also used in official reports by church groups and eventually by the Foreign Affairs Committee.[121]

The missionaries were documenting the very instances the Japanese authorities were denying. Reports and letters amounting to thousands of pages filtered through Japanese censorship, often sent out in the suitcases and food parcels of missionary children studying in the States or China. One staid Presbyterian lady, Alice Butts, carried a number of documents across the border securely concealed in her whale-bone corset.[122]

In all the vast correspondence of the 491 Protestant missionaries in Korea in 1919,[123] only one, Frank Herron Smith, wrote as an apologist for Japan. Smith, a Methodist working with Japanese in Korea, said of himself, "I stand alone."[124] But he clearly saw the independence movement for what it was. He wrote, "The Koreans frankly do not much want reforms. They want their freedom and would be glad if Japan went so far that the world would necessarily turn against her."[125]

Frank Schofield, who had continued to send photographs out of the country as well as signed letters to the Japanese press denouncing the administration's mishandling of the situation, eventually had to leave Korea to avoid police reprisal.[126] According to a friend, Schofield also harbored in his basement "some Koreans who were putting out patriotic literature, a very risky business."[127] The friend, Bolling Reynolds, then principal of a mission school in Chunju, was doing some harboring of his own, hiding in his attic an elderly lame man active in the movement who was being sought by police; Reynolds later helped him to escape "in a small boat up the river."[128]

Kim Tai-Won, who was decorated for his services during the Sam-Il movement, disguised himself as a farmer to distribute copies of the *Independence News* to villagers throughout Chungchong province. Mr. Kim told a friend that he received the news sheets in Seoul regularly and secretly from Methodist missionary James Dale Van Buskirk. Dr. Van Buskirk was on the staff of Severence Hospital which was searched thoroughly by the police who were looking for, but were never able to find, contraband mimeograph equipment.[129] The doctor also treated Ewha graduate Helen Kim who was suffering from TB and was believed to be too sick to survive imprisonment; the Van Buskirks, with various other missionaries, helped to support and conceal her for several years.

The one missionary brought to trial for subversive conduct was Presbyterian E.M. Mowry, principal of two church elementary grammar schools and lecturer at the boys' academy in Pyongyang.

According to Samuel Moffett's account to U.S. Consul Leo Bergholz, on April 4 at 4:30 p.m. when most of the missionaries were gathered for a prayer meeting at the Holdcroft home, a cordon of police and gendarmes suddenly picketed the Presbyterian compound and began to search the residences. The two older Moffett boys saw the Japanese hit, kick and punch their father's secretary, and strike him across the face with a whip. Police searching an empty building on the premises found two copies of a mimeographed Korean notice on thin paper that had been rolled into a small ball and thrown away. A detective told Moffett that a student had admitted that he and several others had taken Moffett's mimeograph machine and printed notices in the empty building when the missionary was away.

At the Mowrys', a grammar school teacher and a student who had just been released from jail were arrested. Indeed, most of the Koreans found on the compound, students, secretaries and gardeners, were seized and beaten although, Moffett said, "so far as I know there was nothing wrong with any of them being on our places or in our houses."[130] After going through the seminary dormitories and confiscating several mimeograph machines, the Japanese marched off with their captives.

That evening a messenger was sent to escort Moffett and Mowry to the police station. After close questioning, Moffett was allowed to leave about midnight; Mowry, however, was not released. The following morning Mowry's secretary, Yi Po-Sik, who had been hiding the day before, gave himself up to the police. When Charles Bernheisel and Robert McMurtrie went to the police station to inquire about Mowry they were told he had been found guilty and sent to prison. The police refused to divulge the charges against him, and the two missionaries went to the prison where they were instructed to see the public procurator, who said he could not yet specify the charges but gave them permission to see him. Mowry was kept in a cell to himself, was well treated and allowed to have his own bedding, seals and magazines sent in, though not permitted a cot, chair or his medicine.[131]

The missionary's trial, in the form of a hearing which came up suddenly on April 19, was conducted in Korean and Japanese. By Japanese law he had the right to have a lawyer but he was not told the date of the trial until the afternoon before, and then was advised that it was not customary to secure a lawyer "except in grave cases."[132]

Samuel Moffett translated the proceedings for the report to the mission board. Mowry, who was 39 years old, and had come to Korea from Mansfield, Ohio, in 1909, was finally charged with his crime: "knowing that the police were searching for them you gave permission for [five] boys to remain in your house."

The procurator ended the hearing with a short speech. "There is no doubt guilt in this case even though you say you did not know it was wrong. It is impossible not to suspect Christianity in this matter and you concealed those who agitated for independence. Your crime is a grave one but on one side your taking in employees and students who had no place to go was in a sense a manifestation of human kindness. I demand a sentence of six months imprisonment and think that you should look on this as a light sentence."

The courtroom spectators were shocked to see the wicker

basket, traditionally used for Japanese criminals, placed over Mowry's head before he was led from the courtroom.[133]

Judgment was shortly rendered, and Mowry was sentenced to six months at hard labor. An appeal was filed and the missionary was released on bail the same day.

The *Peking Daily News*, quick to see that Japan had made a tactical error, printed a congratulatory editorial on April 24, 1919: "We are delighted to see that the Rev. Mr. Mowry has been sentenced to six months' imprisonment with hard labor in connection with the movement in Korea. We rejoice because whether the verdict be sustained or not, by the time the appeal can be heard . . . every five-cent Sunday school in America, every tin-roofed tabernacle from California to Carolina, from the Lakes to the Gulf, will be having lessons or sermons on the subject . . . every newspaper will be full of it . . .

"The arrest and condemnation of an American missionary will be a splendid advertisement for the Korean cause. If the Japanese authorities had been sitting up nights trying to find a way of advertising their failure in Korea they could not have devised a better way of so doing than by arresting and condemning Mr. Mowry."

Mowry's appeal trial was held in Seoul in May, and he was acquitted.

Mowry and all the missionaries had come face to face with the question, how does Christianity relate to politics, or for that matter, to life? Korean church leaders had attempted to maintain a firm distinction between institutional and individual participation in the independence movement. The use of church facilities was forbidden and political discussion was avoided in church meetings. Demonstrations were considered a political and not a church-sponsored activity. The Japanese authorities, however, failed to grasp the distinction; they saw organized Christian participation, demonstrations starting from churches, rallies led by pastors and church bells ringing to convene the demonstrators. Certainly the jails were full of Christians.[134]

The missionaries, too, were ambiguous about their apolitical stance and eventually adopted the motto, "No neutrality for brutality." In Korea, once again moral neutrality had been rejected as the missionaries struggled with the business of being *in* but not *of* the world.

EPILOGUE

Just as the missionaries struggled with the problem of being in but not of the world, they were in the position of being in but not of Korea. There was no way the missionaries could totally separate themselves from the cultural baggage they brought with them, within them. Yet as they lived many years in Korea, making an effort to identify with and to understand Korean people and thought, they picked up some new cultural baggage.

They served as a bridge between two cultures. As Ruth Compton, niece of Methodist missionary Jeannette Walter, wrote, "Long before the days of 'exchange programs,' extensive travel, and intercultural programs, Aunt Jean provided us with all of these. When Korea was a little known country in the world, it was part of our life in a small Kansas town."[1]

The missionary made an imprint on those Koreans with whom he had contact, students, parishioners, friends. Expatriate Korean writer Younghill Kang wrote of meeting an aging missionary: "He greeted me in his grave, pleasant way, in words of an excellent Korean. More than any exiled countryman, he reminded me of the country I had left. . . . His life for the most part had been spent in Korea, and he had recently buried his Canadian missionary-wife in Korean soil. The remote peace of Asia mingled with the steadfast faith of the Christian on his brow."

The encounter moved Kang to cite from Browning's *Abt Vogler* as a sort of missionary creed:

> Therefore to whom turn I but to thee, the ineffable Name?
> Builder and maker, thou, of houses not made with hands.
> What, have fear of change from thee who art ever the same?
> Doubt that thy power can fill the heart that thy power expands?

There shall never be one lost good! What was, shall live as before.
The evil is null, is naught, is silence implying sound;
What was good shall be good, with, for evil, so much good more;
On earth the broken arcs; in the heaven, a perfect round.

"Perhaps such a quotation," wrote Kang, "is the best commentary I could make upon this other world, the world of the old-fashioned missionary . . . which has necessarily influenced my destiny profoundly."[2]

The missionaries were themselves broken arcs, by no means perfect, any more than were the cultures from which and to which they came. Delving into their histories, one can find a few scandals, many shortcomings and a lot of firm-minded individuals beset by sin. They were very much aware of their failures, and were exceedingly hard on themselves. In fact, perhaps their greatest fault was not being more lavish in applying God's forgiveness, which they generously preached, to themselves and to their colleagues.

Yet theirs were wonderful lives and wonderful work. That unlikely first Protestant missionary, Horace Allen, recognized it at the end. He wrote Horace Underwood in December 1905, from the United States, "I am glad to be out of politics. It is dirty work and I never intended to get into it. You are in the best work after all, for when a man can feel that everything he does is for the good of someone else, he can have a satisfaction that is rare."[3]

It was good work, well done. As "ideas with skins on," the missionaries went about their business and God's, teaching the revolutionary and world-shaking principles of Christ which they themselves understood only in part. The power in their actions and teachings was not just within them, but beyond them; it was the power of God at work in the world. In studying the missionaries' coming to Korea, one learns of Christ's incarnation; in their love relationships, one sees a bridegroom and the church called the bride.

In social change one sees the liberating Christ. In education, one hears the Teacher, and in medical work encounters the Great Physician; in the Great Revival, one meets Christ the Baptizer, the Renewer, and in the 1919 movement confronts Christ the non-violent revolutionary. The story of the missionaries is truly His story, the story of God working in human history through very human instruments indeed.

The pioneer missionaries attempted great things and accomplished much. If, in retrospect, they seem larger than life, it is both because of the Spirit within them and because they grew to meet the demands of their day; they rose to the occasion. They themselves talked not so much of what they had accomplished as of what they had received; if others spoke of their sacrifices, they preferred to testify of their blessings. They would be the first to say that from the Koreans' generous acceptance, kindness and love, they learned grace. No one said it was easy, but quite a few said it was fun.

The work begun by the Protestant missionaries and their Korean colleagues is far from finished; it continues in schools, hospitals, churches, reform movements, concern for human rights and social justice, and especially, in individual lives. It is the same power and Spirit at work.

FOOTNOTES

NOTES FOR CHAPTER I

1 William E. Henthorn, *A History of Korea* (New York, The Free Press, 1971), p. 220.

2 James Dale Van Buskirk, *Korea, Land of the Dawn* (Toronto, Missionary Education Movement of the U.S. and Canada, 1931), p. 11.

3 Younghill Kang, *East Goes West* (London, Charles Scribners Sons Ltd., 1937), pp. 192–193, refers to the Western insistence on historical truth as "factual sincerity." In contrast, he says, "A gentleman says what is respectable and decent to say."

4 *James Scarth Gale and His History of the Korean People*, a new edition of the *History* together with a biography and annotated bibliographies by Richard Rutt (Seoul, Royal Asiatic Society and Taewon Publishing Co., 1972), p. 93.

5 *Ibid*, p. 94.

6 *With Tommy Tompkins in Korea* (New York, Fleming H. Revell Co., 1905), pp. 49–50.

7 George Paik, *The History of Protestant Missions in Korea*, footnote, p. 17. Allen Clark, *Avison of Korea, the Life of Oliver R. Avison, M.D.* (Seoul, Yonsei University Press, 1979), page 26.

8 Isop Hong, "Modern Korean Thought," *Korea, Its Land, People and Culture of all Ages* (Seoul, Hakwon-Sa Ltd., 1960), p. 320.

9 Paik, p. 33.

10 *Ibid*, p. 35.

11 *Ibid.*

12 Charles Allen Clark, *Religions of Old Korea* (Seoul, Christian Literature Society, 1961), p. 240.

13 Rhodes, p. 61.

14 Clark, pp. 244–246.

15 Rhodes, p. 69.

16 Paik, pp. 40–42.

17 Joseph H. Longford, *The Story of Korea* (London, T. Fisher Unwin, 1911), pp. 282–284.

18 Paik, p. 42.

19 Kim Yongbok, "The Tonghak School," *Korea, Its Land, People* etc., p. 68.

20 Yi Kyu-Tae, *Modern Transformation of Korea*, p. 42.

21 Kim Yongbok, p. 69.

[22] Gale, *Korea in Transition*, p. 95.
[23] Sidney Lewis Gulick, *The East and the West: A Study of Their Psychic and Cultural Characteristics* (Tokyo, Charles E. Tuttle, 1961), p. 65.
[24] Kim Young-Kwun, ed. *Handbook of Korea* (Seoul, Korea Overseas Information Service, 1978), p. 200.
[25] Kang, *The Grass Roof* (New York, Charles Scribners Sons, 1931), p. 59.
[26] Martina Deuchler, "The Tradition: Women During the Yi Dynasty," *Virtues in Conflict* (Seoul, Royal Asiatic Society and Samwha Publishing Co., 1977), p. 25.
[27] Spencer J. Palmer, *Korea and Christianity: The Problem of Identification with Tradition* (Seoul, Hollym Corp., 1967), pp. 40-41.
[28] Longford, pp. 32-33
[29] John Paton Davies, "America and East Asia," *Foreign Affairs*, January 1977, p. 368.
[30] "Yang" is the Korean word for Western, "kui" or "kwi" is demon or devil, both from Chinese characters. Horace G. Underwood II suggests that when early New England seamen identified themselves as Yankees, the Chinese said, "Well, if you say so yourselves . . . "!
[31] Gale, *Korea in Transition*, pp. 128-129.
[32] Malcolm Fenwick, *The Church of Christ in Korea* (Seoul, Baptist Publications, 1967 reprint of 1911 edition), pp. 9-10.
[33] Fenwick, pp. 49-56.
[34] Henry Loomis letter, May 30, 1883, *The Korea Mission Field*, July 1937, pp. 139-141.
[35] George Paik, footnote, p. 78.
[36] *Korea Mission Field*, July 1937, pp. 139-141.
[37] Rhodes, p. 12; Paik, p, 84.
[38] Paik, p. 82; Annual Report of the Missionary Society of the Methodist Episcopal Church, 1884, p. 204; R.S. Maclay, "Korea's Permit to Christianity," *The Missionary Review of the World*, vol. 9, no. 8, August 1895, p. 287.
[39] Paik, pp. 82-83.
[40] *M.E. North Report*, 1884, pp. 204-205.
[41] George Heber Jones, *Korea: The Land, People and Customs* (Cincinnati, Jennings & Graham, 1907), p. 66.
[42] Kim, *Women of Korea*, p. 204.
[43] *Ibid*, p. 219.
[44] Mrs. William B. Scranton letter to Alice Appenzeller, 1934.
[45] W.A. Noble, "Pioneers of Korea," *Within the Gate* (Seoul, YMCA Press, 1934), pp. 29-30.
[46] Lillias H. Underwood, *Underwood of Korea* (New York, Fleming Revell Co., 1918) p. 25.
[47] *Ibid*, p. 28.
[48] Horace G. Underwood, "Reminiscences," paper read in Pyongyang on August 27, 1909, *Quarto-Centennial* Papers, pp. 98-99.
[49] Underwood letter to Ellinwood, Yokohama, Feb. 18, 1885.
[50] William Elliot Griffis, *A Modern Pioneer: The Life Story of Henry G. Appenzeller* (New York, Fleming Revell Co., 1912), pp. 70-71.
[51] Reid-Appenzeller correspondence, Missionary Research Library, Union Theological Seminary, New York.
[52] Griffis, p. 59; also *Within the Gate*, p. 8.

53 James Gale, *The Vanguard* (New York, Fleming Revell Co., 1904), p. 91.
54 Griffis, p. 213.

NOTES FOR CHAPTER II

1 William Elliot Griffis, *A Modern Pioneer.*
2 Scranton paper read at the Decennial celebration of the founding of the Protestant Missions, *Korean Repository,* vol. 5, July 1898, p. 257.
3 Mary F. Scranton, "Woman's Work in Korea," *Korean Repository,* vol. 3, January 1896, pp. 2–3.
4 *Ibid,* p. 3.
5 Appenzeller diary, April 2, 1885.
6 Sherwood Hall, *With Stethoscope in Asia* (McLean, Va., MCL Associates, 1978), p. 27.
7 Allen letter to Ellinwood, Oct. 1, 1884.
8 Lillias Underwood, *Fifteen Years Among the Top-Knots* (New York, American Tract Society, 1904, Royal Asiatic Society Reprint, 1977), p. 3.
9 F.S. Miller, "Reminiscences by Some of the Senior Missionaries," *The Fiftieth Anniversary Celebration* (Seoul, Presbyterian Mission, 1934), p. 50.
10 Appenzeller letter to his father, July 20, 1885.
11 Annie Baird, *Fifty Helps for the Beginner in the Use of the Korean Language,* 4th edition (Yokohama, Fukuin Printing Ltd., 1911), p. 95.
12 Annie Baird, *Inside Views of Mission Life* (Philadelphia, Westminster Press, 1913), pp. 28–30.
13 John Fairbank, *The United States and China* (Cambridge, Harvard University Press, 1962), p. 40.
14 Allen letter to Ellinwood, June 23, 1885.
15 *Underwood of Korea,* p. 43.
16 Leonora H. Egan, "Lillie in Korea," *Fifteen Years among the Top-Knots,* Seoul, Royal Asiatic Society reprint, 1977, p. 388.
17 Ellers to Ellinwood, July 25, 1886.
18 Heron to Ellinwood, September 14, 1886.
19 Allen diary, December 20, 1885.
20 Heron to Ellinwood, August 27, 1886.
21 Underwood to Ellinwood, September 17, 1886.
22 Allen to Ellinwood, September 7, 1886.
23 Ellinwood to Heron, November 2, 1886.
24 A copy of the Underwood plan was sent to Ellinwood.
25 Allen to Ellinwood, January 3, 1887.
26 Hepburn to Ellinwood, February 19, 1887.
27 Allen to Ellinwood, April 25, 1887.
28 Scranton wrote Heron on April 18, 1887 and Heron sent a copy of the letter to Ellinwood.
29 Gilmore to Board of Foreign Missions board member Dr. Wells, May 21, 1887.
30 Allen to Ellinwood, August 22, 1887.
31 Allen to Ellinwood, February 10, 1887: "Mr. Underwood is *not* sick. Yet he is going to use $150 . . . as a pleasure trip to Yokohama. The only redeeming feature of the trip is that he may perhaps get a wife."

32 Allen to Ellinwood, September 5, 1887.
33 Appenzeller to Reid, January 3, 1887.
34 Copy of the Foreign Office's reply sent by Underwood to Ellinwood on February 15, 1886.
35 Heron to Ellinwood, February 12, 1886.
36 Allen to Ellinwood, May 31, 1886.
37 Underwood to Ellinwood, July 9, 1886.
38 Appenzeller diary, February 21, 1887.
39 *Ibid,* May 12, 1887.
40 Appenzeller to Bishop Moore, June 11, 1901; Everett Hunt, *Protestant Pioneers in Korea,* p. 72.
41 Appenzeller to Wadsworth, February 14, 1887.
42 Appenzeller diary, February 21, 1887.
43 *Ibid,* October 11, 1887. On December 4, 1887, the third anniversary of the 1884 emeute, he baptized two more Pae Jae students.
44 Heron to Ellinwood, February 13, 1887.
45 Ellinwood to Underwood, May 4, 1887.
46 Allen wrote Ellinwood on October 28, 1886 that he had been made a nobleman of the second rank, the same that Moellendorff held and higher than any other foreigner. "It is not a decoration this time but real rank as I am nominally governor of a district north of here."
47 Underwood to Allen, January 27, 1886; copy to Ellinwood.
48 Underwood to Ellinwood, November 29, 1887.
49 Ross' account of his experiences with the Koreans was written for *Missionary Review of the World,* vol. 3, no. 4, April, 1890, and was reprinted in *The Korea Mission Field,* Seoul, July 1937, pp. 134–139.
50 George Paik, *The History of Protestant Missions in Korea,* p. 52.
51 Ross, p. 137.
52 *Ibid,* pp. 138–139.
53 Underwood to Ellinwood, November 29, 1887.
54 Appenzeller diary, October 31, 1887.
55 *Ibid,* December 25, 1887.
56 Mattie Wilcox Noble, *Victorious Lives of Early Christians* (Seoul, Christian Literature Society, 1927), p. 1.
57 *Ibid,* pp. 114–115.
58 Daniel Gifford, *Everyday Life in Korea,* p. 134.
59 *The History of Protestant Missions in Korea,* pp. 208, 282.
60 Underwood to Hepburn, February 6, 1888.
61 Heron to Ellinwood, July 23, 1888.
62 *Ibid.*
63 Copy of Appenzeller's letter to his board in his diary, August 12, 1887.
64 In 1887 the Allens received $1,400 salary; the Herons $1,300; Underwood $800; Annie Ellers $800—Presbyterian mission budget, August 1888. The married Methodist missionaries received $1,200 plus $100 for each child, unmarried ladies $600 plus $150 "for incidentals;" both missions provided housing, but the Methodists also provided "heavy furniture." S. L. Baldwin, Methodist mission board member to Ellinwood, October, 1888.
65 Annie Heron Gale, "Dawn in the Land of Morning Calm," *Michigan Quarterly Review,* p. 146.
66 Heron to Ellinwood, April 11, 1888.

67 *Op. Cit.*, p. 149.
68 Leonora Egan, *Fifteen Years Among the Top-Knots*, p. 376–377.
69 *Ibid*, p. 380.
70 Heron to Ellinwood, April 11, 1888.
71 Underwood to Ellinwood, May 21, 1888.
72 Paul A. Cohen, *China and Christianity*, Harvard University Press, 1963.
73 Allen to board of foreign missions, June 22, 1888.
74 Allen to Ellinwood, August 29, 1888.
75 Leonora Egan, pp. 383–384.
76 Lillias Underwood, *With Tommy Tompkins in Korea*, p. 38.
77 *Op. Cit.*, p. 388.
78 Heron to Ellinwood, November 6, 1888.
79 Lillias Underwood, *Fifteen Years Among the Top-Knots*, p. 34.
80 *Ibid*, pp. 35–36.
81 *Ibid*, p. 37.
82 *Underwood of Korea*, p. 64.
83 *Op. Cit.*, p. 56.
84 *Underwood of Korea*, p. 89.
85 *Op. Cit.*, p. 43.
86 *Ibid*, p. 42.
87 Robert Townsend, *Up the Organization*, Knopf.
88 Gifford to Ellinwood, October 21, 1890.
89 Moffett to Ellinwood, March 18, 1890.
90 *Ibid*.
91 *Ibid*.
92 Underwood to Ellinwood, March 27, 1891.
93 Moffett to Ellinwood, September 15, 1890.
94 Ellinwood to Baird, October 1, 1891.
95 Appenzeller to Methodist board, April 1, 1889.
96 *Ibid*.
97 Gifford to Ellinwood, February 9, 1891.
98 Moffett to Ellinwood, February 11, 1891.
99 Allen to Ellinwood, February 23, 1891.
100 *Korean Repository*, vol. 4, March 1897, p. 88.
101 Moffett to Ellinwood, March 25, 1891.
102 Moffett to Ellinwood, May 21, 1891.
103 Ellinwood to Underwood, May 11, 1891.
104 Allen to Ellinwood, October 23, 1891.
105 Allen to Ellinwood, February 23, 1891.
106 Heard to William Baird, copy to Ellinwood, July 29, 1891.
107 Allen to Ellinwood, February 23, 1891.
108 Vinton to Ellinwood, May 20, 1891.
109 Vinton to Ellinwood, August 27, 1891.
110 Allen to Ellinwood, July 3, 1891.
111 *Fifteen Years*, p. 102.
112 Malcolm Fenwick, *The Church of Christ in Korea*, p. 12.
113 George Paik, p. 222.
114 Ellinwood to Underwood, May 8, 1893.
115 *Underwood of Korea*, pp. 127-128.
116 Paik, p. 223.
117 Gifford to Ellinwood, July 22, 1893.

NOTES FOR CHAPTER III

1 Samuel H. Moffett collection.

2 James E. Adams, "Rolls of the Mission's Dead," *Quarto-Centennial* (Pyongyang, Presbyterian Mission, 1909), pp. 118-119.

3 Samuel Moore to Ellinwood, March 22, 1893.

4 Moore to Ellinwood, December 28, 1893.

5 Rhodes, p. 104.

6 Moore to Allen, March 13, 1900.

7 Butcher Pak, *The Church at Home and Abroad,* August 1896, pp. 115-116; Allen Clark, *Avison of Korea,* pp. 97-102. Avison remembered Pak's illness as cholera.

8 Yi, *Modern Transformation of Korea,* p. 46.

9 Samuel Moore, "The Butchers of Korea," *Korean Repository,* vol. 5, April 1898, p. 129.

10 *Korea and Her Neighbours,* p. 172.

11 Moore to Ellinwood, April 21, 1895.

12 *Ibid,* June 7, 1895.

13 Rhodes, p. 101.

14 Harriet E. Pollard, The History of the Missionary Enterprise of the Presbyterian Church U.S.A. in Korea with Special Emphasis on the Personnel, (unpublished master's thesis for Northwestern University, 1927), p. 32; Roy E. Shearer, *Wildfire: Church Growth in Korea* (Grand Rapids, Eerdmans Publishing Co., 1966), pp. 89-90.

15 *Korean Repository,* vol. 5, April 1898, p. 128.

16 *Ibid,* pp. 131-132.

17 *Modern Transformation of Korea,* p. 42.

18 Adams, "Rolls of the Mission's Dead," p. 119.

19 *Within the Gate,* p. 78.

20 Janice Vere Hilburn, "A Popular Korean Product," *Light of the East* (Seoul, Sahm-Bo Publishing Co., 1972), p. 180.

21 *My 40 Year Fight for Korea,* p. 15.

22 *Ibid,* pp. 224-225.

23 Moose, *Village Life in Korea,* p. 233; Sherwood Hall, *Stethoscope in Asia,* p. 547.

24 *Korea and Her Neighbors,* p. 118.

25 *The Grass Roof,* pp. 55-57

26 Joseph Longford, *The Story of Korea,* p. 42.

27 Appenzeller diary, March 15, 1888.

28 *Within the Gate,* p. 47.

29 Bernheisel letter, December 1924, Samuel H. Moffett collection.

30 "A Leaf from my Journal," *Korea Review,* vol. 1, March 1901, pp. 111-112.

31 Ellen C. Parsons, *Fifteen Years in the Korean Mission,* p. 19.

32 "Woman's Work in Korea," *Korean Repository,* vol. 3, January 1896, p. 5.

33 *Ibid,* March, 1894.

34 *Ibid,* February 5, 1902.

35 *Ibid,* February 14, 1902.

36 Bernheisel letter, December 13, 1902, Samuel H. Moffett collection.

[37] *Ibid*, December 4, 1928.
[38] *Victorious Lives of Early Christians in Korea* (Seoul, Christian Literature Society, 1927), pp. 104–105.
[39] *Ibid*, p. 105.

NOTES FOR CHAPTER IV

[1] James Van Buskirk, *Land of the Dawn* (Toronto, Missionary Education Movement, 1931), p. 125.
[2] Kim, *Women of Korea*, p. 218.
[3] *Korea Review*, vol. 2, February 1902, pp. 55–56.
[4] Martina Deuchler, "The Tradition: Women During the Yi Dynasty," *Virtues in Conflict*, p. 7.
[5] *Korean Repository*, vol. 3, January 1896, p. 4.
[6] Yi, *Modern Transformation of Korea*, p. 116.
[7] Kim, *Women of Korea*, p. 226.
[8] *Op. cit.*, p. 113.
[9] Graham Lee letter, October 9, 1892, Samuel H. Moffett collection.
[10] Hugh Brown to Ellinwood, May 3, 1892.
[11] *Korea from its Capital*, p. 300.
[12] *The Gospel in All Lands*, 1888, p. 373.
[13] Blacker, *The Japanese Enlightenment*, p. 85.
[14] Louisa Rothweiler, *Korean Repository*, vol. 1, March 1892, p. 89.
[15] *Ibid.*
[16] Induk Pahk, *September Monkey*, pp. 47–48
[17] *Op. Cit.*, p. 93.
[18] *Ibid.*
[19] Pahk, *September Monkey*, pp. 48–49.
[20] Yim, *My 40 Year Fight for Korea*, p. 27.
[21] Charles Bernheisel letter, June 1907, Moffett collection.
[22] Helen Kim, *Within the Gate*, p. 78.
[23] *Ibid*, p. 80.
[24] Kim, *Women of Korea*, pp. 225–226; Stokes, *History of Methodist Missions in Korea, 1885–1930, p. 207.*
[25] Kim, *Grace Sufficient*, p. 31.
[26] Shin Hu-Dam, 1724, quoted by Donald L. Baker, "The Martyrdom of Paul Yun: Western Religion and Eastern Ritual in Eighteenth Century Korea," Royal Asiatic Society *Transactions*, 1979, pp. 36–37.
[27] M.B. Stokes, "Methodist Evangelism," *Within the Gate*, p. 106.
[28] *Korean Repository*, vol. 3, July 1896, p. 282.
[29] *Village Life in Korea*, pp. 125–126.
[30] Paik, p. 131.
[31] Annie Baird letter to her family, September 12, 1892.
[32] "Reminiscences by Some of the Senior Missionaries," The 50th Anniversary Celebration papers, Seoul, Northern Presbyterian Mission, 1934, pp. 50–51.

33 *The History of Protestant Missions in Korea 1832–1910*, p. 229.

34 Hunt, *Protestant Pioneers in Korea*, pp. 258–259.

35 Baird, *William M. Baird of Korea*, p. 115.

36 *Ibid.*

37 Baird, *William M. Baird of Korea*, p. 121.

38 William Scott, *Canadians in Korea*, 1975, p. 26.

39 Weems, *Hulbert's History of Korea*, vol. 1, pp. 36–37.

40 H.D. Appenzeller, *Within the Gate*, pp. 88–89.

41 *Korea Review*, vol. 2, November 1902, p. 508.

42 *Michigan and Korea 1899–1914*, p. 122.

43 *Ibid.*

44 Paik, p. 310.

45 Bernheisel letter, June 1906, Moffett collection.

46 Becker, *Michigan and Korea*, p. 156.

47 *Korea Review*, vol. 6, p. 353.

48 Stokes, *History of Methodist Missions in Korea*, pp. 214–215.

49 Hugh Heung-Wo Cynn, *The Rebirth of Korea*, p. 102.

50 James Earnest Fisher, *Democracy and Mission Education in Korea*, p. 50.

51 Paik, p. 236.

52 Fisher, pp. 41–60.

53 In Jong You, The Impact of the American Protestant Missions on Korean Education from 1805 to 1932, unpublished dissertation, University of North Carolina School of Education, Chapel Hill, 1967, pp. 254–256.

54 Paik, p. 407.

NOTES FOR CHAPTER V

1 "The Korean Doctor and His Methods," *Korean Repository*, vol. 2, May 1895, p. 188.

2 "The Beginnings of Medical Work in Korea," *Korea Repository*, vol. 1, December 1892, p. 356.

3 Charles Stokes, *History of Methodist Missions in Korea, 1885–1930*, p. 70.

4 *With Stethoscope in Asia*, p. 42.

5 M.E. North Report, 1886, p. 276.

6 Paik, p. 124.

7 Stokes, p. 101.

8 Vinton to Ellinwood, January 19, 1892.

9 *Avison of Korea*, p. 84.

10 *Ibid*, p. 87–88.

11 *Ibid*, p. 111.

12 *Ibid*, p. 112.

13 Ellinwood to Samuel Moffett, December 21, 1900.

14 Avison, letter from St. Louis to the Presbyterian Board of Foreign Missions, May 19, 1900.

15 *Avison of Korea*, p. 118.

16 *Korea Review*, vol. 1, September 1901, pp. 459–460.

17 *Ibid*, vol. 6, February 1906, p. 66.

18 *Avison of Korea*, p. 120.

19 Kim, *Women of Korea*, p. 274.
20 *Avison of Korea*, p. 129.
21 *Ibid*, p. 127.
22 Allen to Ellinwood, October 8, 1884.
23 Scranton to Bishop Fowler, September 3, 1889.
24 *Korean Repository*, vol. 3, June 1896, p. 240.
25 "Results of Medical Missions in Korea," *Missionary Review of the World*, September 1901, p. 690; Paik, p. 331.
26 *Challenge and Crisis in Missionary Medicine*, pp. 18–19.
27 Scott, *Canadians in Korea*, p. 63.
28 Quarto-Centennial papers, p. 38.
29 Brown, *Mission to Korea*, pp. 126–127.
30 Quarto-Centennial papers, p. 43.
31 Stokes, p. 164.
32 *Ibid.*
33 *Ibid*, p. 217.
34 Sallie Swallen letter to her daughter, August 30, 1914.
35 Conversation with Gertrude Swallen Voelkel, Duarte, February 1980.
36 Conversation with Dr. Clark's daughter, Carter Clark Settle, Kwangju, Korea, October 14, 1982.
37 Conversatons with Richard Baird and Charles Stokes.
38 *Avison of Korea*, p. 123.
39 Conversations with Richard Baird, Gertrude Swallen Voelkel, Duarte.
40 *Ibid.*
41 *One Hundred Years*, p. 439.
42 J.F. Preston, "Korea," *The Missionary*, June 1909, p. 320; *Mission to Korea*, p. 62.
43 Anabel Major Nisbet, *Day in and Day out in Korea*, p. 86.
44 *Mission to Korea*, p. 235.

NOTES FOR CHAPTER VI

1 Charles Stokes, pp. 112–113; Roy Shearer, *Wildfire*, p. 175.
2 Moffett to Ellinwood, October 20, 1890.
3 Elizabeth McCully, *A Corn of Wheat or the Life of the Rev. W.J. McKenzie of Korea* (Toronto, Westminster Co. Ltd., 1903), p. 71.
4 *Ibid*, pp. 165–166.
5 Scott, *Canadians in Korea*, p. 32.
6 *Fifteen Years Among the Top-Knots*, pp. 124–125.
7 *Korean Repository*, vol. 2, August 1895, p. 296.
8 *Fifteen Years*, p. 125.
9 McKenzie letter to O.R. Avison, pp. 221–222; *Korean Repository*, vol. 2, August 1895, pp. 308–309.
10 Jones letter to Appenzeller, n.d., Appenzeller papers, Missionary Research Library, Union Theological Seminary, New York.
11 *Fifteen Years*, pp. 125–126.
12 Moffett to Ellinwood, January 12, 1894.
13 *Ibid.*
14 *Ibid*, July 30, 1894.
15 *Korea and Her Neighbours*, pp. 311–312.

16 *Ibid*, pp. 347-349.
17 *Ibid*, p. 348.
18 *Ibid*, p. 349.
19 George Heber Jones, Rise of the Church in Korea, manuscript, 1914, pp. 86-87, Missionary Research Library, Union Theological Seminary, New York.
20 Shearer, *Wildfire*, pp. 117-118.
21 Moffett to Ellinwood, June 27, 1898.
22 C.C. Vinton, "The Latest Advance in Korea," *Missionary Review of the World*, vol. 13, no. 5, May 1900, p. 367.
23 Jones, *The Asiatic Fields* (New York, Eaton and Mains, 1904), p. 73.
24 *Korea in Transition*, pp. 133-155.
25 Jones papers, Missionary Research Library, Union Theological Seminary, New York.
26 Sallie Swallen letter to her sister, December 17, 1912.
27 Nisbet, *Day in and Day Out in Korea*, pp. 69-70.
28 Sallie Swallen letter to her mother, January 1898.
29 Gale, *The Vanguard*, p. 261.
30 Kim, *Grace Sufficient*, p. 10.
31 *Within the Gate*, p. 69.
32 *William M. Baird of Korea*, p. 239.
33 *Inside Views of Misison Life*, (Philadelphia, Westminster Press, 1913), pp. 129-131.
34 Shearer, *Wildfire*, p. 150.
35 *Korean Repository*, vol. 2, October 1895, p. 384.
36 *Ibid*, December 1895, p. 484.
37 *Korea Mission Field*, vol. 5, January 1909, p. 10.
38 Kim, *Grace Sufficient*, p. 14.
39 Kay Cooper, "The Bible Woman," *Korea Magazine*, vol. 1, January 1917, p. 8.
40 *Victorious Lives*, p. 109.
41 *Ibid*, p. 38.
42 *Within the Gate*, p. 70.
43 Samuel Hugh Moffett, *Christians of Korea*, p. 58.
44 W.A. Noble, "The North Korea District," *The Gospel in All Lands*, 1902, p. 92.
45 *History of Protestant Missions in Korea*, pp. 293-294.
46 Stokes, *History of Methodist Missions*, p. 119.
47 Horace G. Underwood, *Call of Korea*, pp. 173-174.
48 *Wildfire*, p. 9.
49 Appenzeller letter, July 4, 1890, Missionary Research Library, Union Theological Seminary, New York.
50 *Undiplomatic Memories*, p. 96.
51 Methodist Church South Report for 1905, p. 39.
52 Methodist Episcopal South Korea Mission Minutes, 1903, p. 25; Stokes, p. 188.
53 *Korea Review*, vol. 6, February 1906, pp. 69-70.
54 "A Notable Meeting," *The Missionary*, January 1907, p. 21.
55 *Gold in Korea*, p. 62.
56 *Ibid*, p. 63.
57 *Ibid*, pp. 64-65.

58 *Ibid*, p. 66.
59 Bernheisel letter, February 25, 1907.
60 Ruth Appenzeller Knight, tape to the author, July, 1977.
61 *Gold in Korea*, p. 68.
62 Bernheisel letter, February 25, 1907.
63 "The Spirit Among Pyeng Yang Students," *Korea Mission Field*, vol. 3, May 1907, pp. 65-67.
64 M.E. North Report for 1907, p. 419.
65 *Michigan and Korea 1899-1914*, p. 115.
66 *Gold in Korea*, p. 71.
67 Rise of the Church in Korea, p. 74.
68 Scott, *Canadians in Korea*, p. 57

NOTES FOR CHAPTER VII

1 Hugh Heung-Wu Cynn, *The Rebirth of Korea*, p. 83.
2 Quoted by Denis and Peggy Warner, *The Tide at Sunrise: A History of the Russo-Japanese War*, 1904-1905, p. 85.
3 Carmen Blacker, *The Japanese Enlightenment: A Study of the Writings of Fukuzawa Yukichi* (Cambridge, Cambridge University Press, 1964), pp. 135-136.
4 *Ibid.*
5 Cynn, pp. 163-164.
6 *Ibid*, p. 165.
7 Allen to the Secretary of State, July 18, 1898, State Department Archives.
8 *Ibid*, November 18, 1899. See Fred Harrington's *God, Mammon and the Japanese*, p. 302, for Allen's warnings to the State Department and his quarrel with Theodore Roosevelt.
9 Woon-Sang Choi, *The Fall of the Hermit Kingdom*, pp. 44, 53.
10 *Korea Review*, vol. 5, April 1905, p. 150.
11 *Ibid*, p. 137.
12 *Korea Review*, vol. 5, March 1905, p. 112.
13 *Ibid*, p. 113.
14 *Ibid*, vol. 5, May 1905, p. 194.
15 *Ibid*, vol. 5, July 1905, p. 271.
16 McKenzie, *The Tragedy of Korea*, p. 133; Woon-Sang Choi, p. 46.
17 *Tragedy of Korea*, p. 135; Choi, pp. 47-48.
18 Willard Straight, diary entry for Nov. 18, 1905, quoted in Herbert Croly's *Willard Straight* (McMillan Co., New York, 1925), p. 182.
19 *Korea Review*, vol. 5, Nov. 1905, pp. 427-428.
20 *Ibid*, vol. 6, Jan. 1906, p. 7. Lillias Underwood wrote Min's eulogy for the *Korea Review*; Min had been the palace representative at the Underwood's wedding in 1889.
21 *Ibid*, p. 9.
22 *Modern Transformation of Korea*, pp. 26-27.
23 *The Korea Review*, vol. 6, July 1906, p. 273.
24 *Ibid*, vol. 4, May 1904, p. 220; vol. 5, Feb. 1905, p. 78.
25 *Ibid*, vol. 6, Feb. 1906, p. 199.
26 Henderson, *Korea Under Japanese Colonial Rule*, ed. Andrew C. Nahm (Center for Korean Studies, Western Michigan University, 1973), p. 263.

27 *Ibid*, p. 262.
28 *Korea Review*, vol. 6, Oct. 1906, p. 394.
29 J. McRee Elrod, *An Index to English Language Periodical Literature Published in Korea 1890–1904*, p. xi.
30 *Korea Review*, Vol. 6, pp. 351–352, 360.
31 "Opium in Korea," *Korea Review*, vol. 6, July 1906, pp. 248–251.
32 *The Tragedy of Korea*, pp. 152–155.
33 *Ibid*, p. 149.
34 *Korea Review*, vol. 6, July 1906, p. 278.
35 In the fall of 1905 Kojong sent Syngman Rhee and Homer Hulbert to Washington to appeal to President Theodore Roosevelt to intervene in Korea's behalf.
36 *The Tragedy of Korea*, pp. 158–159.
37 *Ibid*, p. 161.
38 *Gold in Korea*, p. 12.
39 *The Tragedy of Korea*, p. 170.
40 Edwin Reischauer, *The United States and Japan*, Third Edition, p. 482.
41 *The Tragedy of Korea*, p. 188.
42 *Ibid*, pp. 200–201.
43 *Ibid*, p. 202.
44 *Ibid*, p. 203.
45 *History of Protestant Missions in Korea*, p. 329.
46 *Korea Review*, vol. 6, August 1906, pp. 290–291.
47 Bernheisel letter, January 1909.
48 Scranton letter to A.B. Leonard, May 15, 1905, microfilm, United Methodist World Mission office, New York.
49 Walter Smith letter to Arthur Judson Brown, Jan. 30, 1908.
50 *History of the Methodist Missions in Korea 1885–1930*, p. 232.
51 Quoted by Samuel H. Moffett, *Christians of Korea*, pp. 66–67.
52 Harriet Pollard, p. 86.
53 Report of Chinju station, June 30, 1911.
54 Arthur Judson Brown, *One Hundred Years*, pp. 460–462.
55 Bernheisel letter, May 1916, Moffett collection.
56 Woo-Keun Han, *The History of Korea*, pp. 467–468.
57 See *Tragedy of Korea*, p. 152; George McGrane, *Korea's Tragic Hours*, p. 70; "Korean Settlers in Siberia," Isabella Bishop, *Korea and Her Neighbours*, pp. 223–238.
58 *The Tragedy of Korea*, p. 261.
59 Ruth Benedict, *The Chrysanthemum and the Sword: Patterns of Japanese Culture* (Boston, Houghton Mifflin Co., 1946), p. 21.
60 Yung-Chung Kim, ed., *Women of Korea*, p. 260.
61 Louise Yim, *My Forty Year Fight for Korea*.
62 Woo-Keun Han, *The History of Korea*, p. 473.
63 *Women of Korea*, p. 233.
64 Hugh Heung-Wo Cynn, *The Rebirth of Korea*, pp. 15–16.
65 *My Forty Year Fight*, p. 101.
66 Report of Walter C. Erdman and Gordon Holdcroft. April 7, 1919 from Tokyo to their board, and memories of Lee Kap-Song quoted by Spencer J. Palmer in *Korea and Christianity*, pp. 135–138.
67 *Ibid*, p. 136.
68 *Ibid*, p. 137.

[69] *My Forty Year Fight*, p. 104.
[70] F.A. McKenzie, *Korea's Fight for Freedom*, pp. 245–246.
[71] Quoted by Samuel Hugh Moffett, "There is No Cheap Hope," *Korea Calling*, Oct. 1979, p. 3; a similar account is in *Rebirth of Korea*, p. 79.
[72] The declaration is printed in full in F.A. McKenzie's *Korea's Fight for Freedom*, pp. 247–250, and in Cynn's *Rebirth of Korea*, pp. 19–23.
[73] Translation of placards calling for non-violence from the 1919 papers on microfilm, Presbyterian Historical Society in Philadelphia.
[74] Helen Kim, *Grace Sufficient*, p. 42.
[75] Edith Kerr and George Anderson, unpublished history, *The Australian Presbyterian Mission in Korea, 1889–1941*, p. 21.
[77] Kim, *op. cit.*
[78] *Women of Korea, pp. 260–261.*
[79] *My Forty Year Fight*, pp. 120–121.
[80] *Korea's Fight for Freedom*, p. 253.
[81] *Women of Korea*, p. 261.
[82] *Ibid*, p. 262.
[83] Richard Rutt, *James Scarth Gale and His History of the Korean People*, p. 65.
[84] Yong-Ock Park, "The Women's Modernization Movement in Korea," *Virtues in Conflict*, p. 105.
[85] *The Rebirth of Korea*, p. 65.
[86] *Ibid*, p. 55.
[87] *Ibid*, p. 47.
[88] *Ibid*, p. 49.
[89] *Ibid*, p. 91.
[90] *My Forty Year Fight*, p. 141.
[91] *A Handbook of Korea*, 1978 ed. (Seoul, Korea Overseas Information Service), p. 94; *My Forty Year Fight*, p. 120.
[92] *The Rebirth of Korea*, p. 66.
[93] Erdman, Holdcroft letter, April 7, 1919.
[94] Quoted by Roy Shearer, *Wildfire*, p. 65.
[95] G.T. Brown, *Mission to Korea*, p. 111.
[96] Quoted by Cynn, *Rebirth of Korea*, pp. 178–180.
[97] G.T. Brown, *Mission to Korea*, pp. 110–111.
[98] *Ibid.*
[99] *Op. Cit.*, p. 180.
[100] *Wildfire*, p. 66.
[101] *Korea and Christianity*, p. 138.
[102] Osgood, p. 295; *Mission to Korea*, pp. 117–118.
[103] Rutt, *James Scarth Gale and His History of the Korean People*, p. 319.
[104] Frank W. Schofield, "What Happened on Sam Il Day March 1, 1919," *The Feel of Korea* (Seoul, Hollym, 1966), pp. 276–277.
[105] *Episodes*, pp. 62–66.
[106] *Ibid.*
[107] *Ibid.*
[108] Forty-One Years in Korea, unpublished manuscript, pp. 76–84, Moffett collection.
[109] Samuel H. Moffett, "The Independence Movement and the Missionaries," *Transactions*, Royal Asiatic Society, Korea Branch, vol. 54, 1979, pp.

14-15; Frank Baldwin, "Missionaries and the March First Movement: Can Moral Men be Neutral?" *Korea Under Japanese Colonial Rule*, pp. 198-199.

110 Moffett, p. 30.

111 *Ibid*, p. 14.

112 Forty-One Years in Korea, p. 76; letter, April 4, 1919.

113 Moffett, p. 14.

114 John Thomas statement, 1919 papers, Presbyterian Historical Society, Philadelphia.

115 Erdman-Holdcroft letter to Presbyterian mission board, April 7, 1919.

116 Moffett, pp. 17-20.

117 Erdman-Holdcroft letter, April 7, 1919.

118 *Ibid.*

119 1919 papers, Presbyterian Historical Society.

120 Erdman, Holdcroft letter, April 7, 1919.

121 Moffett, pp. 22-23.

122 *Ibid*, p. 25.

123 *Ibid*, p. 13, 30.

124 Smith letter to Gulick, Oct. 15, 1919.

125 *Ibid.*

126 J. Ernest Fisher, "March First 1919 and the Missionaries," *Korea Calling*, vol. 14, March 1975, p. 3.

127 *Ibid.*

128 *Ibid.*

129 *Ibid.*

130 Moffett account to American Consul Bergholz, microfilmed 1919 papers, Presbyterian Historical Society.

131 Charles Bernheisel to Bergholz, 1919 papers.

132 Moffett letter to Presbyterian board, April 21, 1919.

133 *Ibid.*

134 Baldwin, p. 198.

NOTES FOR EPILOGUE

1 *Aunt Jean*, p. 288.

2 *East Goes West*, p. 97.

3 H.N. Allen papers, New York Public Library

Index

1. 1st impressions of Korea P. 57-58
2. The origin of Baptism (strict) P. 64-65